Evaluating e-Learning

How can novice e-learning researchers and postgraduate learners develop rigorous plans to study the effectiveness of technology-enhanced learning environments? How can practitioners gather and portray evidence of the impact of e-learning? How can the average educator who teaches online, without experience in evaluating emerging technologies, build on what is successful and modify what is not?

By unpacking the e-learning life cycle and focusing on learning, not technology, *Evaluating e-Learning* attempts to resolve some of the complexity inherent in evaluating the effectiveness of e-learning. The book presents practical advice in the form of an evaluation framework and a scaffolded approach to the design of an e-learning research study, using divide-and-conquer techniques to reduce complexity. It adapts and builds on familiar research methodology to offer a robust and accessible approach that can ensure effective evaluation of a wide range of innovative initiatives, including those covered in other books in the *Connecting with e-Learning* series.

Readers will find this jargon-free guide is a must-have resource that provides the proper tools for evaluating e-learning practice with ease.

Rob Phillips is Associate Professor in the Educational Development Unit at Murdoch University, Perth, Western Australia. He has worked as a researcher and academic at universities in Australia and Germany since 1982, and has a background in theoretical chemistry and computer science. He has worked with educational technology since 1992, designing and project managing educational technology development projects across most discipline areas. Currently, he provides professional development and mentoring for academic staff in the scholarship of learning and teaching. Current research interests include university policy issues; evaluation research in e-learning; making creative and innovative use of technology; academic analytics; and project management in educational innovations. Rob has a strong publication record, and is active in the management of two journals: the *Australasian Journal of Educational Technology* and *Research in Learning Technology*. He is a life member and past-president (1996–2000) of the Australasian Society for Computers in Learning in Tertiary Education (ascilite) and is a fellow of the Higher Education Research and Development Society of Australasia. He was an executive member of the Australasian Council on Open, Distance and E-learning (ACODE) from 2004–2006, and received a 2007 Australian Learning and Teaching Council Citation for Outstanding Contribution to Student Learning.

Carmel McNaught is Director and Chair Professor in the Centre for Learning Enhancement And Research (CLEAR) at The Chinese University of Hong Kong. Since the early 1970s, Carmel has worked in higher education in Australasia and southern Africa in the fields of chemistry, science education, second-language learning, e-learning, and higher-education curriculum and policy matters. Current research interests include evaluation of innovation in higher education, strategies for embedding learning support into the curriculum, and understanding the broader implementation of the use of technology in higher education. She is actively involved in several professional organizations and is a Fellow of the Association for the Advancement of Computers in Education; is a university quality-assurance auditor for both Australia and Hong Kong; is on the editorial board of 13 international journals; and is a prolific author whose recent publications and activities can be viewed at http://www.cuhk.edu.hk/clear/people/Carmel.htm

Gregor Kennedy is Director of e-Learning and Associate Professor of Educational Technology in the Centre for the Study of Higher Education at The University of Melbourne. His current work involves leading the university's strategy in technology-enhanced learning and teaching, supporting staff in the use of learning technologies, and undertaking research in the area of e-Learning. He has a background in psychology and has spent the past 15 years conducting and overseeing research and development in educational technology in higher education. His research interests include use of technology by staff and students, contemporary learning design and emerging technologies, approaches to educational technology research and evaluation, computer-based interactivity and engagement, and the use of electronic measures for educational research and evaluation. He has published widely in these areas. He is a long-standing member of the Australasian Society for Computers in Learning in Tertiary Education (ascilite) and is an editorial board member of *Australasian Journal of Educational Technology*.

Connecting with e-Learning series
Edited by Allison Littlejohn and Chris Pegler

e-Learning is rapidly becoming a key component of campus-based education as well as a cornerstone of distance learning. However, although e-learning is an increasingly essential skill for effective teaching, it remains challenging for most teachers in higher and further education. There are four major reasons for this:

- Learners increasingly expect effective application of technologies; this can be intimidating to teachers/lecturers who are novices at using these technologies themselves.
- Already under pressure for time, teachers need to understand how to design an appropriate blend of online and offline learning activities; otherwise their learners may end up working unproductively and unhappily.
- Courses need to be created sustainably, so that learning materials can be easily generated, stored, retrieved and repurposed.
- Teachers/lecturers are understandably uncertain about how to invest their time and effort in a fast-moving field.

This exciting new series provides relevant guides for both newcomers to teaching in higher and further education and experienced teachers/lecturers who are developing their practice online. Featuring practical, accessible advice that draws on recent research and the experiences of expert practitioners, each book is structured, accessible and relevant to teachers and lecturers worldwide.

Books in the series include:

The Power of Role-based e-Learning
Sandra Wills, Elyssebeth Leigh and Albert Ip

A Guide to Authentic e-Learning
Jan Herrington, Thomas C. Reeves and Ron Oliver

Preparing for Blended e-Learning
Allison Littlejohn and Chris Pegler

The Educational Potential of e-Portfolios: Supporting Personal Development and Reflective Learning
Lorraine Stefani, Robin Mason and Chris Pegler

The website for this series is **connecting-with-elearning.com**

Evaluating e-Learning
Guiding Research and Practice

**Rob Phillips, Carmel McNaught
and Gregor Kennedy**

Routledge
Taylor & Francis Group

NEW YORK AND LONDON

First published 2012
by Routledge
711 Third Avenue, New York, NY 10017

Simultaneously published in the UK
by Routledge
2 Park Square, Milton Park, Abingdon, Oxon OX14 4RN

Routledge is an imprint of the Taylor & Francis Group, an informa business

Typeset in Minion Pro by
RefineCatch Ltd, Bungay, Suffolk, UK

Library of Congress Cataloging in Publication Data
Phillips, Rob, 1954–
    Evaluating e-learning: guiding research and practice/Rob Phillips,
    Carmel McNaught, Gregor Kennedy.
        p. cm. — (Connecting with e-learning)
    Includes bibliographical references and index.
    1. Computer-assisted instruction—Evaluation. 2. Web-based
    instruction—Evaluation. 3. Distance education—Evaluation.
    I. McNaught, Carmel, 1950– II. Kennedy, Gregor. III. Title.
    LB1028.3.P475 2011
    378.1'7344678—dc22   2010052667

ISBN: 978-0-415-88193-7 (hbk)
ISBN: 978-0-415-88194-4 (pbk)
ISBN: 978-0-203-81336-2 (ebk)

This book would not have been possible without the support of our families, colleagues and students.

Contents

Figures

Tables

Series Editors' Foreword

Evaluating e-Learning: Guiding Research and Practice is the fifth book to be published in the *Connecting with e-Learning* series. We selected this topic because we place considerable importance on the subject matter. In sponsoring this proposal for the series, and throughout the negotiation around the contents of the book, we have gained confidence that there is a re-focus in the field on methodology and that this topic is a vital addition to our series.

Readers will be aware of the current emphasis around the world on costs – benefits and value for money in education and other public-sector services. Within this changing context, evaluation of e-learning effectiveness, and learning from what we have invested time, effort and resources in, is even more critically important than before.

As with other books in the series, the authors are known internationally, not only for innovation in e-learning practice, but also for their deep experience of – and commitment to maintaining contact with – wider learning and teaching concerns. They have been dedicated to ensuring that the book has staying power and remains focused on the bigger issues – not being distracted by technological fads and fashions, while acknowledging the influence that these have. Every aspect of this book has been subject to careful consideration, with the intent of creating an accessible and helpful guide to evaluation for those involved at all levels of e-learning – whether academics, managers or educational technologists. It provides necessary guidance and support for those who have never previously been involved in research methods, and a robust framework for adapting methods which may already be familiar to some readers to examine e-learning.

We have enjoyed our involvement of the development of this book and regard it as a necessary cornerstone of the series. We firmly believe that evaluation is an essential foundation for effective e-learning practice.

Allison Littlejohn
Caledonia Academy, Glasgow Caledonian University, UK
Chris Pegler
Institute of Educational Technology, Open University, UK

Foreword

The undertaking of an evaluation of any educational initiative is a complex task. Because of the addition of the technology component, with the attendant training and technical support issues, an evaluation of an e-learning initiative can be very daunting. In *Evaluating e-Learning: Guiding Research and Practice*, Rob Phillips, Carmel McNaught and Gregor Kennedy provide a 'divide and conquer' approach to the topic. They use the Learning Environment, Learning Processes and Learning Outcomes (LEPO) framework and the e-learning life cycle to deconstruct the conduct of an e-learning evaluation-research study into five general forms: *baseline analysis, design evaluation, project-management evaluation, formative evaluation* and *effectiveness research*.

This book provides not only a good theoretical basis for evaluating e-learning initiatives; it is also a practical resource. The authors' 'divide and conquer' approach allows an iterative presentation of current theory followed by a discussion of practical issues. As we proceed through this theory-to-practice approach in each chapter, there is a feeling of a protégé being coached by a mentor.

The authors provide an excellent review of the literature in the area of evaluation of e-learning. They talk about this endeavour as "evaluation research" which they use "simply to capture the idea that investigations of e-learning will often involve a mix of evaluation and research activities that can be applied throughout the e-learning life cycle. When it comes to e-learning investigations, there is typically an ebb and flow between making judgements about the e-learning environment and developing a greater understanding of learning in that environment" (Chapter 4, p. 50).

Those who espouse a particular epistemological approach will find the authors' approach a challenge as they are committed to a pragmatic approach to evaluation research. We are encouraged to use a mix of different methods: "we advocate using a mixture of qualitative and quantitative data sources using methods which are most appropriate to the evaluation questions posed" (Chapter 2, p. 21). They ask us to combine the best features of different approaches to evaluation in order to design an appropriate evaluation protocol that fits the specific program being evaluated. This is where it becomes apparent that the authors have 'been there, done that, worn the T-shirt until it was a rag'. There are lots of examples of 'what works' and, often more importantly 'what doesn't work'. They refer to themselves as pragmatic evaluators, which means that they borrow techniques and philosophical ideas from whatever theory fits the current project being evaluated. Throughout, we are encouraged to think hard about alternative explanations for what we observe.

Cutting to the chase – if I were undertaking an evaluation of an e-learning initiative for the first time, this would be my bible. If I were asked to teach a course on the evaluation of e-learning, this would be my textbook. Finally, if I were evaluating e-learning initiatives, this would be a major reference in my library.

T. Craig Montgomerie
Professor Emeritus, Department of Educational Psychology
The University of Alberta

Preface

Why Did We Write this Book?

The use of technology to enhance learning has moved from being explored by a minority of academic technophiles to being a mainstream concern in educational institutions worldwide. A large proportion of educational courses/programs in the developed world now has some e-learning component, and there is increasing uptake in the developing world. This book is timely in that, despite large investments in e-learning worldwide, teachers and institutions are still grappling with how best to gather and portray evidence of the impact of e-learning.

Our primary concern is with learning – and we want to contest a consistent theme in the field of e-learning that principles for effective learning design *depend on* the technology that is used and hence that, as technologies evolve, so too do learning-design principles. We believe there is more stability in the field of e-learning and that we can make informed decisions about how best to use a range of technologies to support learning that will stand the test of time.

In the book, we explore the nature of learning, and provide a robust framework for evaluation and a set of methods that will assist practitioners and researchers to gather and interpret evidence to enrich their understanding of how a broad range of technologies can be used in constructing effective learning environments. We regard our framework and suggested evaluation strategies as being a set of tools that are broadly applicable to any educational context; our focus on technology-supported contexts is, as stated earlier, because of the ubiquity of technology in higher and further education, and the need to gain a stronger evidence base about its effectiveness.

Evaluation of the effectiveness of e-learning environments is a complex issue, and there is no simple and certain answer about whether a certain application of e-learning has had an effect on learning. Part of the complexity arises from a lack of clarity about the meaning of the terms 'e-learning' and 'evaluation', and the nature of research into e-learning – issues that this book will unpack.

What is the Scope of the Book?

The book aims to provide a step-by-step guide on how to design and conduct an e-learning evaluation study. This book addresses acknowledged weaknesses in the quality of research into education, and therefore e-learning. Our aim is to contribute to 'strengthening' educational research by:

- unpacking and clarifying terms which are used imprecisely;
- recognizing the need for rigorous research and providing practical guidance about how to do this;
- recognizing that there are multiple approaches to educational research, and critiquing approaches which are used less thoughtfully than they should be;
- recognizing that developing e-learning is a creative design endeavour, and evaluation and research approaches should be appropriate to that sort of endeavour;
- promoting a holistic approach that incorporates all components of the teaching and learning environment, while also addressing contextual learning processes.

Who Should Read this Book?

We envisage a broad readership for the book. Specifically, it is aimed at both practitioners involved in developing and implementing e-learning in higher and further education, and educational researchers seeking to understand how we can gain evidence of learning and how learning might be supported by a range of technologies.

This book is intended to be used in both formal and informal learning settings. In formal settings in postgraduate courses, the readership is likely to be academics, developers, managers or support staff involved in, or seeking to be involved in, e-learning or blended learning. This may range from tertiary educators using commercial virtual learning environments or learning management systems, to corporate staff developing e-learning products.

The readership in informal learning settings is made up of anyone concerned with e-learning! This includes:

- developers and project managers of e-learning materials;
- tertiary teachers who wish to conduct research at varying levels of rigour into how their students learn in a particular e-learning environment;
- teachers developing their existing practice for online and blended learning for new markets, including employment-based, off-campus environments;
- experienced practitioners seeking to evaluate the use of e-learning in varied fields of endeavour;
- educational researchers in the field of e-learning.

There is a clear interface between this book and the growing interest in, and literature on, the scholarship of teaching and learning. The book provides tools that readers can use to evaluate innovation in a scholarly fashion, to publish their results and to contribute to the rigour of e-learning research and practice.

This is a book for all levels of e-learning practitioners and researchers in higher and further education. We have focused on providing a book with a minimum of jargon, where contested terms are clearly defined.

What is in the Book?

This book is divided into three parts: an overview, a theoretical section and a practical section.

Part I contains an introductory chapter which gives a broad overview of issues surrounding the evaluation of the effectiveness of e-learning environments. The term 'e-learning' is unpacked, and the cyclical nature of e-learning development and evaluation is highlighted.

In Chapter 2 we provide an overview of the process of evaluation. We discuss the need for multiple sources of data and careful interpretation of what the data might mean. We link a framework of 'tips' for doing evaluation to the remaining chapters in the book. We end Chapter 2 with an orientation for academic teachers who wish to get started in evaluation by exploring three key questions that teachers often ask about their teaching and their students' learning.

Part II of the book provides a scholarly background to evaluation of e-learning. Chapter 3 unpacks the implications of the statement: Students learn within *learning environments*, going through *learning processes* in order to achieve *learning outcomes*. We present and justify a conceptual framework which combines the learning environment, process and outcomes in a way which covers various contexts and draws together other frameworks. This framework is used to guide discussion in later chapters.

Chapter 4 explores the nature of educational evaluation, and looks at evaluation of e-learning through four scenarios, which are threaded through later chapters. By working through the scenarios, we establish that there is a research component to e-learning evaluation, and we introduce the term *evaluation research* to illustrate that what is commonly called e-learning evaluation is actually a mixture of evaluation and research. We then explore the nature of research through various disciplinary and trans-disciplinary viewpoints, concluding with some examples of our own work which indicate that a variety of approaches is appropriate.

Chapter 5 builds on Chapter 4 in recognizing that research approaches need to be clearly described and justified. We go back to 'first principles' in discussing the phenomenon being studied, what is meant by theory, and the need for disciplined inquiry in addressing clear research goals. We explore these concepts further in terms of several paradigms of inquiry, recommending a pragmatic paradigm which draws on the strengths of the others. Chapter 5 then explores issues relating to methodologies, before presenting a set of principles for high-quality educational research.

In the final chapter of Part II (Chapter 6) we draw together the findings of the earlier chapters in this section to discuss evaluation and research approaches suitable for e-learning. We return to our scenarios and establish that, like e-learning development itself, e-learning evaluation research is a cyclical process. We suggest that design-based research offers a valuable perspective that suits a pragmatic, mixed-methods approach to evaluation research. However, we also recognize that other approaches are suitable for particular contexts, and discuss these approaches.

In Part III, we focus on the actual process of e-learning evaluation and research, grounding it on the theoretical issues discussed in Part II. We start in Chapter 7 by unpacking a diagram of the process of conducting an evaluation-research study. This discussion acts as an advance organizer for the chapters that follow.

Chapter 8 explores evaluation research across different phases of the e-learning life cycle, returning to the scenarios introduced in Chapter 4. Five distinct evaluation and research 'forms' are identified, with differing emphases at different stages in the e-learning life cycle. Four of these forms are discussed in detail in terms of the learning framework presented in Chapter 3.

In Chapter 9, we turn our attention to practical considerations associated with conducting an evaluation, in particular providing advice on common data-collection techniques, and how instruments to collect data might be devised and used. It also offers some suggestions about how to analyse data once it has been collected. Reliability, validity and how to present data to an audience are also considered. In passing, we note that this book is not a research methods book. While we provide an overview of methodologies and methods which might be appropriate, we refer readers to the research-methods literature to carry out the legwork of the study.

Chapter 10 treats the fifth evaluation form from Chapter 8, the evaluation of the project management of an e-learning innovation. This is treated separately because it is logically a different type of evaluation, but is nevertheless not well represented in the literature.

Chapter 11 extends the discussion to wider issues, such as sustainability, dissemination and institutionalization. Finally, we round off the book with a 'Top Ten' set of take-home messages for our readers.

How Did We Come to Write the Book?

The work that has led to this book began more than a decade ago as a project of the Australasian Society for Computers in Learning in Tertiary Education (ascilite). The Australian government funded the project to support a number of university staff across Australia who had developed technology-enhanced innovations, and wanted to evaluate how effective they were. The project participants were guided by mentors experienced in evaluation, assisted by a draft evaluation handbook (Phillips, Bain, McNaught, Rice & Tripp, 2000) detailing a framework which focused attention on student learning as well as technology. A mini-project model was used, with small evaluation teams supported by evaluation mentors. The draft handbook has been built on substantially in this book, informed by a further decade of scholarship into evaluation of, and research into, what is now commonly called e-learning.

In noting the history behind this book, we wish to warmly acknowledge the colleagues, teachers and students that, collectively, we have worked with and learned from over more decades than we may like to admit. In writing this book, we have further refined and extended our own understanding of learning and of evaluation – usually in long Skype conversations across Australia and to Hong Kong. One of the privileges of being an academic is that we belong to a community of scholars who can support and learn from each other, and this book is a good case to illustrate this point. It is appropriate that technology has mediated the writing of this book – that our in-depth discussions have not been circumscribed by national boundaries and, indeed, they have been enhanced by the focus and immediacy of technology. The result is a book that we hand to fellow practitioners and researchers to assist them in their own work and their future contributions to the field of e-learning. It is in this way that knowledge grows and future generations of learners benefit.

Acknowledgements

This book did not emerge like a butterfly from a chrysalis. It is more appropriate to view the evolution of this book in terms of a decade-long life cycle of a literary 'insect', from embryo to larva, to pupa, to imago. The embryo was the project described in the previous section conducted under the auspices of ascilite, and funded by the Commonwealth Universities Teaching and Staff Development fund. The caterpillar phase began with the writing of the 'evaluation handbook' for this project. We particularly acknowledge the contributions of John Bain, Mary Rice and David Tripp in developing that manuscript, and we appreciate the permission given by the copyright holder, now the Australian Learning and Teaching Council, to draw from that work.

We also drew on two short articles written for a United Kingdom audience. One (Phillips & Gilding, 2002) was written on behalf of the Association for Learning Technology and the Learning and Teaching Support Network (now the Higher Education Academy). The second (Phillips, 2005a) was written for the Institute for Learning and Research Technology at the University of Bristol. We acknowledge the permission of the copyright holders to draw from these works.

The larval phase of the book concluded with an effort in 2002, assisted ably by Tony Gilding, to turn the unfinished handbook into a publishable book. When we could not find a publisher, the book entered a pupation phase.

The pupa remained dormant until we made contact with the series editors, Allison Littlejohn and Chris Pegler. We went through a rigorous and scholarly process in developing the book proposal, and we had long and fruitful email discussions about various chapter drafts. As the chrysalis was transforming, it was assisted by conversations with, and feedback from, Barney Dalgarno, Jan Herrington, Tom Carey, Doug Kennedy, Sean O'Beirne, Chris Jones and Shane Dawson, as well as various research assistants and postgraduate students: Pauline Roberts, Ioanna Ioannou and the research staff at the Centre for Learning Enhancement And Research at The Chinese University of Hong Kong. We also acknowledge the generosity of Tom Reeves and Educational Technology Publications in providing permission to reproduce figures.

A year ago, we weren't completely clear about what sort of insect would appear from its cocoon. Would it be a moth, functional and grey, with a tendency to fly towards the flame of the newest technology? Or would it be a butterfly, striking and inspiring? We think it has become a butterfly – a butterfly that has been supported, protected and encouraged by our partners and young children: Rita; David; and Caitlin, Audrey and Finbar, respectively.

Finally, throughout its life cycle, the butterfly was nourished by various funding bodies in Australia and Hong Kong.

Rob Phillips, Perth
Carmel McNaught, Hong Kong
Gregor Kennedy, Melbourne
June 2011

I
Setting the Scene

1
e-Learning, Learning and Evaluation

1.1 Introduction

In this chapter we will provide a brief history of e-learning, emphasizing the notion that using technology in an educational setting involves conscious design decisions. These design decisions must involve considerations of how learners learn, and so we will establish some key characteristics of learning which, we believe, should be used to guide the design of technology-enhanced learning (or 'e-learning') environments. We will explore the shorthand term 'e-learning' that will be used throughout the book by introducing the concept of an e-learning life cycle. We will firmly establish our position, which is that the focus needs to be on learning, not technology, and that there are a number of ways in which a range of technologies can assist learners to learn.

Questions such as the following naturally arise when one designs any learning environment for learners: "How do we know that the overall learning environment or context – with its technology components, whatever they may be – supports learning? Is this the best way to organize the learning environment?" These are evaluation questions and the central thrust of the book is to provide pragmatic advice to teachers about how to answer such questions. Good evaluation is systematic and scholarly; it involves data collection and careful reflection on the implications of the data.

Overall, this book attempts to resolve some of the complexity of evaluation of the effectiveness of e-learning, by unpacking the e-learning life cycle and the types of evaluation and research that are appropriate at any given part of the life cycle. It also presents practical advice in the form of an evaluation framework and a scaffolded approach to the design of an e-learning research study.

1.2 What is e-Learning?

Computers have been used for education and training since the 1960s, and increasingly since the 1990s. Large and increasing amounts of money have been spent worldwide on the development of computer applications designed to assist people to learn. In the 1990s, learning software tended to be authored as multimedia-rich, monolithic applications, addressing learning needs across a period of time, often several weeks. Among many terms, such 'courseware' was called 'interactive multimedia', 'computer-based learning' (Phillips, 1997), 'computer-facilitated learning' (McNaught, Phillips, Rossiter & Winn, 2000) and 'interactive learning systems' (Reeves & Hedberg, 2003). The authoring software used at that time made it expensive to adapt material to other purposes and to update it for changed information.

With the advent of the World Wide Web in the mid-1990s, it became possible to develop courseware (hyperlinked web pages) which was much more adaptable, and less expensive to create, but which lacked the educational and multimedia richness of the earlier monolithic applications, primarily because of difficulties in delivering large media files over the Internet, which at that stage had very limited bandwidth. Shortly thereafter, the first learning-management systems appeared on the market. These applications delivered web pages to learners and provided online interactive tools that allowed learners to interact with course materials, other learners and their teachers, but primarily only using text.

Bandwidth increases in the early 2000s enabled effective interaction and multimedia capabilities to be provided over the web. At the same time, the 'learning object' movement started to gain momentum, driven largely by the American military's requirement to provide reusable and adaptable training content for its staff (Advanced Distributed Learning, 2003), independent of the computer system being used.

A large number of terms has been used to describe the range of these computer applications over the last two decades. A current favourite is technology-enhanced learning; however, while enhanced learning is the intention, it is not always the practice and, in a book about evaluation, we have chosen to use the more neutral term *e-learning*. While we will argue in Chapter 3 that there are semantic nuances surrounding the term e-learning which make it problematic, we will continue to use the term in this book, because it is a useful shorthand and widely accepted. We choose to use, as one among many, the definition of Littlejohn and Pegler (2007, p. 15): "the process of learning and teaching with computers and other associated technologies, particularly through use of the Internet".

For several years, proponents of e-learning have used the term in a 'one size fits all' fashion, despite its use in a range of contexts. We agree with Friesen (2009, p. 4) that e-learning has "come to represent a useful shorthand for a range of different orientations to ... the use of technologies in education and learning. Often the precise way that the term e-learning is used is dependent on the author's particular purposes or specific research agenda". Because the term is often used without explicating the underlying assumptions of the author, understanding e-learning is hampered, leading to confusion on the part of practitioners and policy-makers.

e-Learning is primarily a branch of the discipline of education. However, it also brings in influences from other fields, including computer engineering, information technology, design and media studies. "It is *inter* disciplinary in that it seeks to combine and explore the *inter* connections between new and different approaches from different fields and specializations; it is *multi* disciplinary in that it simultaneously tries to respect the *multiplicity* of differences that can separate one research approach from another" (Friesen, 2009, p. 12). Its multidisciplinary nature and its rapid evolution have led to individual researchers taking different approaches to evaluation and research, derived from their individual contexts and often with little reflection on the appropriateness of that approach to the task of evaluating e-learning.

An important factor underpinning the arguments presented in this book is that e-learning results from a design activity, where the outcome of the design activity is an e-learning *artefact*. We take a broad view of the interpretation of artefact to mean both tools developed using information and communication technologies (ICTs) and tasks designed through these tools (see section 1.5, p. 9 for further discussion on this). Research into designed artefacts has an extra element not present when researching natural phenomena – that is, whether the designed artefact functions as it was designed, or can be improved. This element of improvement is not present in traditional science research into natural phenomena, but is present in artificial sciences such as engineering, architecture, computer science, and e-learning. These ideas will be explored further in section 6.3, p. 87.

Indeed, in this book, we will emphasize evaluation of the effectiveness of a designed and constructed e-learning environment, purposefully including one or more artefacts. Such an environment might perhaps be used in a number of different contexts.

1.3 Key Characteristics of Learning

In recent years, a consensus has emerged about the type of learning environment that is likely to support learners to develop thinking skills such as critical thinking and problem solving in order to become knowledge workers. Such learning environments are the design outcome of a largely constructivist pedagogical philosophy, adoption of a deep approach to learning and a learner-centred approach to teaching, and outcomes-centred subject design (Phillips, 2005b). It is not the intention of this section to provide a comprehensive summary of learning theories; what we would like to provide are some key principles about learning that will be used progressively in the book to anchor our comments about designing and evaluating effective learning experiences.

More specific advice is provided by a report from the National Research Council in the United States of America (USA) into how people learn (Bransford, Brown & Cocking, 1999, 2000). Among the key findings of this comprehensive review of research, several themes stand out as having most relevance to tertiary education.

An important goal of tertiary education is for novices to become experts in particular discipline areas. Bransford and colleagues distinguished a key difference between novices and experts, which is that experts have in-depth and organized content knowledge. This enables them to see relationships and patterns between pieces of information, and also to retrieve important parts of their knowledge relatively easily. In essence, an expert has a well-organized, personal knowledge network.

This finding has important implications for universities. For tertiary learners to become experts, they need to attain a deep, organized and contextualized understanding of their discipline – and the learning environment needs to support this. It is much easier to develop a knowledge network if knowledge is organized by fundamental principles, as this enables learners to categorize and interrelate areas of understanding in ways that make sense to them.

A further factor noted by Bransford and colleagues is that for learning to be effective, it needs to be transferable to other contexts. To know 'about' something is not sufficient; one needs to know how to use knowledge in new situations that arise. So, learners need to see knowledge not as a fixed commodity, but rather as something to be extended and utilized. In addition, learners are most successful when they see themselves as being active agents in the process of gaining and using knowledge.

These characteristics closely match those of 'deep approaches to learning' reported in the tertiary learning literature (Biggs, 1999; Gibbs, 1992; Ramsden, 1988, 1992). Learners who adopt a deep approach to learning are interested in the topic and actively try to understand key concepts. Once these key concepts are understood, an attempt is made to link together the concepts to make a coherent whole. Then new knowledge can be related to previous knowledge and to personal experiences, and thus integrated into a personal knowledge network.

The 'approaches to learning' research has identified several key principles about how teachers should design and teach to increase the likelihood that learners adopt a deep approach to learning. Three key ideas are as follows:

1. Transmission approaches lead to surface learning.
2. Depth of learning is determined by the nature of the learning tasks.
3. Surface and deep approaches are reactions to the teaching environment.

However, the situation is more complex and the motivation of individual learners is a critical factor. Many readers may remember boring, didactic learning environments where they were, nevertheless, engaged by the topic and adopted a deep approach to learning; they may also remember interactive learning activities that did not engage them, perhaps because of conflicting demands on their attention. Teasing out how best to design for learning is always complex and involves a degree of compromise (Goodyear, 2009). Perhaps the most fundamental principle is that the modern university teacher needs to design flexible learning experiences that support diverse groups of learners as they learn how to learn.

Well-designed learning tasks become an important precursor for effective learning to take place. A learning activity is "an interaction between a learner and an environment (optionally involving other learners, practitioners, resources, tools and services) to achieve a planned learning outcome. Under this definition, task, content and context *are* fundamentally inseparable" (Beetham, 2004). We will also distinguish between *learning tasks* and *learning activities*, according to Goodyear's (2009) insightful definition: "Tasks are what teachers set. Activities are what students actually do" (p. 13).

However, while the interrelatedness and holistic nature of this description of learning tasks and learning activities is important to bear in mind, some analysis is needed in order to be able to suggest principles and strategies to teachers about how to decide whether learning tasks are well designed or not in any particular learning context.

Learning tasks are usually planned in terms of outcomes or objectives. Allan contended that there are "fundamental conceptual differences between outcome-led design and the traditional university approach which emphasizes input and process" (Allan, 1996, p. 104). The modern university teacher needs to design effective learning tasks, and to "facilitate their productive use by the student" (Laurillard, 2002b, p. 24). This argument leads us to think of learning as having three components: the learning environment designed for learners to use; the learning processes used by students (how they learn); and the learning outcomes that students can demonstrate (what they learn).

These ideas are discussed further in Chapter 3, where a conceptual model is developed which characterizes learning in terms of the interactions between learners, teachers and the learning environment, learning processes and learning outcomes. These ideas are fundamental to the structure of this book.

1.4 Evaluating Learning and e-Learning

Evaluation is a term that is often used imprecisely, with different meanings in different contexts. This section seeks to unpack the various meanings of 'evaluation' in an educational context, and clarify the way that we interpret the term in this book, as well as setting the scope of what is covered in this book.

There are numerous ways that the term 'evaluation' is used in higher education. There is also a cultural element to definitions of 'evaluation'. In education textbooks originating in the USA, 'evaluation' is used in the sense of making judgements about assessable learner work. In this book, we follow the United Kingdom (UK) convention, describing the process whereby teachers set specific tasks to judge the extent to which learners can demonstrate learning outcomes as 'assessment' and the term 'evaluation', in the sense of making judgements about how effective the design of the learning environment is for supporting learning. As this book is on e-learning evaluation, we will concentrate on learning environments involving e-learning artefacts (discussed further in section 1.5 on the following page).

The previous section has indicated the importance of well-designed learning tasks to engage learners in productive learning processes. The e-learning artefacts that we design act as tools which facilitate learning activities, which learners can use in developing their own understandings (Von Brevern, 2004).

The history of e-learning over decades is littered with examples of products promoted as ends in themselves which would revolutionize education. However, when technologies are viewed as tools, the fallacy in this argument is revealed. Maslow (1970, cited in Jensen and Kiley, 2005) "is credited with the notion that if the only tool people have is a hammer, they tend to see and respond to everything as if it were a nail", an analogy also used by Reeves and Hedberg (2003, p. 35). While few people would claim that it is sensible for a tradesperson to use just one tool, this occurs relatively frequently with educational technology.

We argue in this book that e-learning evaluation should focus on holistically evaluating learning environments, rather than just evaluating the technologies which contribute to the environment. While there is still an element of evaluating the tools, e-learning evaluation is increasingly about how well these tools are used to facilitate an effective learning environment. In the developed world, at least, ICT use has become embedded throughout education.

In the 1990s, technical issues were a major component of evaluating e-learning. Authoring tools were immature, hardware was slow when handling multimedia elements, screen sizes were small, and Internet connectivity was slow and intermittent. People were also grappling with how best to apply these technologies to learning situations. However, over the last decade, technological issues have reduced in importance as the tools have matured. New tools largely build on the underlying multimedia and networking capabilities developed over the last two decades, and combine features of, or link between, existing tools. We do acknowledge that new technological tools are continually evolving, and there is an element of technical evaluation and research of these tools; however, the thrust of this book is not on technology per se but on making informed decisions about the design of learning environments.

Since the approach we promote in this book focuses on holistically evaluating the way a student learns in a given environment – which may use one or more technological tools – many aspects of our approach could also be applied in a technology-free environment. In other words, many of the approaches developed in this book in an e-learning context could be applied to other educational innovations.

1.4.1 Other Instances of Evaluation and Research into e-Learning

There are some instances of evaluation which will *not* be covered in this book.

An institution might want to evaluate the roll-out of a strategic initiative – for example, the implementation of an e-learning strategic plan – to see if it was worth the money expended and if it achieved its goals. This is an evaluation of a *program*, and we are not interested in this per se, although some elements of program evaluation are used to set the scene in Chapter 4.

Selection decisions, at an institutional or individual level, can also be informed by evaluation. At an institutional level, an evaluation might be carried out to select the most appropriate e-learning system to implement, for example, an e-portfolio system. Individually, an academic might use evaluation to select the most appropriate of several published educational resources for the given teaching context, for example, a textbook or a physics simulation learning object.

In addition, evaluation might be used in terms of evaluating teaching quality, for example, implemented through the surveys of learner satisfaction carried out at many institutions. Survey results can be aggregated to provide institutional indicators of quality, and they can also be used to affirm or improve individual practice, but they are beyond the scope of this book.

Also beyond the scope of this book, apart from passing mention in Chapter 11, are evaluations of the institutionalization and sustainability of e-learning innovations as they are implemented on a broad scale, and also the impact that evaluation data might have on institutional e-learning policy.

We also recognize that there are different aspects of research into e-learning, some of which are beyond the scope of this book. Conole and Oliver (2007a) and Friesen (2009) recognized the complexity of this emerging multi- and interdisciplinary field, and identified four distinct types of e-learning research: pedagogical, organizational, technical and socio-cultural. Our interest is mainly pedagogical, with a brief foray into organizational matters in Chapter 11. There is also a hard, computer-science aspect to e-learning research, with technical work on emerging approaches and specifications. At the same time, communications and culture researchers shine a postmodern lens on how technology facilitates or hinders human communication and collaboration.

In this book, we are pragmatically interested in the *effectiveness* of e-learning, and we will discuss this in detail in subsequent chapters. However, before we do that, we need to clarify what we mean by e-learning artefacts and the e-learning life cycle.

1.5 Types of e-Learning Artefacts

In section 1.2, we introduced the idea of e-learning artefacts, designed instances of technology which can be used as tools to facilitate learning. This section takes that discussion a little further.

e-Learning artefacts have had various forms over the last two (or more) decades. This section outlines some generic types of e-learning artefacts which will be used to illustrate discussion throughout this book. The specific characteristics of each of the generic types lead to variations in the forms of evaluation carried out.

One concept we have used in developing this distinction is in the scale at which the artefact is designed, using the distinction between macro-, meso- and micro-levels of educational design, where the timeframe of use is weeks or months, days or weeks, and minutes or hours, respectively (Goodyear, 2009; Jones, Dirckinck-Holmfeld & Lindström, 2006).

1.5.1 Interactive Learning Systems

As outlined earlier, early e-learning artefacts tended to be monolithic applications which provided content, interaction and navigation within the same product, often delivered on CD-Rom. We will call these sorts of artefacts *interactive learning systems*. Early web-based systems also tended to incorporate content and navigation within a self-contained product, and we characterize these as interactive learning systems as well. Interactive learning systems are still developed and used, but, increasingly, content is sourced from a database rather than being hard-coded. However, these systems are arguably less prevalent than other types of e-learning artefacts. Interactive learning systems tend to be designed for use by individuals (and sometimes small groups) for largely independent learning, where learners interact with the computer and resources on the computer. Interactive learning systems correspond to a meso-level of educational design, typically being used over several weeks to facilitate learning on a particular topic.

Educational games are one particular example of interactive learning systems where there are good theoretical frameworks (e.g. Amory, 2007) and a strong research community. We will not explore games per se, and just note in passing that the frameworks and methods advocated in this book apply very well to games environments.

1.5.2 Generic Learning Tools

A second type of e-learning artefact arose with the development of *generic learning tools*, which can be defined as generic artefacts made up of a set of component tools to enable the management of content and navigation between pages of content. While interactive learning systems are learning environments in themselves, generic learning tools facilitate the design of learning environments. A learning environment might incorporate a number of tools which enable learners to interact with the system (e.g. using online quizzes), and to interact with each other through a range of communication tools.

Commercial and open-source learning-management systems (also called virtual learning environments in the UK) are currently the most widespread examples of generic learning tools. However, other tools with similar characteristics are maturing or emerging, including learning-design/activity-management systems, e-portfolio systems, blogging engines and other Web 2.0 systems.

Generic learning tools tend to support the integration of a range of learning tasks, and tend to reflect the nature of face-to-face learning and teaching activities, where learners interact with online resources, their teachers and other learners.

Generic learning tools correspond to a macro-level of educational design, typically being used over several months to facilitate learning in a unit of study over a semester. They tend to be used in blended learning environments (Littlejohn & Pegler, 2007), mixing online and face-to-face study.

1.5.3 Learning Objects

The third type of e-learning artefact distinguished here is the *learning object*. While there is no commonly agreed definition of learning object – see, for example, Edwards, Rai, Phillips and Fung (2007) – they are generally small, self-contained artefacts, designed to address a specific learning objective, usually a single lesson about a particular concept. They are, therefore, at the micro-level of educational design, tending to be associated with a single learning activity.

Much has been written about learning objects in the first years of the 21st century (e.g. Chapters 7–9 of Conole & Oliver, 2007b; Lockyer, Bennett, Agostinho & Harper, 2009). A driver for the development of learning objects as small, self-contained modules was the difficulty in adapting interactive learning systems for new purposes (repurposing). This hampered the reusability of expensive resources in other contexts. The thinking was that small modules addressing single concepts could be developed that could then be reassembled for use in a variety of contexts.

Learning-object repositories have been developed to facilitate the sharing and reuse of learning objects. Some of these repositories have been established with the explicit aim of widening access to educational resources; the Open University's OpenLearn site (http://openlearn.open.ac.uk) and the Massachusetts Institute of Technology OpenCourseWare site (http://ocw.mit.edu/index.htm) are well-known examples of open educational resource sites. While the term 'open educational resource' has become popular, we will retain the more general term, learning object. Both the Multimedia Educational Resource for Learning and Online Teaching (MERLOT; http://www.merlot.org) and the Digital Library for Earth System Education (DLESE; http://www.dlese.org) repositories have associated user communities that appear to support growth and re-use. However, many repositories have been unsuccessful, for reasons identified in McNaught (2007) and O'Reilly, Lefoe, Philip and Parrish (2010).

Learning objects can be aggregated together into interactive learning systems, or integrated with other learning activities in learning environments facilitated through generic learning tools.

1.6 The e-Learning Artefact Life Cycle

e-Learning is a design field (Reeves, 2006a), and e-learning artefacts need to be designed and developed. The development of e-learning artefacts is a complex, multidisciplinary process, proceeding through multiple design, development and evaluation cycles. The e-learning design and project-management literature (Duncan, 1996; England & Finney, 1999; Howell, 1992; Phillips, 1997) decomposes the development process into a series of steps. One characterization of the development cycle consists of a number of phases:

- analysing the requirements;
- specifying the design;
- development;
- implementation.

At each phase evaluation can lead to revisiting an earlier stage. At some stage in the development cycle, an artefact is deemed to be suitable for widespread use and it is implemented and then maintained through further cycles of development.

However, e-learning evaluation and research can commence at various stages of the e-learning artefact life cycle, with three generic cases. The e-learning artefact may:

- exist only in conceptual form and need to be developed from scratch, with evaluation at each stage;
- have been sourced from a repository, but it is unclear how well it functions in a new context and what modifications may be needed (repurposing);
- have been used in a given context, but it is unclear how well it functions as designed, and there is little rigorous evidence of its effectiveness.

In any case, an e-learning artefact needs to be embedded into a learning environment which encompasses the needs of the learner and the desired learning outcomes. Developing an interactive learning system, or a learning object, may have a more technical focus than developing a learning environment from a generic learning tool. This is because the former two involve developing or repurposing an e-learning artefact, while the use of a generic learning tool focuses attention more explicitly on the design of learning activities. This will be discussed further in Chapter 8.

1.7 Summary

This introductory chapter has provided a broad overview of issues surrounding the evaluation of the effectiveness of e-learning environments. Our primary concern is with learning and our focus is on gathering and interpreting evidence that might assist practitioners and researchers to understand how a range of technologies can be used in constructing effective learning environments. We have discussed various uses of the term e-learning (often in the context of trying to innovate in some aspect of teaching and learning), and described three types of e-learning artefacts: interactive learning systems; generic learning tools; and learning objects. Finally, we have highlighted the cyclical nature of e-learning development and evaluation.

In the next chapter we will explore a pragmatic overview of the evaluation process that we hope will act as a referential framework for the more theoretical and detailed chapters that follow in Part II.

2
Evaluation as Part of a Teacher's Role

This chapter is intended to offer practitioners and early-career researchers a 'taster' of what they can learn from this book. It is meant to set the scene for exploring why and how evaluation of an educational innovation is a normal part of the process of teaching. In addition, we want to demystify evaluation and show that it can be applied in a low-stakes, efficient manner.

2.1 The Process of Evaluation

As human beings, we naturally ask questions about how useful and how valuable our activities are. We can think of evaluation as a process of considerably sharpening this natural activity of checking on our ongoing work. A more formal definition is to think of evaluation as 'providing information to make decisions about the product or process' being investigated.

There is an ongoing argument in this book that evaluation is a multi-faceted activity. Even seemingly simple questions (e.g. 'Does this approach assist learners in understanding real-world applications of X?') are complex in nature and, almost always, multiple methods of data collection are needed in order to get a useful answer. When many people think about evaluating the effect of an e-learning innovation, they think of 'asking the students', usually by giving them a survey. While learners' perceptions about the merit of an e-learning innovation are valuable, they are only one source of data, and relying on perceptions alone can give a false impression.

For example, in a study where groups of learners created their own interactive videos for language learning (De Souza, Fardon & Phillips, 2002), half of the students stated that they had not learned any language through this process. Seen on its own, this perception may have convinced the teaching staff to discontinue the approach. However, other evidence from video 'out-takes' showed that student teams were indeed engaging deeply with the language, but because of the challenge of learning new technology, they were unaware of this.

A further example relates to an interactive videodisk study in the early 1990s (Laurillard, 2002a). Students using this videodisk to study physics were found to perform significantly better in exams than students had in previous years. However, when a subsequent researcher went to ask the students what happened, they said that the videodisk was so bad that they had to get together in self-study groups, and go to the library together, and this was the source of their better performance.

The previous example from the UK is very similar to the experience one of us had in Australia in the late 1990s when online tutorials were just becoming popular. A microeconomics resource pack of textual information in PowerPoint and low-level multiple-choice questions was given very high ratings by the students, who also performed well in examinations. However, in a focus-group meeting, the students admitted that they preferred self-study or study in groups because they found that attending classes with the teacher of the course was unpleasant.

Now, we are *not* advocating poor teaching or poorly designed e-learning environments in order to get learners to develop good study techniques! Rather, we want to emphasize that one needs to probe carefully in an evaluation exercise and seek a number of perspectives, through a number of sources of data. This is illustrated in Figure 2.1. We will return in detail to the strategies for carrying out an evaluation in Part II of the book.

In Chapter 1 we introduced the e-learning artefact life cycle, and this life cycle is a central metaphor throughout the book. Evaluation is a reflective and ongoing process which has a different emphasis at each stage of the e-learning life cycle, but which has the same general steps. The steps are listed briefly below.

- Identify the problem or phenomenon to be investigated.
- Work out some questions to ask.
- Decide who should be asked (the participants).
- Determine the sources of data (evaluation strategies) to be used.
- Develop an evaluation plan.
- Collect data.
- Analyse the data.
- Decide what actions are needed, and make changes to the learning environment.
- Start again.

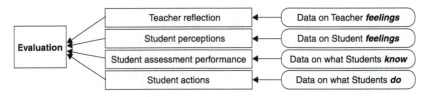

Figure 2.1 Sources of evaluation data.

This can be done with varying levels of formality. It can be done relatively informally, as a reflective practitioner (cf. Foreman-Peck & Winch, 2010), or it can be done as a rigorous evaluation researcher, as we discuss in the remainder of this book.

2.2 Practical and Simple Tips for Your Evaluation

There are many guides to evaluation in the literature. One overview, written by one of us (Phillips & Gilding, 2002), contains a list of practical tips. This list is presented below, together with links to where each aspect is treated in more detail later in the book.

- Take small steps: don't try to understand everything at once.
- Be a reflective practitioner: remember you are evaluating the use of technology-enhanced learning in order to improve your learners' learning experiences and, indirectly, your teaching. *See Chapters 3 and 6.*
- Use a cycle of understanding and improving: think formatively rather than summatively. *See Chapters 4 and 6.*
- Try to understand and be comfortable with your personal paradigm of teaching and learning: question some of the assumptions underpinning the paradigm. *See Chapter 3.*
- Critically question whether your disciplinary research paradigm is applicable to evaluations of the effectiveness of ICT on learning. Often we use traditions that may not be suitable for the new learning environment. *See Chapter 5.*
- Write down why you designed the teaching activities and use of e-learning in the way that you did, and why these are likely to lead to the learning outcomes you require. *See Chapter 8.*
- Think of ways in which your evaluation (research) can go beyond learner perceptions. *See Chapter 4.*
- Use experimental and quasi-experimental techniques cautiously, as they are problematic. It is difficult to keep elements of the learning experience constant between groups and different learning contexts. *See Chapter 6.*
- Evaluate learning in the whole teaching and learning context, not just the ICT itself. *See Chapter 3.*
- Examine not only *what* students learn, but *how* they learn: reflect on the relation between learning process and outcomes. *See Chapters 3 and 8.*
- Focus on questions to ask, and how best to get answers to these questions. *See Chapter 8.*
- Use an evaluation matrix to organize and manage the evaluation study. *See Chapter 8.*
- Start again – remember that teaching with ICT is a craft that we refine over time.

Regarding the final point, it is helpful to see cycles of evaluation as going through phases. The first trial of an innovation might have a key aim of reassuring the teacher that the e-learning artefact works as intended. This can be a 'quick and dirty' evaluation, or it could be more complete and be conceptualized as formative evaluation. The second trial, conceptualized as 'ongoing' evaluation, could be seeking evidence at a deeper level, perhaps questioning the assumptions of cycle 1, perhaps collecting data to inform the teacher's own practice. Further cycles might focus more on data about learning outcomes, and could result in scholarly publication to inform the field of e-learning.

Committed academic teachers take every opportunity to fine-tune their teaching and resources with each new cohort of learners. For a reflective practitioner, a summative evaluation of one offering of a unit often has formative consequences for the next offering.

2.3 How to Start

Before an investigation of the success of an e-learning innovation can begin, both the criteria for success and the questions of interest associated with these criteria need to be clarified. Obviously, one criterion that can be used to judge the effectiveness of an e-learning innovation is student learning. We briefly distinguished in Chapter 1 between learning outcomes (what is ultimately produced in terms of learners' achievement) and the learning processes involved with the learning experience. There is little point in developing courseware and implementing e-learning unless it ultimately encourages learning.

We can contrast questions that have a strong focus on learning processes and learning outcomes with the aims of many evaluation studies published in the literature. That is, in current evaluation studies there is often a reliance on learner opinion (Did they like it?) and insufficient focus on whether the innovation has resulted in a learning enhancement of some kind (Did they learn well in this context? With these resources?). Learners might like an e-learning innovation because it's easy and they don't have to do any work, but this doesn't mean that they learn from it.

If the processes involved in learners achieving learning outcomes are used as criteria of success or effectiveness, we need some way to judge the extent to which outcomes are demonstrated. While a plethora of different research questions can be asked in relation to these criteria, in our experience three questions commonly emerge from educators (lecturers, tutors, curriculum co-ordinators and developers) just starting to investigate the educational effectiveness of e-learning and learning outcomes:

1. How does the (new) innovation using e-learning compare with the old course?
2. What are students learning from the new course?
3. How do students learn from the e-learning components in my course?

When presented with the first question, *How does the (new) innovation using e-learning compare with the old course?*, the topic of interest is whether or not one method of instruction 'out-performs' the other. Traditionally, researchers investigating this question have attempted to compare learning outcomes with or without the e-learning innovation, using experimental designs and randomized controlled trials. There is a popular perception in academia that these approaches are the most desirable and rigorous way to conduct empirical research. In Chapters 4–6, we unpack the characteristics of evaluation and research and identify a range of valid research approaches, of which the randomized controlled trial is just one.

If a change is made to a learning environment, and if an improvement in outcomes is observed after the change, then it is attractive to assume that the improvement can be attributed to that change. However, such clear pathways of causality are hard to establish when considered more deeply.

Let us explore how a comparative study could be designed using a hypothetical example in the area of science education. DNA transcription is a concept which often proves difficult for undergraduate biomedical science students to grasp, and is traditionally taught through a series of lectures. Course co-ordinators in biomedical science thought they might be able to capitalize on the capabilities of multimedia to teach students about the concepts and processes involved in DNA transcription. An e-learning module on DNA transcription was developed, which utilized animations and feedback questions in a learner-centred, self-paced learning environment. After the introduction of the module in the course, the co-ordinators were interested in whether the e-learning module enabled students to understand the concepts and processes associated with DNA transcription better than when they were taught the same content in lectures.

To investigate this question using a randomized controlled experiment, the course co-ordinators would first need to have a solid theoretical framework about how or why multimedia – particularly the use of graphical representations, animations and feedback – would be beneficial to learners who were learning conceptually difficult material. A cohort of biomedical science students could then randomly be divided in two and a comparative study could be performed. One group would receive the 'traditional instruction' and the other would receive the learning module on DNA transcription. Ethical issues would need to be considered here and a 'cross-over' design would need to be employed to ensure all learners received both forms of instruction. Pre- and post-tests could be used to assess learners' understanding, and differences between pre- and post-tests could be used as the dependent variable in a statistical analysis.

While it is feasible to carry out such an experiment, when considered more closely, its value can easily be questioned. If, indeed, the expected difference was found between groups it is very difficult – if not impossible – to attribute this difference to the e-learning module itself. This is because the change that was made to the learning environment was not only associated with the e-learning module. When the new learning program was introduced into the learning environment, a number of other factors that are likely to impact on learning were also changed. These could include, but are not restricted to, the learning design of tasks students were asked to complete, the role of the teachers in the classroom, the amount of interaction between students, and between students and their teachers. Given that these variables were not controlled across groups in the experimental design, it is difficult to make valid comparisons between the two groups. The two groups were effectively experiencing two different learning *systems* rather than experiencing the same system with one variable changed (the e-learning module).

While we will discuss this further in Chapter 6, it is important to recognize that when comparative studies employing experimental designs are used in e-learning research, typically *two different complex learning systems* are being compared (Salomon, 1991). Thus, instead of studying 'patterns of differences', we are studying 'differences in patterns' (Rowe, 1996). In such circumstances, the ultimate goal of experimental studies – to determine causality through the control of variables across treatment and control groups – becomes untenable. This, in large part, accounts for the thousands of previous comparative e-learning studies that have shown no significant difference between the treatment and control groups.

It may, therefore, be more appropriate to ask the second question, *What are students learning from the new course?* This is also predominantly concerned with learning *outcomes*, but without any comparisons. Once again, we need some way to assess what students have learned – their intended learning outcomes. Alternatively, some researchers have investigated unintended learning outcomes, not restricting their research focus to what is desired or expected of learners.

Quantitatively, this question can be addressed through a pre-test/post-test design, usually involving objective test questions, for example, multiple-choice questions. Learners are given a pre-test before they engage with the e-learning environment to test their base knowledge or understanding of the content area. Learners then access the e-learning environment and perform the required learning tasks. When they are finished, learners complete a post-test on the content area. The pre- and post-tests should have close correspondence to ensure the two scores can be validly compared through statistical tests. However, when the topic being studied is conceptually difficult, it may not be simple to develop multiple-choice questions which validly assess learning outcomes in a non-superficial way. Quantitative approaches also rarely reveal how or why a learner reaches a certain understanding.

A more descriptive methodology using qualitative methods could be employed in order to inform the researcher about what learners thought they had learned and what skills learners were seen to develop. It is often valuable to interview learners about what led them to particular understandings.

In this book, we advocate using a mixture of qualitative and quantitative data sources using methods which are most appropriate to the evaluation questions posed. In answering the question of 'what are students learning', we might:

- undertake a peer review of the assessment task to ensure that it appropriately assesses the desired learning outcome;
- analyse learner performance in the assessment, through both individual assessment items and overall grades;
- interview a sample of learners about what they understood and why.

This last consideration takes us into a discussion of the third question, *How do students learn from the e-learning components in my course?* This does not focus so much on the achievement of learning outcomes as on an understanding of the educational *processes* underlying the achievement of these outcomes (or lack thereof). Possible antecedents or concomitants to students' learning outcomes may be drawn from many areas within the learning environment. Many researchers have investigated this question without assessing learning outcomes at all, content to focus their attention on the patterns of relationships between the components of the learning environment – e.g. the characteristics of the learner, the design characteristics of the e-learning environment, and contextual factors.

Largely qualitative approaches are more appropriate to shed light on this question, asking learners what they thought of their learning experience, what they thought was beneficial and supported their learning, and what did not assist them. From techniques such as focus groups, interviews and observations, researchers can build a detailed picture of how learners interacted with the e-learning environment and how elements in the learning environment seemed to affect the learning process. While this approach does not enable the researcher to predict learning outcomes, it does provide a rich analysis of how individual learners interact with the learning environment.

A recurring theme of the preceding discussion is that the learning environment needs to be treated holistically, as a system. This is at odds with many current evaluation studies, where there is an 'atomizing' of the learning under investigation. Looking at learning gains that might occur over an hour or two is rather artificial. Our focus should be on the overall learning experience, and this means being aware of the entire learning context. This implies that teachers need to reflect on the idea that their students' learning may depend on what takes place beyond any individual course or, certainly, individual lessons. It is important to recognize that learning takes place in informal settings, outside of classrooms.

What matters is how learners develop the overall capabilities required in the discipline or context in question, and how a large number of learning experiences work together to assist learners in developing those capabilities. Researching and evaluating e-learning environments in this context is a complex undertaking which this book tries to address.

Despite this complexity, we are not saying that teachers using e-learning approaches should not evaluate their work. There is a place for relatively informal evaluations which can help a teacher to improve their teaching and improve the design of the learning environment.

However, we claim that more rigorous approaches are needed to optimize improvements in learning. Evaluation of learning is a key area of focus in this book and clear evaluation of the ways in which technology might enhance learning is our rationale for writing it.

In order to answer these learning-focused questions, we need to unpack our understanding of a number of aspects of evaluating e-learning. The rest of this book should enable readers to build a solid framework (informed by both theory and practical experience) that they can use for future work in evaluating e-learning.

Chapter 3 unpacks the implications of the statement: Students learn within *learning environments*, going through *learning processes* in order to achieve *learning outcomes*. We will then explore the relationship between educational evaluation and research (Chapter 4) which will lead us to consider in some depth research paradigms and methodologies (Chapter 5). In the final chapter of Part II (Chapter 6) we focus on evaluation and research approaches suitable for e-learning. We suggest that design-based research offers a valuable perspective that suits a pragmatic, mixed-methods approach to evaluation research.

In Part III we focus on the practical conduct of evaluation that is grounded in appropriate theoretical perspectives. An advance organizer for Part III will be at the end of Chapter 6.

II
Theory

3

The Learning Environment, Learning Processes and Learning Outcomes (LEPO) Framework

3.1 Introduction

In section 1.3, we summarized some key characteristics of learning in tertiary contexts, based on a constructivist pedagogical philosophy. Characteristics which we identified included: deep approaches to learning, learning to become experts, transferring knowledge learned to new contexts, the importance of motivation, and the engagement of learners with well-designed learning activities. Nevertheless, despite substantial research over many years about how learners learn, our understanding of that process is incomplete. Educational research has produced a myriad of 'theories' and frameworks – see, for example, Dyke, Conole, Ravenscroft and de Freitas (2007) for a useful discussion. However, many of these are quite narrowly focused, and few of them have broad applicability.

This chapter attempts to lift the 'lens' on learning to a more general level by integrating concepts from other frameworks to arrive at a broad description of what occurs in learning and teaching environments. Our aim is to develop a generalized and integrated conceptual framework for learning, a "metaview of the key themes that emerge ... with specific reference to e-learning" (Dyke et al., 2007, p. 84).

This discussion considers learning in general, but with a 'leaning' towards e-learning, because so much of the current work in learning is associated with the use of various technologies. However, we limit the scope by considering only the higher-education sector. The level of our discussion is broadly within the field of education rather than, for example, cognitive psychology or neuroscience, although these disciplines may enrich the framework once it has been refined at a conceptual level.

Our emphasis is on learning as a process rather than teaching as an activity, but it includes both the activities of teaching and the design of learning environments. Our contention is that there is a lack of clarity about learning in its broadest form. While teachers and teaching have a role in learning, they are only part of the picture.

Most of the learning that students do does not occur in lectures. Very little of it actually occurs when students are face-to-face with their teachers. Students may be involved in worthwhile study activity while they are in lectures (listening carefully, making notes, etc.). But most of the sense-making, conceptual change, development of real understanding, ability to apply knowledge in new situations, honing of skills, etc. – what we really mean by learning – occurs at other times and in other places.

(Goodyear, 2009, p. 9)

3.2 Learning

Learning may be defined as the process of developing a "new ability to do something, and/or an understanding of something that was previously not understood" (Goodyear & Retalis, 2010, p. 6). However, there can be many interpretations of the word 'learning' and these meanings cloud discussion about it. Grammatically, 'learning' has three forms. The first is as a noun, with two distinct definitions in *The Cambridge Online Dictionary* (n.d.):

- "the activity of obtaining knowledge";
- "knowledge obtained by study".

The former definition is clearly related to activities which learners undertake in order to develop their understanding – a process. The latter definition relates to a product or outcome constructed by the learner which can be demonstrated to others as evidence of acquired level(s) of understanding. The noun 'learning' can also function in an adjectival manner (gerund) by modifying another noun, for example, the learning process. Learning can also be used as the present participle of the verb (I am learning), and this present participle can also be used in an adverbial sense (e.g. the learner practised hard, learning how to do a titration). The semantic nuances surrounding 'learning' can lead to different interpretations of what is meant by emergent terms such as e-learning and m-learning, making it difficult to develop a shared understanding of these emerging areas of scholarship.

Learning can be formal, in an educational context where learners take the role of students, working towards some sort of qualification. It can be informal, something which, arguably, all humans do regularly, as they solve problems presented by day-to-day life. Learning may also be implicit, "situations where complex information is acquired effortlessly" (Goodyear & Retalis, 2010, p. 7), such as language learning by young children.

However, it would be inaccurate to claim that only formal learning occurs in an institutional educational context. While many learners at all levels of education attend classes taught by teachers, they also work on their own and in groups outside of class to develop their understanding of the subject area. This is informal learning in a formal setting. Learners at university also informally develop their human capacities, which may or may not be triggered by activities in their formal classes, at coffee shops and other drinking establishments.

3.3 The Learning Environment, Learning Processes and Learning Outcomes (LEPO) Framework

We conceptualize learning as having three components: the environment which facilitates learning (*learning environment*), the activities which are part of learning (*learning processes*) and the knowledge, behaviours, skills or understanding which can be demonstrated (*learning outcomes*). Two general actors interact with these three components, the *learner* and the *teacher*, and all components exist in a broader, *educational context*. For convenience, we have called this the LEPO (Learning Environment, Processes, Outcomes) framework. The interactions between the five elements of the framework are modelled in Figure 3.1. This framework is derived from, and encompasses, existing models of learning as well as research about the characteristics of learners and teachers. The relationship of these other models to the LEPO framework will be discussed in subsequent sections. Each of the five components has its own characteristics, which will also be discussed below.

At the highest level, Figure 3.1 indicates that learning environments facilitate learning processes, and these lead to learning outcomes, which, in turn, determine the learning environment. The model also indicates that teachers design learning environments, facilitate learning processes and assess learning outcomes, while learners work within learning environments, engage in

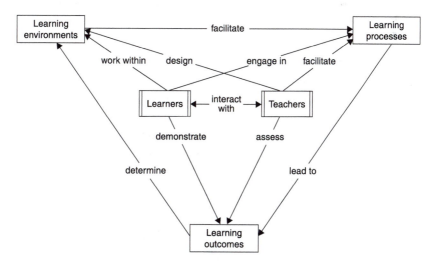

Figure 3.1 Model of the LEPO framework, showing the interrelationships between learning environments, learning processes, learning outcomes, and the roles of learners and teachers.

learning processes and demonstrate learning outcomes, as well as interacting with their teachers.

3.4 The Origins of the LEPO Framework

The LEPO model is informed by a range of work in higher education and e-learning research. However, it draws particularly on five pieces of scholarship:

1. Biggs' Presage, Process, Product (3-P) model (1989);
2. Laurillard's conversational framework (2002b);
3. The Learning-centred Evaluation Framework initially conceived by Bain (1999);
4. Reeves and Reeves' model for interactive learning on the web (1997);
5. Goodyear's problem space of educational design (Ellis & Goodyear, 2010).

These works will be summarized briefly here to provide context for the rest of the discussion.

3.4.1 Biggs' 3-P Model

Biggs (1989) conceived of learning as having three components: Presage, Process and Product, which can be broadly interpreted as what happens before, during and after learning. The Presage component has two aspects, 'student factors' and 'teaching context', while the process and product components are analogous to the learning processes and learning outcomes components of the LEPO framework.

3.4.2 Laurillard's Conversational Framework

Laurillard's conversational framework (2002b) approaches learning pragmatically, arguing that there are four main aspects of learning and teaching:

Discussion	between the teacher and learner at the level of descriptions;
Interaction	between the learner and the teacher, mediated by tasks and resources designed by the teacher;
Adaptation	of the learning environment by the teacher and action by the learner;
Reflection	on the learner's performance by both teacher and learner.

Phillips and Luca (2000) extended this model to include discussions between learners. A revision of the extended framework is provided in Figure 3.2. Laurillard's schema is based on forming an information-rich environment in which the learner is able to discover knowledge, but the discovery is supported

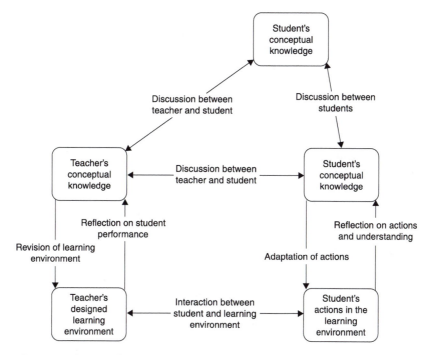

Figure 3.2 The extended Laurillard conversational framework.

and scaffolded by extra guidance functions which provide support and feedback for subsequent learning.

Teachers and learners are explicit in Laurillard's model. Furthermore, the left-hand side of Figure 3.2 has similarities to the learning environment; the right hand-side represents learning outcomes, and the arrows correspond to learning processes.

3.4.3 Learning-centred Evaluation Framework

Bain (1999) proposed a framework for evaluating the effectiveness of e-learning, based on earlier work by Alexander and Hedberg (1994), and later developed by Reeves and Hedberg (2003), that mapped phases of evaluation to the phases of an e-learning development project. Bain's (1999) innovation was to add a second dimension, that of the learning environment, learning processes and learning outcome, in planning research and evaluation into e-learning. This work was subsequently extended under the name Learning-centred Evaluation Framework by Phillips, Bain, McNaught, Rice and Tripp (2000).

In this work, we have extended our earlier work to more holistically incorporate elements of other frameworks, and to better account for the complexity of current e-learning environments.

3.4.4 Reeves Model for Interactive Learning on the Web

Reeves and Reeves (1997) proposed a model for interactive learning on the web which shares many similarities with the LEPO framework and with Biggs' 3-P model. This model is summarized in Table 3.1. It posits that learners bring certain attributes to their study (a set of input conditions analogous to the learner characteristics in the LEPO model) and engage in learning processes; this engagement results in an output (learning outcomes in the LEPO framework).

Table 3.1 Components of the Reeves and Reeves (1997) 'Process model of interactive learning on the web'

Input	Process	Output
Cultural habits of mind	Opportunity to construct learning	Knowledge and skills
Aptitude and individual differences	Task ownership	Robust mental models
Origin of motivation	Sense of audience Collaborative support Teacher support Metacognitive support	Higher-order outcomes

3.4.5 Goodyear's Problem Space of Educational Design

Goodyear and colleagues have been investigating new conceptions of educational design: "the set of practices involved in constructing representations of how people should be helped to learn in various circumstances" (Goodyear & Retalis, 2010, p. 10). The logical evolution of this model is described in Ellis and Goodyear (2009). Learning processes are central to this scheme, through various activities which lead to learning outcomes. Learning activities are supported by learning tasks and tools and artefacts, and through social interactions with people. The activity takes place in a study situation (an educational context) and it is supported through extrinsic and intrinsic feedback. Goodyear uses the concept of an activity system to refer to the complex interaction of learners and teachers with learning environments, processes and outcomes. While most elements of the LEPO framework are represented in the Goodyear model, the teacher is only peripherally present.

Given this background on the LEPO framework, we will now examine its components in detail.

3.5 Components of the LEPO Framework

3.5.1 Learning Environment

The learning environment provides the context in which the learner works. It is informed by the desired learning outcomes, and it specifies the content and resources (both traditional and electronic) which support this design. It also encompasses physical and virtual spaces, and the nature of any e-learning artefacts. In addition, the learning environment specifies the teacher's design of the learning and assessment tasks which will facilitate the learning processes undertaken by learners.

The learning environment as conceived here draws from the 'teaching context'/situational aspect of the presage component of Biggs' 3-P model, although it is arguably broader. The learning environment is also analogous with the 'designed learning environment' component of Laurillard's (2002b) conversational framework.

The learning environment should be designed with the characteristics of the learners it is designed for in mind – this aspect will be explored below. The learning environment shares characteristics with what Goodyear and Ellis (2010) termed *teaching-as-design*, "the planning work involved in setting good learning tasks, creating supportive learning environments and helping learners share their efforts in learning teams or learning communities" (pp. 110–111).

An overarching characteristic of learning environments is that they are designed, in line with the Goodyear model, and they can therefore be described. Sometimes this description is informal, and sometimes it is detailed. When a learning environment is well defined, it is easier to evaluate whether it functions as it was designed, and therefore whether it can lead to its desired outcomes (cf. Chapter 8). However, a degree of flexibility is essential in order to support individual learners' learning needs, and allow useful unintended outcomes to be explored.

As noted in section 1.5, the learning environment may be specified at macro-, meso- or micro-levels of design, depending on the timeframe of the planned activities. At the macro-level, the learning environment is typically expressed in a 'study guide', a document which specifies the overarching activities and context of a unit of study, including the desired learning outcomes, assessment activities and deadlines, and content to be covered. At a meso-level, the learning environment may specify a particular learning task in detail. For example, an experiment or field trip which may run over several days might be described in a laboratory manual. At a micro-level, learners may engage with an e-learning simulation which covers a conceptually difficult area. The design of this simulation would typically be specified in detail, while learners would also be given specific guidance about how to use and interact with it, including the tasks they are required to undertake.

Apart from issues of timescale, consideration of these three levels leads us to a second distinction between elements of the learning environment. These are between the *curriculum design* (in this case at a macro-level: the context, desired learning outcomes, assessment and content), the *learning design* (the meso-level specification of one learning task) and the *design of any learning object type e-learning artefacts* (in this case at a micro-level). This three-way distinction will be useful in Chapter 8.

In a nutshell, the curriculum focuses on what to learn, and the learning design focuses on how the curriculum can be taught, especially on what learning tasks the learners engage in.

3.5.1.1 CURRICULUM DESIGN

Curriculum is yet another contested term in educational discourse (Fraser & Bosanquet, 2006). Conole and Oliver distinguished between four uses of the term:

1. curriculum as 'content' (syllabus);
2. curriculum as plan (either at the level of lesson or course);
3. curriculum as planned process (pedagogy);
4. the hidden curriculum (political or value-based influences that remain unstated).

(Oliver, 2003, cited in Conole, Oliver, Littlejohn & Harvey, 2007, p. 102)

Hicks (2007) reviewed different meanings of the term, reporting that curriculum encompasses what is to be learned, why it is to be learned, where and when it is to be learned and how it is to be assessed. He also included a further element under 'curriculum': how what is to be learned is planned to be taught. We choose to treat that element as a separate, *learning design* component of the learning environment.

Hicks leaned towards a definition of curriculum which encompassed the whole educational environment, that is, all aspects of the LEPO framework, recognizing that others use 'curriculum' to refer to a coherent set of units/courses across a degree program (e.g. the undergraduate curriculum).

In this work, we use 'curriculum' as Bain (1999) did, constraining it to that part of the learning environment which specifies the context, the desired learning outcomes, assessment tasks and content.

3.5.1.2 LEARNING DESIGN

In section 1.3, we highlighted the importance of tasks and learning activities in developing deep understanding in learners. We need carefully to review some terms here in order to facilitate productive discussion later. In Chapter 1 we defined learning tasks (what the teacher designs) and learning activities (what the learner actually does) as being interactions between a learner and an environment.

Beetham (2004), Goodyear (2009) and Oliver (1999) all conceived of an interlinking between tasks, content and context, resources and tools. The design of learning tasks forms a crucial part of the learning environment. As we suggested above, we use the term *learning design* to refer to this design process. Bain (1999) called this the *teaching for learning* analysis.

Learning design is at the centre of Goodyear's (2009) framework for educational design. This framework draws on the content and resources specified in the curriculum-design phase, and specifies the learning tasks that we wish learners to engage with. Modelling languages and systems (Botturi & Stubbs, 2008; Dalziel, 2003; IMS Global Learning Consortium, 2010) have emerged to specify learning designs as time-sequenced activities performed by *actors*, typically learners and teachers. Goodyear and Retalis (2010) have taken this idea further with their work on *design patterns* and *pattern languages*. Similarly, Conole et al. (2007) have presented a detailed taxonomy of learning activities to assist in the development of a shared vocabulary around learning designs.

The point we want to make here is that learning design is an important part of the learning environment, no matter how it is specified.

3.5.1.3 DESIGN OF AN e-LEARNING ARTEFACT

Learning design considers the embedding of tasks within the entire learning environment. Some of those tasks may be facilitated by e-learning artefacts. As discussed in section 1.6, sometimes an e-learning artefact may already exist, either as a generic learning tool or as a learning object sourced from elsewhere. In other cases, the e-learning artefact may not exist at the start of an e-learning development project, and its behaviour needs to be specified as part of the design of the e-learning environment. We will return to this aspect of the learning environment in Chapter 8.

In summarizing the components of the learning environment, we turn to the work of Reeves (2006b) who identified eight critical factors impacting on the success of a learning environment: (1) goals; (2) content; (3) instructional design; (4) learner tasks; (5) instructor roles; (6) student roles; (7) technological affordances; and (8) assessment. The first two of these are associated with curriculum design; the seventh with the design of an e-learning artefact; and the others with the learning design.

3.5.2 Learning Processes

In section 3.5.1.2, we began to unpack a conceptual overlap between learning tasks designed as part of the learning environment, and the use of those learning tasks by learners – in other words, learning activities. Learning activities are the ways in which learners engage with the learning environment and the learning tasks embedded in it. But what is the relationship between learning activities and learning processes?

Goodyear's work is helpful in distinguishing between *studying* and *internal learning processes*. Studying is a "set of real-world [learning] activities in which people engage, for the purposes of intentional learning" (Goodyear & Retalis, 2010, p. 8). This is contrasted with the process definition of learning presented in section 3.2: "a set of psychological processes which lead to greater competence or understanding" (p. 8). Goodyear and Retalis posited that "learning processes are tightly bound up with" (p. 12), but are not the same as, studying activity.

There are, therefore, two ways that *learning processes* will be used in this book – the activity of intentional *studying*, and *internal* cognitive processing. We call these contextual learning processes and cognitive learning processes, respectively. Contextual learning processes refer to what the learner actually does, whether intended or not – in other words, participation in learning activities. This includes: interaction with the learning environment; engagement with designed learning tasks; how this engagement occurs (e.g. individually, in groups, as directed by the teacher); and self-directed review and reflection activities.

Cognitive learning processes refer to all cognitive activities that contribute to learning (e.g. problem solving, reflection). They are fundamentally at the level of personal activity, whether through individual cognitive activities or through social engagement with others (Bransford et al., 1999).

We will attempt to be clear about which of these two connotations of learning process we are using as we refer to these concepts in future sections and chapters.

The learning process component of the LEPO framework incorporates the 'approaches to study' component of the 3-P model (Biggs, 1989, 1993). It also draws heavily on Laurillard's (2002b) conversational framework, where learners engage with ideas/concepts/resources to: develop conceptual knowledge; interact with the learning environment designed by their teacher; and discuss their conceptions with their teachers and other learners. The idea of 'learning process' is a core part of Reeves and Reeves' (1997) process dimension, and of Goodyear's (2009) model in the interaction elements around the problem space.

The range of activities characterized as learning processes in the LEPO framework is quite broad. Learning activities can be either teacher-centred or learner-centred, depending on the intentions of the teacher, and formal (learning or assessment activities) or informal. Indeed, the formal teacher-designed tasks are often blended by learners with their own informal ways of studying and thinking. Some examples of learning tasks and activities that clarify this point are:

- participating in lectures, laboratories, tutorials and other scheduled classes;
- participating in group activities in small or large classes;
- listening to lecture recordings;
- doing (and perhaps repeating) formative self-tests;
- preparing assignments for formative or summative assessment;
- taking part in structured discussion activities;
- engaging in individual study/revision;
- doing exercises and examples;

- pre-reading for classes;
- discussing study topics in a learning common room, coffee shop or garden;
- discussing aspects of study.

Learning processes may also be helpfully categorized in terms of the types of interaction learners have within the LEPO framework. Learners can interact with their teachers, other learners and with the learning environment itself (whether through interaction with resources, learning tasks or e-learning artefacts) (Anderson, 2005; Phillips, 2004).

Teaching can assist learners to be more metacognitive and self-regulatory (Bransford et al., 2000). One important role of the teacher in higher education is to assist learners to develop these and other generic lifelong learning skills. Metacognitive strategies, where learners reflect on their actions and understandings, and adapt them accordingly, are also part of the learning process (Laurillard, 2002b). Thus, a useful learning environment is one where the e-learning artefacts (which the examples above show can be very varied in design) support learners to engage in learning activities that will, hopefully, result in the achievement of desired learning outcomes.

3.5.3 Learning Outcomes

For the last decade there has been a wave of writing about '21st-century' skills, often also called 21st-century literacies. Learning 'wish lists' now cover a wide range of desired learning outcomes – for example, discipline-based conceptual knowledge, professional skills, IT and media literacies, independent learning skills, ability to understand and internalize societal beliefs and values, lifelong learning skills, etc. Shulman (2005) coined the phrase "pedagogies of uncertainty" to describe the need for more open learning designs that can assist learners to achieve an ever-growing set of desired learning outcomes.

Learning outcomes refer to the things learners are able to demonstrate as a result of their engagement in a course of study. The term 'learning outcome' is often not used precisely in higher-education practice. There is a fuzziness in the distinction between 'learning outcomes' and 'learning objectives'. At times, both seem to be used interchangeably. Semantically, objectives are what it is intended that learners are able to do after a course of study, and outcomes are what learners can actually do.

Allan (1996, p. 107) analysed the history of these terms and distinguished three types of learning outcomes:

1. Subject-based outcomes, which subsume learning objectives and which are complex, discipline-based, [and] capable of being assessed.
2. Personal transferable outcomes, including acting independently, working with others, using information technology, gathering information, communicating effectively, organizational skills.

3. Generic academic outcomes, [such as] making use of information, thinking critically, analysing, synthesizing ideas and information.

The first of these is discipline-specific, while the others are generic. We will treat them separately below.

Learning outcomes are an explicit part of the Goodyear problem-space model (section 3.4.5). While they are a component of the Biggs 3-P (as 'product') and Reeves (as 'output') models, they are not as well developed in those. Learning outcomes are represented on the right-hand side of Laurillard's conversational framework, at the learner's 'conceptual knowledge' and 'experiential world'.

3.5.3.1 DISCIPLINE-SPECIFIC OUTCOMES

According to Allan (1996) and Eisner (1979), there is little distinction between subject-based outcomes and learning objectives, other than the distinction between intention and demonstration noted above. They took them to be broad enough to enable deep learning and specific enough to be assessable. This contrasts with an earlier use of 'learning objective' in a narrow, behavioural sense. Because this narrow perception of the term is still prevalent, we have chosen to use the terms *learning outcome(s)* and *desired learning outcome(s)* in this book.

Learning outcomes correspond to the 'knowledge obtained by study' definition of learning given in section 3.2. It is the product of student learning processes. But what is 'knowledge' in this context? Without delving too far into epistemology, and starting with an everyday source, the wikipedia definition is helpful: "Learning is acquiring new knowledge, behaviours, skills, values, preferences or understanding, and may involve synthesizing different types of information."

This definition encompasses different dimensions of 'knowing', and various classification schemes (taxonomies) have been developed to identify levels of knowledge and understanding. Two will be discussed here: Bloom's cognitive, psychomotor and affective domains; and Biggs' SOLO taxonomy.

Bloom's cognitive, psychomotor and affective domains. Bloom's work has been widely used in education. He categorized cognitive and conceptual understandings (cognitive domain: Anderson & Krathwohl, 2001; Bloom, 1956; Krathwohl, 2002); physical behaviours and skills (psychomotor domain: Harrow, 1972); and professional skills, a range of literacies and learning skills, as well as societal beliefs and values (affective domain: Krathwohl, Bloom & Masia, 1964).

The original Bloom's taxonomy (1956) has been revised to account for a richer understanding of 'knowledge' (Anderson & Krathwohl, 2001; Krathwohl, 2002). It now distinguishes between four forms of knowledge: *factual knowledge, conceptual knowledge, procedural knowledge* and *metacognitive knowledge,* as a second dimension against a revised first dimension of cognitive reasoning, which, in increasing levels of complexity, involves *remembering, understanding, applying, analysing, evaluating* and *creating*. Anderson and Krathwohl (2001) described factual knowledge as "knowledge of discrete, isolated content elements"; conceptual knowledge as involving "more complex, organized knowledge forms"; procedural knowledge as "knowledge of how to do something"; and metacognitive knowledge as involving "knowledge about cognition in general as well as awareness of one's own cognition" (p. 27).

Biggs' SOLO taxonomy. The 'Structure of Observed Learning Outcomes' (SOLO) taxonomy (Biggs, 1999; Biggs & Collis, 1982) is a systematic way of describing levels of performance. More than Bloom's taxonomy, it focuses on the quality of the work learners produce when they are trying to solve problems or explain complex concepts.

The SOLO taxonomy describes a learner's understanding of a subject in five levels of increasing complexity. We have used a simplified set of labels for the levels originally devised by Biggs.

Single point. Little recognition of appropriate concept or relevant processing of information.

Multiple unrelated points. Preliminary processing but question not approached appropriately.

Intermediate. Some aspects of question addressed but no relationship shown between facts or concepts.

Logically related answer. Several concepts are integrated so coherent whole has meaning.

Unanticipated extension. Coherent whole is generalized to a higher level of abstraction.

No matter which taxonomy is chosen, subject-based outcomes should require demonstration of the range of specified knowledge and skills. This is discussed further in Chapter 8.

3.5.3.2 Generic Learning Outcomes

Generic learning outcomes are also called variously generic skills, graduate attributes, 21st-century skills and competencies.

The contemporary world requires university graduates to have a range of other skills to be successful knowledge workers and citizens. These are Allan's (1996) personal transferable and generic academic outcomes, including a range of interpersonal skills, literacies and learning skills. Learning skills texts (cf. Marshall, 2006; Marshall & Rowland, 2006) place a strong emphasis on developing capabilities such as organizational, planning and time-management skills, as well as critical thinking and metacognitive skills. These generic learning outcomes combine with subject-based knowledge to produce the 'expertise' of a graduate (Bransford et al., 1999). However, Barrie (2005) recognized "that some generic outcomes are complex interwoven aspects of human ability, which are difficult to explicitly teach or assess in traditional university experiences" (p. 3). These include societal beliefs and values, lifelong learning skills and ethical perspectives.

Studies of the effectiveness of e-learning may also be concerned with the intended or unintentional development of generic skills in learners.

3.5.4 Learners

When undertaking educational research it is easy to view learners as a homogenous group, rather than as individual human beings with distinct lives outside of their study commitments. The LEPO framework recognizes that learners have individual characteristics that can influence how they learn. Some of the models described above, particularly Biggs' 3-P model, explicitly recognize that learners bring their existing, individual characteristics, prior knowledge, needs, motivations and expectations into the context of their learning.

The research literature in educational psychology has contributed greatly to our understanding of how individual characteristics can impact on learning processes and outcomes. For example, in the area of achievement motivation, Pintrich and Schrauben (1992) developed a social cognitive model of learner motivation that recognizes "students' beliefs (cognitions, perceptions) about themselves and [that] the task or classroom environments act as mediators of their [learning] behaviour" (p. 151). More specifically, Pintrich and Schrauben identified attributes such as self-efficacy, task value, achievement goals and locus of control as important contributors to students' involvement in learning. Like other researchers who have developed models of students' approaches to learning (cf. Biggs, 1989, 1993; Entwistle, Hanley & Hounsell, 1979), Pintrich and Schrauben do not see these characteristics as fixed entities, but rather as predispositions that are able to change according to the attributes and features of a specific social and educational context.

In addition to these more intra-individual characteristics, learners come to university with their own unique set of circumstances and situations. Learners' socio-economic background, their familial and cultural history, their current employment and living situation, and their relationship status may all influence their beliefs about how they should engage with university learning and how they should operate in various educational contexts.

It is, of course, impossible to account for the large range of individual learner characteristics while evaluating e-learning in higher education. Nonetheless, it is important to recognize the diversity inherent in learner cohorts and, where possible, actively build this knowledge into research and evaluation studies through the use of theoretically based quantitative or qualitative approaches. Moreover, exploratory strategies that use methods such as interviews and focus groups are often particularly useful in uncovering complex individual learner characteristics and their possible impact on learners' learning experiences.

3.5.5 Teachers

The role of teachers in learning environments has also tended to be downplayed in some educational research. However, the LEPO framework foregrounds the role of teachers, recognizing their role in *designing* learning environments, *facilitating* learning processes and *assessing* learning outcomes.

The LEPO framework views the term 'teacher' broadly. It should not be interpreted to mean a single teacher; it can include teams of teachers and/or tutors, as well as people supporting teachers (teaching assistants, librarians, e-learning advisors and instructional/educational designers).

Teachers are explicitly present on the left side of the Laurillard model (Figure 3.2), in the design and improvement of the learning environment. The 3-P model also sees a role for teachers as designers of the learning environment. Goodyear and Ellis (2010) foregrounded the concept of teaching as design. They accepted the constructivist view that a modern teacher should be a 'guide on the side' to facilitate learning, but they proposed an expanded design role, which they called a 'team with a scheme', a role which they claim might be difficult to fulfil individually.

The Laurillard and Reeves models both acknowledge that the teacher has a role to facilitate understanding by learners. However, the role of teachers as assessors of learning outcomes is not explicit in any of the models.

Beliefs about how teaching is done at university are deeply entrenched in the university worldview (Ballard & Clanchy, 1988), and these beliefs are often accepted uncritically. Just as we have emphasized individual differences between learners, we need to acknowledge in our evaluation designs that university teachers have a wide range of beliefs about, and approaches to, teaching. Unfortunately, there is insufficient debate and recognition of this rich diversity in many universities and a didactic approach to teaching is often uncritically accepted as the norm.

Many university staff have limited teaching experience when they start to teach, and they tend to teach as they were taught. Developing from a background in disciplinary research, many will have deep contextual knowledge and expertise, but may have variable expertise in teaching. Bransford et al. (2000) found that disciplinary expertise was no guarantee of ability to teach others about their area of expertise. As well as varying abilities in explaining core concepts, teachers have varying abilities to perform in class and to motivate learners to learn.

There are numerous lists of principles of good teaching. Chickering and Gamson's (1987) set of seven principles for good practice in undergraduate education is a classic, often-cited example. Such lists have been found to work cross-culturally (e.g. Kember, Ma, McNaught & 18 exemplary teachers, 2006;

Kember & McNaught, 2007) and have usefully informed decades of academic staff development.

However, lists such as these are often silent on beliefs about teaching. Indeed, Biggs is quite explicit that his model of curriculum alignment (e.g. Biggs, 2003) is 'neutral' with respect to indicating any 'preferred' conceptions about what constitutes good teaching. The personal beliefs and mental models of lecturers (Bain & McNaught, 2006; Pratt & Associates, 1998; Steel, 2009) strongly influence the ways that teachers structure their learning environments and facilitate the embedded learning processes. The relationship between beliefs and practice is complex and not linear. Bain and McNaught's (2006) analysis of 22 cases of teachers who successfully used technology in higher education resulted in five belief–practice clusters – ranging from 'thoughtful instructors' to 'situated knowledge negotiators'. They concluded that "dichotomous descriptions appear to be insufficient if we want to understand how teachers interpret the possibilities of using technology in their teaching and then make decisions about how they might actually use technology" (p. 111). For any teacher, it is the coherence between beliefs and practice that seems crucial: each teacher needs to operate within an educational scenario that he or she personally understands and feels comfortable in. Within this 'comfort zone' there is a broad range of strategies that might support the successful design of effective learning environments.

3.5.6 The Educational Context

The learning and teaching activities embodied in the LEPO framework exist within a broader educational context, described by Cobb, Confrey, DiSessa, Lehrer and Schauble (2003, p. 9) as "a learning ecology – a complex interacting system involving multiple elements of different types and levels". Its characteristics include the campus setting (with both physical and policy dimensions), the structure of the degree program and the learner's individual units of study. While most studies on evaluating the effectiveness of student learning remain within the ambit of the formal curriculum, Ellis and Goodyear's (2009) metaphor of an ecosystem – echoing Cobb et al.'s (2003) earlier ecological reference – enables the wider context of the university to be seen as naturally linked to the formal curriculum experience of learners.

The organizational layers that pertain to understanding the totality of the educational context are:

- specifically designed courses within discipline-oriented programs;
- the departmental milieu in which local policies, priorities of the departmental head or chairperson, and views of colleagues interrelate;
- the university-level environment where strategic vision, funding models, infrastructure, computing facilities, technical support, and policies related to e-learning all have influence;

- the nature of the institution in terms of whether it is on-campus, distance, branded as elite and/or has a strong focus on equity groups, etc.;
- deeper institutional identity enacted in governance structures – for example, whether a corporate or collegial identity exists (McNaught & Vogel, 2006);
- the wider political and governmental context of the country or nation.

We will return to these broad issues in Chapter 11 when we consider the sustainability of e-learning innovations, and how the results of evaluation studies at a local level can work together with institutional research to inform the development of coherent and useful policies on the role of e-learning for the support of learning and development.

3.6 Synergies with the LEPO Framework

The LEPO framework, while attempting to incorporate all aspects of learning, is pedagogically inclusive, in that it does not prescribe how learners and teachers interact with learning environments, processes and outcomes. At the same time, it is a very broad framework, enabling the inclusion of other models and frameworks as subsets of the LEPO 'whole'. In this section, we consider how other pedagogical frameworks map onto the LEPO framework.

Other approaches, which focus on deep construction of knowledge, also fit within the LEPO framework. Brown, Collins and Duguid (1989) proposed a model of teaching based on "the notion of learning knowledge and skills in contexts that reflect the way the knowledge will be useful in real life" (p. 2). This *situated learning* model (also called cognitive apprenticeship) has been extended in recent years by the notion of authentic learning (Herrington & Oliver, 2000; Herrington, Reeves & Oliver, 2009) with the following characteristics:

- provide authentic contexts that reflect the way the knowledge will be used in real life;
- provide authentic activities;
- provide access to expert performances and the modelling of processes;
- provide multiple roles and perspectives;
- support collaborative construction of knowledge;
- promote reflection to enable abstractions to be formed;
- promote articulation to enable tacit knowledge to be made explicit;
- provide coaching and scaffolding by the teacher at critical times;
- provide for authentic assessment of learning within the tasks.

These characteristics provide particular guidance for the design of the learning environment, particularly in terms of learning design and the types of tasks chosen, and the role of the teacher in supporting those tasks.

Not all learning problems can be treated using an authentic or 'apprentice-ship' model. In abstract fields it is not sensible to use a situated-learning approach. For example, we cannot experience a chemical reaction at the molecular scale, so we cannot simulate this real-world environment. The 'cognitive flexibility theory' (Spiro, Coulson, Feltovich & Anderson, 1988) shares some similarities with situated learning, but it is applicable to abstract situations. Cognitive flexibility theory advocates:

- using multiple knowledge representations;
- linking abstract concepts in cases to depict knowledge in use;
- demonstrating the conceptual interconnectedness or web-like nature of complex knowledge;
- emphasizing knowledge assembly rather than reproductive memory;
- introducing both conceptual complexity and domain complexity early.

Once again, these are characteristics of the learning environment, specifically of the learning design. The situated-learning, authentic-learning and cognitive-flexibility models fit within the LEPO framework. They simply provide more detailed prescription about how particular learning environments might be designed to suit particular contexts. We would argue that this is the case for other conceptual learning frameworks.

3.7 Summary

This chapter has presented a generalized and integrated conceptual framework for learning, with five components: the learning environment, learning processes, learning outcomes, learner characteristics and teacher characteristics. The LEPO framework is broad and pedagogically inclusive; it covers a range of contexts, and it is consistent with, and encompasses, other frameworks of learning. We do not claim that the LEPO framework supersedes other models of learning; each of the others has its own foci and strengths. What it does, however, is provide a view of learning which integrates elements of other conceptual models in one generalized framework.

The LEPO framework can contribute to improved educational design of learning and teaching environments, by focusing attention on all aspects of learning, while allowing educational designers to choose specific strategies most appropriate to the learning context.

At the same time, the LEPO framework can contribute to more rigorous educational research and evaluation. The LEPO framework is conceptual, not theoretical – it is non-predictive (see Chapter 5). However, specific predictive theories could be embedded within LEPO and tested in its context, which holistically considers the whole learning and teaching environment. We will return to the LEPO framework in Chapter 8, when we discuss the specifics of evaluating e-learning across the e-learning life cycle.

But, first, we want to explore what we mean by evaluating the effectiveness of e-learning. This is the subject of the next chapter.

4

What is Meant by Educational Evaluation and Research?

4.1 Introduction

Now that we've described the LEPO framework, let's examine the process of evaluation in more detail. In section 1.4, we summarized various evaluation scenarios in higher education, concluding that our focus in this book is on evaluating the effectiveness of e-learning, but not evaluating strategic initiatives, selecting products or resources, evaluating teaching quality, nor evaluating the sustainability of broader e-learning initiatives.

This chapter provides a brief overview of the literature on evaluation, with a summary of *program evaluation*, and some definitions that will be helpful in the presentation of the following arguments. Similarly, we review various approaches to evaluation, which then support our subsequent and more specific discussion of e-learning evaluation across the e-learning life cycle. This analysis will establish that there is clearly a research component to studies that consider the effectiveness of e-learning. This leads us into a discussion of how 'research' is interpreted differently in different disciplines, and an analysis of the broad types of research which are appropriate for e-learning. This sets the scene for further discussion of this issue in Chapter 6.

4.2 Educational Evaluation

As we noted in Chapter 2, human beings naturally ask questions about how valuable their activities are. We can think of evaluation as a process of considerably sharpening this natural activity of checking on our ongoing work. Chapter 1 introduced the idea that the term 'evaluation' is used in different ways in different contexts. This chapter takes that discussion a little further by seeking to unpack the characteristics of evaluation in an education context, in order to identify clearly the scope of this work, and discuss overlaps with other areas of scholarship.

4.2.1 Defining Educational Evaluation

There are numerous definitions of 'evaluation' in the literature and it can be difficult to find a universally accepted view of what it is. Regardless, most definitions of evaluation encompass notions of making judgements about the value or worth of something. For example, the Joint Committee on Standards for Educational Evaluation defined evaluation as the "systematic investigation of the worth or merit of an object" (1994). With such a definition there is an implication that judgements are made against a pre-defined set of standards or criteria. A drawback of this assumption is that unanticipated issues which arise from any enterprise are in danger of being overlooked if evaluation is based on preordained criteria. More recent definitions have gone beyond 'merit or worth' to encompass "production of knowledge based on systematic enquiry to assist decision-making" (Owens, 2006, p. 18.) about whatever is being evaluated. A further definition that we find useful because it recognizes the stages of a project is: "Evaluation is any activity that throughout the planning and delivery of innovative programmes enables those involved to learn and make judgements about the starting assumptions, implementation processes and outcomes of the innovation concerned" (Stern, 1990, cited in Jackson, 1998).

Evaluation is an applied form of social research, "the primary purpose of which is not to discover new knowledge, as is the case with basic research, but to study the effectiveness with which existing knowledge is used to inform and guide practical action" (Clarke & Dawson, 1999, p. 2). Evaluation employs research techniques as a means of systematically generating the necessary information, and uses similar criteria to judge the quality of the evidence. However, it differs from other forms of social research in its audience, goals and its practical orientation (Clarke & Dawson, 1999; Trochim, 2006), as well as in making judgements about the value of what is being evaluated.

One of the more common evaluation approaches is called *program evaluation* which has a substantial literature base, particularly in the USA (cf. Clarke & Dawson, 1999; Guba & Lincoln, 1989; Owen, 2006; Patton, 1990, 1997; Payne, 1994; Worthen, Sanders & Fitzpatrick, 1997). Program evaluation is typically used to systematically evaluate initiatives – or programs – that are large-scale activities designed to elicit broad changes in society. For example, a program evaluation may be used to determine the value and worth of initiatives in public health or the criminal justice system, and the example of an institution gathering evidence about the implementation its e-learning strategic plan provided in section 1.4 is a case of program evaluation within education.

While our explanation of program evaluation could suggest that most educational evaluations will fit within this approach, this is not the case, as not all educational innovations can be seen as 'programs'. For example, many e-learning initiatives are more specific in their focus and are better considered as relatively discrete *projects* rather than broad educational programs. Projects are temporary activities, with fixed end-dates and budgets and specific goals to produce a single deliverable (Baume, Martin & Yorke, 2002). Projects can vary in scale. Developments in interactive learning systems may involve substantial amounts of funding over years, while some learning environments produced with generic learning tools may be developed by individual practitioners with minimal funding and a lack of formality. Even though program and project evaluations may use similar methods, the questions asked of ongoing programs are likely to be different from those asked about individual educational innovation projects.

4.2.2 Types of Evaluation

Many different judgements can be made in evaluation, which has led to a range of evaluation types and models, each with different goals. We will not discuss these in detail here and interested readers are directed to standard textbooks on this topic (for example, Worthen et al., 1997). However, we think it would be useful to introduce briefly some general types of evaluation that will underpin the development of our arguments in later chapters.

A long-standing distinction in evaluation has been between *formative* and *summative* evaluation (Worthen et al., 1997). The fundamental goal of formative evaluation is to provide information to refine and improve the object being studied. Formative evaluation looks for weaknesses in the design of an innovation and in the processes associated with its implementation. In an e-learning context, this information can assist the ongoing design, development and implementation process. Summative evaluations focus on the outcomes of the innovation (project) and seek to determine a project's value and worth by determining "its overall effectiveness or impact" (Clarke & Dawson, 1999, p. 8). Evaluators have found the characterizing of these two types of evaluation helpful in the context of the e-learning life cycle, as one type can be aligned with the design and development of innovation (formative) and the other can aligned with an innovation after it has been implemented and used (summative).

However, this simple dichotomy has been found to be inadequate for the complexity of modern evaluation practice and the multifaceted nature of e-learning. A number of researchers have developed taxonomies that delineate different types of evaluation of e-learning (Alexander & Hedberg, 1994; Bain, 1999; Draper, Brown, Henderson & McAteer, 1996; Gunn, 1999; Phillips et al., 2000; Reeves, 1989; Reeves & Hedberg, 2003; Reeves & Lent, 1984). The nature of these taxonomies is illustrated by some examples. Reeves (1989) suggested six levels of evaluation which include project documentation, assessment of the worth of project objectives, formative evaluation, immediate effectiveness evaluation, impact evaluation and cost effectiveness. Draper et al. (1996) proposed that evaluation of educational technology could have a formative, summative, illuminative or integrative focus as well as fulfilling the purpose of quality audit, assessment or assurance. Finally, in an update of Reeves' earlier work, Reeves and Hedberg (2003) articulated a systems-based approach to the evaluation of interactive learning. They proposed an evaluation framework that includes review, needs assessment, formative-, effectiveness- and impact-evaluation.

An important caveat about any overarching evaluation framework is that the division between the types of evaluation it describes is somewhat artificial. That is, the evaluation types are not mutually exclusive, either conceptually or methodologically. A clear and often-cited example of this is that a single evaluation study can fulfil both formative and summative purposes. A practitioner may carry out an investigation that has the dual aims of improving the educational design of an e-learning environment *and* determining its effectiveness. This notwithstanding, it is still helpful to see each type of evaluation as conceptually distinct, fulfilling different purposes and responding to different evaluation needs.

4.3 e-Learning Evaluation

In this book, we are primarily interested in the effectiveness of e-learning artefacts and learning environments that have been designed using e-learning artefacts. This interest extends across the e-learning life cycle introduced in Chapter 1 and will be illustrated by four scenarios which reflect different phases of the e-learning life cycle. The object being evaluated is the e-learning environment, where this has been designed to facilitate a mixture of learning processes and outcomes.

The following paragraphs will explore these scenarios in more detail, building on concepts established earlier. In summary, these concepts are:

- An e-learning artefact has one of three forms: an interactive learning system; a generic learning tool; or a learning object – each with similar but slightly different characteristics.
- A learning environment is built from one or more e-learning artefacts, and can be contextualized by the designed learning tasks and the desired learning outcomes.
- Learners engage with the learning environment and learning tasks as part of their learning processes.
- Learners can demonstrate learning outcomes.

Table 4.1 outlines four evaluation scenarios which reflect four phases of the life cycle of an e-learning project, from initial exploration, through development, to a mature e-learning environment. We present these scenarios to help structure a discussion of how evaluation can be used across the e-learning life cycle. These scenarios will be revisited at different stages of the book, notably in Chapter 6 and Chapter 8.

Table 4.1 Four educational evaluation scenarios

Scenario	Description	Questions	Judgement/ decision
A	Evaluating the potential of a new technology for use in learning and teaching	How does this new technology work? How could it be used in learning and teaching?	Potential use
B	Evaluating the development of an e-learning artefact	How effective was the conduct of the project? Does the e-learning artefact function technically as designed?	Project quality
C	Evaluating ways to improve a designed e-learning environment	Does the e-learning environment function as designed? How can it be improved?	Improvement Formative
D	Evaluating the effectiveness of an e-learning environment	*What* do learners learn from the e-learning environment? *How* do learners learn from the e-learning environment?	Impact Summative

Scenario A refers to the situation where a new technology with educational potential comes on to the market (a relevant example at the time of writing was micro-blogging, e.g. Twitter). It is appropriate for a teacher to evaluate how he or she might use this technology for teaching and how learners might use this for learning. This will involve trialling, exploration and observation, asking, 'How does this new technology work?' and 'Is this tool worth investigating further?' Initial exploration may be followed by a period of experimentation, asking, 'How can I use it? Can I use it to do x?'

Scenario B corresponds to the evaluation of the conduct of a project to develop an e-learning artefact from scratch (section 1.6). It may follow from satisfactory outcomes from scenario A, but it may also arise from the identification of a teaching and learning problem that an existing e-learning artefact might be able to address. That is, it may be a learning-driven, rather than technology-driven, activity. Evaluation of scenario B is closely aligned with the development of an e-learning artefact. As such, it maps on to Stern's (1990) definition of evaluation, which involves making judgements about the starting assumptions, implementation processes and outcomes of the innovation.

There are two aspects to this scenario, evaluating the conduct of the project itself and evaluating the artefact that is the project deliverable. The former, which we call project-management evaluation, is concerned with areas such as the quality of the project-management processes, the project documentation and the communication between team members. (We will explore the evaluation of the conduct of an e-learning project more fully in Chapter 10.) The latter is often associated with usability testing and considers questions such as 'Does the e-learning artefact function as designed and intended?' and 'Can learners interact with and navigate around as they need to?' If a project is well designed and implemented, project-management evaluation will confirm this and the project is likely to produce usable deliverables. However, these two types of evaluation will not directly provide information about the quality of these deliverables, nor their effectiveness in a learning environment. These are the focus of later cycles of evaluation.

As described in section 1.6, e-learning artefacts, whether developed from scratch, sourced from elsewhere or derived from generic learning tools, need to be thoughtfully embedded into learning environments. Scenario C describes a phase in which the integration of the e-learning artefact within a particular learning environment is judged to be sufficiently mature to evaluate in real life in classrooms or virtual environments. It then becomes appropriate to evaluate whether the e-learning environment functions as designed. The goal is to improve the learning environment through formative evaluation, and evaluation centres, not on the technology per se, but on the way learners use the environment to learn. After sufficient cycles of improvement, the evaluation should lead to a decision that the learning environment functions well and can be used with confidence.

The final scenario (D) in Table 4.1 involves evaluating the effectiveness of a mature e-learning environment, which is known – to a greater or lesser extent – to function as it was designed. With this type of evaluation we focus on learners' learning processes and outcomes, and make judgements about the e-learning environment based on these. As well as contributing to knowledge about the effectiveness of e-learning environments, this type of evaluation will almost certainly identify further ways that the learning environment can be improved, leading to further cycles of development. For example, of the 16 studies reported in Phillips (2002b), while half were more 'summative' in nature, every project reported formative results, identifying ways in which the e-learning environment could be improved. In one project (Daniel, Lockwood, Stewart & McLoughlin, 2002), which sought to evaluate summatively the effectiveness of three CD-Roms funded by large grants over several years, the results were unexpectedly formative. The CD-Roms were not used by learners in the way intended, and the development team had to rethink their design, particularly the way in which the CD-Roms were integrated with other teaching activities.

This example reinforces the earlier point about the interdependency of evaluation phases. We can see from the example above that a nominally summative evaluation can highlight areas for improvement in future cycles of development. Furthermore, it may sometimes be reasonable to combine the evaluation of learning in an e-learning environment with an evaluation of the technical or usability aspects of an e-learning artefact (scenarios B and C). It is also perfectly reasonable to evaluate both improvement and effectiveness (scenarios C and D) at the same time.

While the labelling and ordering of the scenarios in Table 4.1 may suggest that the phases of evaluation should be carried out in a sequential order, this is not the case. There is no need for a lock-step approach to evaluation across the e-learning life cycle. For example, it is relatively common to start an evaluation study such as the one described in scenario C without scenarios A and B being part of a preceding study. This occurs when external evaluators come in to study an e-learning environment developed by a committed teacher. Finally, there is no implication that all four of these phases need be carried out every time a technology-based implementation is considered in a teaching and learning context. In other words, evaluation of e-learning should not be seen as a linear process, but should be viewed as being iterative and context-dependent.

4.3.1 Evaluation, Research and Evaluation Research

The final scenario described above (D) raises a further issue – how an investigation that sets out to 'evaluate' an e-learning artefact or environment may, in fact, gather evidence about how and why an e-learning environment works – that is, how it affects learning. An evaluation of the effectiveness of an e-learning environment may quite easily shed light on *how* learners engaged with the designed learning processes to achieve their results, or *why* some learners achieved at different levels, or *how* some learners used the learning environment to achieve a deeper understanding. While any of these findings could be seen as the outcomes of an *evaluation* study, they could equally be seen as legitimate outcomes of an educational *research* investigation. So the question becomes: Where does educational evaluation stop and educational research begin?

This is a somewhat vexed issue as some authors have argued that providing an explanation of outcomes is not within the remit of evaluation (see Glass & Worthen, 1971). However, others, such as Oliver, Harvey, Conole and Jones (2007), have argued that evaluation and research studies can use similar methods to arrive at similar outcomes, but they can be distinguished based on how those outcomes are used:

> The relationship between evaluation and research more generally remains contested. Evaluation can, in fact, contribute to research as well as providing feedback for changing teaching and learning practice. Both processes use the same methods and study the same things. However, one way to distinguish them is to consider how findings are used. If they are

interpreted by an immediate, local audience and used to support decision making, the study was probably an evaluation; if findings are interpreted in terms of theories and presented as a contribution to knowledge, it was probably research. (Oliver, Harvey et al., 2007, p. 203)

We argue here that studies of the effectiveness of e-learning involve a mixture of evaluation and research, where:

- evaluation is gathering information to help make judgements about the value and worth of an e-learning artefact or environment that can inform decision-making;
- research is gathering information to assist our understanding of how people learn using an e-learning artefact or environment.

For simplicity, we give this the overarching label of *evaluation research*. Our choice resonates with Patton's (1990) definition:

When one examines and judges accomplishments and effectiveness, one is engaged in evaluation. When this examination of effectiveness is conducted systematically and empirically through careful data collection and thoughtful analysis, one is engaged in evaluation research. (p. 11)

However, like many constructs in the social sciences, the term 'evaluation research' has been used with various connotations and meanings. In the late 1960s and early 1970s it was used to distinguish evaluation that employs rigorous, experimental social-science research methodology from other forms of evaluation (Worthen et al., 1997). *No such interpretation is present in our use of the term.*

We use the term evaluation research simply to capture the idea that investigations of e-learning will often involve a mix of evaluation and research activities that can be applied throughout the e-learning life cycle. When it comes to e-learning investigations, there is typically an ebb and flow between making judgements about the e-learning environment and developing a greater understanding of learning in that environment. Furthermore, Chapter 2 indicated that varying levels of rigour can be applied to evaluation activities, while rigour is required in publishable research (for more, see Chapters 5 and 6).

Table 4.2 shows how evaluation research can occur across the e-learning life cycle by demonstrating how each of the scenarios summarized in Table 4.1 can be broken down to support both evaluative and research-based inquiries. Each of the questions in the third column of Table 4.1 is treated separately in Table 4.2, sometimes with both an evaluation and a research component. For example, scenarios B2 and B3 correspond to the second question of scenario B in Table 4.1, with evaluation and research activities respectively. Table 4.2

also explicitly indicates the elements of the LEPO framework which are most relevant at each phase of the e-learning life cycle. That is, in scenario B we are mostly concerned with the learning environment; in scenario C we are concerned with the learning environment and learning processes; and in scenario D we are interested in both learning outcomes and learning processes.

Table 4.2 graphically indicates the balance between evaluation and research for each scenario. Rather than portraying particular evaluation-research activities as purely evaluative or purely research-based, the graphics imply

Table 4.2 Descriptions of evaluation research across the e-learning life cycle

Scenario	Focus	Activity		Goals
A	Exploration	Evaluation ←—|—→ Research		Exploring potential
B1	Learning environment	Evaluation ←|————→ Research		Judgements about the project management
B2	Learning environment	Evaluation ←|————→ Research		Judgements about the usability of the designed e-learning artefact in the context of the particular learning environment
B3	Learning environment	Evaluation ←————|→ Research		Understanding the characteristics of e-learning environments which effectively facilitate learning processes and learning outcomes
C1	Learning environment and learning process	Evaluation ←|————→ Research		Judgements, derived from actual use, about the way the learning environment was designed and how it could be improved
C2	Learning environment and learning process	Evaluation ←————|→ Research		Seeking deeper understanding about ways that learners use and interact with the e-learning environment
D1	Learning process and learning outcome	Evaluation ←|————→ Research		Judgements about whether the e-learning environment works. How effective was it in facilitating its desired outcomes?
D2	Learning process and learning outcome	Evaluation ←————|→ Research		Seeking deeper understanding about how and why the learning environment engaged particular learning processes and led to particular learning outcomes

that there is a variable mixture of each. In other words, we make judgements about the aspects of the learning environment that we more or less understand, and we research the aspects of the learning environment that we do not understand.

For example, in scenario A, we are studying the potential of a new technology for use in teaching and learning involving a mix of evaluation and research. We need both to understand how the technology works and to decide how we can use it, if at all. There is also a level of overlap between scenarios D1 and D2. The approaches taken to determine how effective a learning environment was and understanding how it was effective are very similar. We will unpack these distinctions further in Chapter 8.

However, many aspects of e-learning are relatively well understood. For example, online discussion forums are now an entrenched learning technology and studies over a number of years have provided insight into their effective use (Harasim, Hiltz, Teles & Turoff, 1995; Palloff & Pratt, 1999; Salmon, 2003). However, there are always additional questions that emerge when 'tried and tested' technologies are used in a different context, for example, with learners from a different cultural and/or linguistic background. What might be evaluation in one context may have a stronger research focus in another. So, while in many contexts online discussions are well understood, there is an emerging evaluation-research area in the use of online discussions with Asian learners (McNaught, 2011; McNaught, Cheng & Lam, 2006).

4.4 The Nature of Research

We have argued above that there is a research component to investigating the effectiveness of e-learning artefacts and environments. However, to progress our discussion we need to clarify what we mean by 'research'. At some level, a person who cannot find their car keys and investigates where they might be is conducting research. Like 'evaluation' the term 'research' is used in a variety of ways in academic discourse but, despite this, its meaning is rarely questioned and often it is regarded as universally or even implicitly understood. At most universities an institutional bureaucracy supports research, and academic staff are rewarded for their 'strength' in research. But what exactly is this research? There are many contexts in which research takes place and many different ways in which research is conducted but, unless this diversity of understanding is recognized, it is difficult to have a meaningful dialogue about it. This is what we are attempting here.

Broadly speaking, 'research' is akin to what Shulman (1988) termed *disciplined inquiry*, which can be distinguished "from other sources of opinion or belief [and] is conducted and reported in such a way that the argument can be painstakingly examined" (Cronbach & Suppes, 1969, p. 15). Shulman (1988) viewed academic research as that which is disciplined, systematic, explicit and ethical, whose "data, arguments and reasoning [are] capable of withstanding careful scrutiny by another member of the scientific community" (1988, p. 5). For the purposes of this discussion, we will use the definition of research cited by the Higher Education Funding Council for England:

> 'Research' … is to be understood as original investigation undertaken in order to gain knowledge and understanding. It includes work of direct relevance to the needs of commerce, industry, and to the public and voluntary sectors; scholarship; the invention and generation of ideas, images, performances, artefacts including design, where these lead to new or substantially improved insights; and the use of existing knowledge in experimental development to produce new or substantially improved materials, devices, products and processes, including design and construction. (Research Assessment Exercise, 2008)

Research is undertaken primarily for two reasons:

1. To satisfy human curiosity – that is, to come to a greater or more profound understanding of the world in which we live.
2. To solve problems – that is, to learn to manipulate the world we live in to obtain desirable outcomes.

The multiple purposes of research are discussed further in section 4.5.

In order to achieve high standards in academic research, all researchers and research teams need to draw on a range of generic skills and capabilities including critical-thinking and problem-solving skills, integrity, honesty and reflection throughout the research process, creativity and openness to new ideas, and communication and project-management skills. However, research approaches differ across disciplines, and the following section considers this in order to inform the development of a robust approach to e-learning evaluation research.

4.4.1 Disciplinary Research Differences

The area of 'e-learning' is an interdisciplinary field. Both practice and evaluation research associated with e-learning can draw on a range of discipline areas such as education, sociology, psychology, information technology, computer science, information systems and design, to name just a few. While e-learning is developing as a discipline area, often individual academics have come to e-learning from established disciplines, and have tended to bring with them their particular, discipline-specific research traditions. Shulman (1988) suggested that:

> What distinguishes disciplines from one another is the manner in which they formulate their questions, how they define the content of their domain and organize that content conceptually, and the principles of discovery and verification that constitute the ground rules for creating and testing knowledge in their fields. (Shulman, 1988, p. 5)

Given that it is likely that researchers, evaluators and practitioners in the area of e-learning will often reflect multiple disciplines, and that some of the research traditions of these disciplines will have different ground rules, it is worth considering the characteristics of various disciplinary research approaches, to see which can be appropriately applied to e-learning evaluation research.

The way in which disciplinary differences and research approaches can be distinguished has been the subject of much research itself. For example, Becher (1989), in his work on academic tribes and territories, identified disciplinary differences between types of academic work. Jones, Zenios and Griffiths (2004) subsequently synthesized Becher's textual descriptions and distinguished disciplines across two dimensions: pure versus applied, and hard versus soft. Alternatively, Burkhardt (2006) discussed four research traditions: humanities, sciences, engineering and the arts, which map well to the dimensions proposed by Jones et al. (2004). The four general disciplinary research approaches are presented in Table 4.3, described in terms of their aims, products, characteristics, concerns and outcomes.

From the classifications in Table 4.3, it should be clear that some disciplines (e.g. physics) are referred to as 'hard' disciplines that conduct 'pure' research and aim to create fundamental knowledge and understanding. Research that comes from this tradition typically uses 'hard' data and values the reliability of numbers, and generalizability of findings. Research can be seen as 'blue sky' with less of an emphasis on the application or practical utility of the results. Other disciplines, such as those found within the humanities, also seek knowledge and understanding and can also engage in 'blue sky' research, but are typically 'softer' and less deterministic in their approach. An anthropologist or sociologist might seek to explore and uncover the behavioural and cultural characteristics of a particular community, with no concern for causality, and attempting to discount any preconceptions about that behaviour. Hard–applied disciplines, such as engineering, focus on the practical outcomes of the research process. They are often directed at developing an understanding in order to enhance the way in which something in the world operates. The products or outcomes of this type of research are typically tools and processes that are fit for purpose. For example, an engineer or computer scientist might create and implement a solution to a problem and test its reliability and efficiency. Here, while there is still some sense of discovery, there is an overriding interest in knowing whether the innovation works and why.

Finally, there is the soft–applied quadrant in which educational research is often positioned. Research in this category is often initiated to resolve practical problems or improve professional practice. While researchers such as Burkhardt (2006) claim that, as in the humanities, educational research tends to focus more on critical commentary than on hard evidence, the practical reality is more pluralistic than this. A review of 'educational' journals would reveal that some educational research focuses on questions and employs techniques that

Table 4.3 Disciplinary differences in academic research (derived from Jones et al. (2004) and Burkhardt (2006))

		Pure	*Applied*
Hard		*Pure sciences*, e.g. physics	*Applied sciences*, e.g. engineering
	Aim	• knowledge and fundamental understanding	• practical impact • helping the world work better
	Product	• assertions supported by evidence-based arguments	• tools and/or processes which are fit for purpose
	Characteristics	• cumulative • atomistic (crystalline/tree-like)	• purposive • pragmatic (know-how via hard knowledge)
	Concerned with	• universals • quantities • simplification	• mastery of physical and virtual environment
	Outcomes	• discovery • explanation	• products • techniques
Soft		*Humanities and pure social sciences*, e.g. anthropology, history	*Applied social sciences*, e.g. education and the arts
	Aim	• knowledge and understanding	• practical impact • helping the world work better
	Product	• critical commentary • assertions not backed up by (empirical) evidence	• protocols • procedures • practical guides
	Characteristics	• reiterative • holistic (organic/river-like)	• functional • utilitarian (know-how via soft knowledge)
	Concerned with	• particulars • qualities • complication	• enhancement of (semi-) professional practice
	Outcomes	• understanding • interpretation	• improved practice

are closely aligned with the applied sciences (i.e. hard–applied) while other forms of educational research are more sociological and are clearly aligned with a pure social-science tradition (i.e. pure–soft). There are no easy categorizations here: educational research is diverse and contested; the discipline of education contains a number of viewpoints about what constitutes valid research.

Just as education is difficult to assign to a single disciplinary focus, investigations into e-learning – effectively a subset of educational research – are equally difficult to categorize. We have argued above that investigations of the effectiveness of e-learning can have both an evaluative and a research focus. Because e-learning evaluation research is concerned with practical applications in education as well as with enhancement of professional practice, it can clearly be classified as soft–applied research. However, many e-learning investigations contain a 'hard' element with an 'applied' research focus. Alternatively, some social-science research in e-learning seeks fundamental understanding in complex learning communities, institutions or cultures. So, while disciplinary differences are a useful reminder that research – what it is, how it is done – is often aligned with disciplinary traditions, it may be useful to consider other non-disciplinary ways of categorizing research. This is the focus of the next section, which looks at two non-disciplinary ways of categorizing research. Together with what we have just discussed, they provide us with several lenses through which we can view e-learning evaluation research.

4.5 Research Classifications

4.5.1 Pasteur's Quadrant

In the second half of the 20th century, the accepted way of classifying research was to distinguish between pure (or basic) research and applied research. As indicated in Table 4.3, the primary aim of pure research was to seek fundamental understandings, while applied research was more focused on solving practical problems. Stokes (1997) criticized the pre-eminence of pure research, and argued that the pure–applied distinction was too narrow and did not consider how different types of research might be used. Based on his critique, he proposed a two-dimensional model for classifying research that he called Pasteur's Quadrant (see Table 4.4).

One dimension of Pasteur's Quadrant classified research in terms of the degree to which it reflected a quest for fundamental understanding. Stokes introduced a second dimension to the research classification, which was 'consideration of use'. By using this simple two-by-two classification and providing historical examples from the work of eminent researchers, Stokes (1997) challenged two

Table 4.4 Pasteur's Quadrant

		Consideration of use	
		Low	High
Quest for fundamental understanding	High	1. Pure basic research (Bohr)	2. Use-inspired basic research (Pasteur)
	Low	3.	4. Pure applied research (Edison)

assumptions of the traditional pure–applied dichotomy: (i) that pure research sought fundamental understanding while applied research did not; and (ii) that basic research always preceded applied research.

Stokes provided several examples from the career of microbiologist Louis Pasteur to debunk these assumptions and demonstrate that his work was inspired by both consideration of use and a quest for fundamental understanding (Quadrant 2 in Table 4.4). Similarly, Stokes argued that Neils Bohr's work on atomic structure had no consideration of use, but sought fundamental understanding (Quadrant 1 in Table 4.4). On the other hand, Thomas Edison's inventions applied existing understanding to develop new tools and techniques to solve real-world problems, without any intention of extending that understanding (Quadrant 4).

One might question whether research in Quadrant 3, which has no consideration for use and no quest for fundamental understanding, has any value, or, indeed, is academic research at all. Stokes (1997) characterized this Quadrant as "research that systematically explores *particular* phenomena without having in view either general explanatory objectives or any applied use to which the results will be put" (italics in original; p. 74). The dedicated activities of amateur astronomers and birdwatchers fit into this category, and this type of 'research' may ultimately prove to be of considerable value to other researchers, in other Quadrants, at a later stage.

Reeves and Hedberg (Reeves, 1999; Reeves & Hedberg, 2003) have been vocal critics of much e-learning research, claiming that it is located in this third Quadrant and, as such, has neither quest for understanding nor consideration of use. They have argued for e-learning research to be more use-inspired and socially responsible. In section 4.3.1, we argued that evaluation research into e-learning involves a mixture of judgements (evaluation) and understanding (research). We consider both of these activities to be inspired by use (in Stokes' terms) because we are studying a learning environment as it is used by learners and, through the process of evaluation research, we are aiming to understand better how technology can be applied and used. Furthermore, the research component of evaluation research is clearly intent on a quest for fundamental understanding, while the evaluation component is not.

4.5.2 Boyer's Four Scholarships

One final lens through which to look at academic research is Ernest Boyer's (1990) four different types of scholarship. This analysis was also based on a critique of the post-war emphasis on pure research, which Boyer (1990) called the *scholarship of discovery*. In addition to the scholarship of discovery, Boyer proposed three other types of scholarship: the *scholarship of integration*, the *scholarship of application* and the *scholarship of teaching*.

The *scholarship of discovery* is perhaps the most immediately recognizable of Boyer's classifications, and is aligned with traditional notions of research –

that is, research that pursues new knowledge and fundamental understanding. The scholarship of discovery, therefore, is clearly high on Stokes' (1997) dimension of 'quest for fundamental understanding', and, as it is silent about 'consideration of use', fits squarely in Quadrant 1 (Table 4.4). The *scholarship of integration* involves connecting knowledge and discovery into larger patterns and contexts. This includes interdisciplinary and multidisciplinary research, at the "boundaries where fields converge" (p. 19). As Boyer (1990) explained:

> The distinction we are drawing between 'discovery' and 'integration' can be best understood, perhaps, by the questions posed. Those engaged in discovery ask 'What is to be known, what is yet to be found?' Those engaged in integration ask 'What do the findings mean? Is it possible to interpret what's been discovered in ways that provide a larger, more comprehensive understanding?' (p. 19)

The *scholarship of application* involves engagement in problems that affect individuals, institutions and society, and asks questions such as: 'How can knowledge be responsibly applied to consequential problems? How can it be relevant to society?' This scholarship type is directly analogous to Stokes' (1997) 'consideration of use' dimension. Like Stokes' consideration of use, Boyer's scholarship of application acknowledges that real-world problems can define an agenda for research. Boyer argues that the scholarship of application moves "from theory to practice, and from practice back to theory, which in fact makes theory ... more authentic" (Boyer, 1996, p. 17).

The *scholarship of teaching* is perhaps the hardest to conceptualize. It is not scholarship *about* teaching, but the scholarship *of* teaching. Hutchings and Shulman (1999) distinguished between good teaching and the scholarship of teaching in that the latter: gathers evidence; is informed by current ideas about the field, and teaching in that field; and invites "peer collaboration and review" (p. 13). Furthermore, the scholarship of teaching is public, "open to critique and evaluation and in a form that others can build on" (p. 13); and it involves inquiry into "issues of student learning" (p. 13). The scholarship of teaching goes beyond improving individual classroom practice to advancing teaching practice in general, the focus of various forms of *action inquiry* (Kemmis & McTaggart, 2000; McNiff, Lomax & Whitehead, 2003).

Boyer's four scholarships have some overlaps with Stokes' schema. The scholarship of discovery and the scholarship of application are directly analogous to Stokes' 'fundamental understanding' and 'consideration of use' components, respectively, which are conceived of as separate dimensions by Stokes (1997). On the other hand, the scholarship of integration cuts across Stokes' boundaries, and the scholarship of teaching builds on the other scholarships. As Hutchings and Shulman (1999) explained, scholarship of teaching "is a special case of the scholarship of application and engagement, and frequently entails the discovery of new findings and principles" (p. 15). Boyer's (1990) scholarship of teaching is an eminently suitable lens through which to view evaluation research into e-learning.

4.6 Examples of Evaluation Research into e-Learning

Collectively, we have managed and contributed to many teams developing and researching innovative e-learning applications over many years. This section describes some of these projects and maps them against the general research approaches outlined in previous sections, to demonstrate the diversity of approaches to e-learning evaluation research. These examples cover a significant time period, partly because issues in e-learning evaluation research are enduring, and particularly to indicate the diversity of valid approaches.

Example 1: Virtual reality techniques for veterinary diagnostic imaging

A particular teaching and learning problem led to the development of the e-learning solution which was the focus of this research. A course in veterinary diagnostic imaging was offered at Masters level by distance education. In a face-to-face situation, diagnostic imaging skills are learned in small groups, through gesturing at radiographs around a 'light box', but the traditional, print-based distance-education model was not well suited to the desired learning outcome. First, the packages of hard-copy radiographs sent to learners were bulky and expensive to post. Second, learners were often unable to identify the relevant regions of X-rays, and were unable to receive timely feedback on diagnoses they made.

These issues were addressed by several technological components, progressively developed in three cycles over several years.

1. The QuickTime VR three-dimensional virtual-reality technique was applied to large, two-dimensional X-ray images. This enabled learners to view the whole X-ray on screen, and then zoom in on fine detail within the images with minimal loss of diagnostic clarity, as well as seeing annotations embedded in the images (Phillips, Pospisil & Richardson, 2001).
2. Microsoft Word macros were developed to enable academics to design their own diagnostic self-tests. Learners can enter their answer, click a button and receive a detailed expert answer immediately (Phillips, 2002a).
3. A prototype digital whiteboard was developed to enable text-based discussion and annotation of a shared image (Phillips, Scott & Richardson, 2003).

An evaluation was carried out during each cycle, and the focus was largely on the e-learning artefact, and how it could be improved. However, the research also addressed aspects of the learning environment (accessibility issues and the broader course context), and whether the innovations were addressing the learning process as intended.

A number of sources of data were used to evaluate the usability and effectiveness of the e-learning environment. These included design specifications, expert feedback, learner observation, lecturer feedback, online usage statistics and an email survey of learner experiences.

The rounds of evaluation identified bugs and interface issues which were resolved in subsequent years. Learners found the virtual X-rays were very useful. In the initial round, the quality wasn't quite as high as hard copies, and learners preferred to practise on the virtual images and be assessed on the hard copies. A higher-resolution scanner was used in subsequent years. However, the flexibility of the new approach was a clear benefit. Practising professionals could study for a higher qualification in their own time at their location of choice, without being tied to the piles of hard copies at home.

In terms of the research classifications described in previous sections, this work was a mixture of hard– and soft–applied research, with a strong concern for use, but little quest for fundamental understanding. In Boyer's terms this work involved the scholarship of teaching, with an emphasis on the scholarship of integration, due to the linking of existing ideas in new ways.

Example 2: A longitudinal study of the use of e-cases in veterinary microbiology
The development of e-cases in veterinary microbiology began in the early 1990s at an Australian university. The e-cases were designed for undergraduate learners and integrated into a revised learning design with an expanded set of desired learning outcomes (information management, practical diagnosis of bacterial and fungal animal diseases, team work and communication skills) and more appropriate assessment strategies. Data was collected over a period of seven years and some data collection is ongoing. A brief summary of the data and interpretations is in Table 4.5. The underlying technology is now web-based but a similar learning design with the same e-cases is still in use 20 years later. The overall outcome of the project was that changes in institutional climate worked together with the project's outcomes to influence faculty policy for the design of the veterinary program to include a greater number of problem-based courses with learning designs similar to the veterinary microbiology course. This project highlights the need to think at an institutional or system level in order to achieve lasting benefits (Laurillard, 1999; see also Chapter 11). Further detail can be found in McNaught, Whithear and Browning (1994; 1999) and McNaught, Burd, Whithear, Prescott and Browning (2003).

This was soft–applied research or, in Stokes' terms, a mixture of use-inspired basic research and pure applied research, through a clear quest for understanding together with a pragmatic focus on operational matters. In Boyer's classification, this work involved the scholarship of teaching, with some emphasis on the scholarship of application (innovative e-learning artefact).

Table **4.5** Outline of the longitudinal study of the use of e-cases in veterinary microbiology

Data	Interpretation
Learners' impressions of the learning environment and course design – annual survey (ongoing) and focus groups over three years	Initial reservations but views changed quite quickly to being positive as learners adapted to what was their first experience of e-learning
Learners' perceptions of their learning outcomes – annual survey (ongoing)	Generally positive but feedback has allowed adjustments, e.g. to the length of the e-cases
Assessment data on learning outcomes – analysis of the cognitive demand (Bloom, 1956) of examination items pre- and post-innovation and learners' overall performance (two years)	Evidence that learners do well on assessment which was more demanding than previous assessment designs
Interviews with cohort 2 of the learners two years later when they were in clinical experience	Learning benefits did not last because of the isolated nature of the experience

Example 3: Collaborative writing exercises using a wiki with large classes

This e-learning project was part of a larger study that explored staff and learners' experiences with technology in higher education, and the use of Web 2.0 technologies in teaching and learning (Kennedy, Dalgarno, Bennett et al., 2009). The project involved the design and implementation of a technology-based collaborative writing exercise using a wiki with a large class of first-year psychology learners. Laboratory classes containing between 20 and 30 learners were asked to create collaboratively a wiki-based submission on a key area being covered in the psychology course (motion detection by the visual system). Learners and teachers were provided with extensive technical, administrative and pedagogical support, and learners were given guidance on the basic concepts they should cover in their submission. Learners were encouraged to create scholarly summaries of the key concepts of motion detection using descriptions, reflections, quotes, images, web links and diagrams.

This e-learning environment was one of eight e-learning implementation projects that were evaluated through a cross-case comparison, broadly based on Reeves and Hedberg's (2003) notion of effectiveness evaluation. Quantitative and qualitative data were collected from staff and learners in the areas of knowledge, skills and attitudes. Staff members involved in the learning activity were interviewed on a number of occasions across the semester, and a sample of learners completed an online questionnaire and contributed to focus-group discussions at the conclusion of the exercise. The outcomes of this evaluation were that the e-learning environment was effective (e.g. high task relevancy, encouraged both staff and learners to share and reflect); and identified where learners encountered difficulties (e.g. many learners found it hard to negotiate and manage collaboration and contribution) (cf. Kennedy et al., 2009).

In addition to the use of interviews and questionnaires as tools in this evaluation, metrics that were automatically generated by the wiki were also harvested for a study that sought to investigate the degree to which learners behaved cooperatively and collaboratively in developing their contributions. Electronic measures of the number, timing and scope of contributions made by the learners in the cohort and the content of their wiki comments were the subject of detailed analysis. This analysis showed that while a great number of learners were making a contribution to the activity, evidence of sustained online collaboration was limited (Judd, Kennedy & Cropper, 2010).

Like the previous example, this work can be characterized as soft–applied research in disciplinary terms, but as use-inspired basic research according to Stokes, because the aim was to arrive at evaluation-research outcomes that could inform practice. In Boyer's terms, this work was mainly the scholarship of application with an element of the scholarship of teaching.

4.7 Summary

This chapter discussed the nature of evaluation in the context of this book, noting the characteristics of educational evaluation and the similarities and distinctions between program and project evaluation. We presented various evaluation approaches and models which we applied to four e-learning evaluation scenarios related to the e-learning life cycle.

We established that studies of the effectiveness of e-learning involve a variable mixture of both evaluation and research, and we have called this 'evaluation research'. We then turned our attention to the interpretation of 'research', and discussed how the term is interpreted differently in different disciplines. We presented three models which characterize research in different dimensions: the disciplinary distinctions of Jones et al. (2004) between hard and soft, and pure and applied research; Stokes' (1997) consideration of use, and quest for fundamental understanding; and Boyer's (1990) scholarships of discovery, integration, application and teaching. These acted as lenses through which we can view e-learning evaluation research.

In e-learning evaluation research, the evaluation component involves making judgements about the usability and usefulness of an e-learning environment, while the research component involves a search for fundamental understanding. These two components resonate well with Stokes' (1997) consideration of use, and quest for fundamental understanding. We have also established that e-learning evaluation research can be multidisciplinary, combining a mixture of soft and hard, and applied and pure characteristics. Finally, we established that evaluation research into e-learning is a form of Boyer's (1990) scholarship of teaching, which, in turn, encompasses elements of the scholarship of application, the scholarship of integration and the scholarship of discovery.

In the remainder of this book we will use the terms 'practitioners', 'evaluators', 'researchers' and 'investigators' interchangeably, using the term which seems most appropriate to the context where it is used.

We have argued in this chapter that there is a need to look beyond disciplinary assumptions when conducting e-learning evaluation research. At the same time, we do not claim that there is one *right* approach to evaluation research into e-learning. The examples in the previous section demonstrate that a diversity of approaches is feasible. This makes it important to clarify the context of any evaluation research and justify the approach taken. Different approaches may also be appropriate at different phases of the e-learning life cycle and for different contexts, but those approaches need to be justifiable, rather than applied in an unthinking manner. Chapter 5 explores these issues in a more theoretical way.

5
Research Paradigms and Methodologies

5.1 Introduction

Chapter 4 established that there are many types of research, and there are disciplinary differences between approaches to research. It further established that e-learning evaluation research involves a mixture of making judgements (evaluation) and seeking understanding (research), and that this resonates well with Stokes' (1997) two dimensions of 'consideration of use' and 'quest for fundamental understanding', as well as with Boyer's (1990) notion of the scholarship of teaching.

Chapter 4 also presented broad arguments that there are different approaches to e-learning evaluation research, depending on the stage of the e-learning life cycle that is being investigated. This chapter seeks to provide a more theoretical view of the philosophies and concepts which underpin paradigms of research and the research methodologies which may be associated with them. This is done in order to help readers to recognize their own preferred approaches to research or investigation, and to guide them towards the most appropriate approach for their situation. This chapter addresses issues relevant to educational research in general (with a 'leaning' towards e-learning). Chapter 6 will build on this chapter to explicitly discuss research approaches which are appropriate for e-learning.

We recognize, as Reeves (2000b) did, that "the research goals held by any given [educational] researcher are influenced by many factors including the epistemological views of the investigator, his/her research training, and the dominant research paradigms within his/her line of inquiry" (p. 22). One aim of this chapter is to encourage readers, whether novice or experienced researchers, to take a broader, reflective view of their scholarly practice, so that they can contribute to the improvement of research into e-learning in all its forms. We commence by discussing the definition of the research problem (the phenomenon, research goals and overarching research questions), and then various epistemological and paradigmatic aspects of research, before discussing methodologies.

5.2 Phenomena

By its very nature, research is concerned with increasing human understanding of various phenomena. A phenomenon is an instance of something – an artefact or event that is known through the senses. In many cases, when we think of phenomena we think of everyday phenomena, such as the seasons, gravity and waves on the ocean. These phenomena *exist naturally* in our world and we can observe them. Other phenomena, such as the inner workings of atoms and molecules, cannot be directly observed, but also exist naturally and their behaviour can be measured in various ways. Over the centuries, scientists have investigated and ultimately discovered how many of these natural phenomena work, and this understanding has contributed to the complex society in which we live.

However, phenomena are not restricted to things that exist naturally. Phenomena can be designed; when you consider the ways in which the natural world has been manipulated and controlled over centuries, it is easy to recognize that many phenomena are created by people. Simon (1969) distinguished between *natural sciences*, which concern themselves with discovering how existing things work, such as in the fields of physics, biology and anthropology, and *artificial sciences*. Artificial sciences seek to design artefacts, understand and reflect on them, and ultimately improve their design and use. The fields of engineering, architecture and computer science are quintessential artificial sciences and, under this characterization, e-learning is as well.

When we say that artificial sciences seek to design artefacts, it may give the impression that these are physical 'things'. However, designed artefacts may be either tangible (e.g. an aeroplane, a bridge) or intangible (e.g. a network, a computer program), and they may also be events, such as interactions between people. In an educational context a university class is an event phenomenon: a coming-together of teacher, learners and various resources in a particular setting. Each class is potentially different, and any understanding derived from a given class may be different from an understanding derived from a different class. The diversity of the instances of the phenomenon often mean that: (1) different research approaches may be required to investigate it; and (2) it is difficult to develop generalized descriptions of the phenomenon.

Finally, research into designed phenomena has an extra element not present when researching natural phenomena. A key component of research in the artificial sciences is the consideration of the way in which a 'manufactured' artefact functions, and essentially whether it functions as designed. With natural phenomena, researchers have to take them as they are; but with designed phenomena, there is potential to improve the phenomenon through its design. Thus, research into designed phenomena is not only concerned with the behaviour of that phenomenon, but also with the design and functionality of the artefact which represents the phenomenon. This is an important consideration for e-learning evaluation research.

5.3 Working from a Theoretical Basis

We argued in Chapter 4 that one of the essential drivers of research is human curiosity. Throughout history, researchers have observed something, realized they were unable to explain it or understand how it works, and set about finding this out. The renowned 17th-century physicist and mathematician, Isaac Newton, was (according to legend) in such a situation when an apple fell from a tree on to his head one afternoon. As well as shock, surprise and perhaps pain, he felt curiosity. Why did the apple fall? His previous life experience had told him that everything falls (i.e. it is a phenomenon of nature), but why is this the case and how does it happen? What is the explanation for it?

Newton came up with the idea that a force (gravity) acted on the apple, and this caused it to fall when the stem of the apple broke away from the tree (the force keeping the apple in place). But to understand what was happening he needed evidence, which he obtained by measuring the phenomenon. Newton took lots of measurements of falling objects and was able to determine that the distance travelled by a falling object was proportional to the square of the time taken in falling. From these measurements and sets of data he developed a *theory* that the distance travelled could be expressed as a formula $s = 0.5gt^2$, where s is the distance, t is the time and g is a constant number which represented the constant natural phenomenon of *gravity*.

Newton proposed a *theory* that sought to explain a pervasive natural phenomenon and indeed his theory seemed to explain, within the accuracy of 17th-century instruments, the behaviour of falling objects. His theory predicted, in a scientific fashion, how other falling objects would behave. However, for Newton's theory to be accepted by the scientific community as a valid explanation of the effects of gravity, it needed to be tested and verified, or perhaps, debunked. And only a single instance of the theory *not applying* was needed to invalidate it.

Newton's basic gravitational theory was tested by many scientists in numerous contexts and was shown to predict reliably the behaviour of falling objects. It was also able to be generalized to a range of contexts, even predicting the motion of planets, which led to the development of modern astronomy. In fact, Newton's theory was so generalizable that it became recognized as a *law of nature* by the scientific community until the 20th century. It was only then that Albert Einstein's work pointed out that in some contexts – when velocity approaches the speed of light – Newton's laws became invalid. Most theories are not so broadly applicable that they can be regarded as laws of nature, but they are nevertheless useful within their contextual constraints.

The point of this brief history of gravity research is that Newton proposed a *theory* that sought to explain, in some way that is predictable, a particular phenomenon. The importance of having a theory is that it provides a foundation for research, inquiry and exploration. It sets out explicitly an explanation of some phenomenon that provides a basis for empirical testing. While in

Newton's case he began investigating through curiosity – and a tacit theory of 'falling' – and built his theory on empirical measurement, those who came after him used this original theory as the basis of their research. Most structured empirical research orients itself within a theoretical framework, acknowledging and building on theory and empirical research that has come before.

However, unlike the theory proposed by Newton, the phenomena under investigation in education are usually more difficult to measure and too complex to be reduced to mathematical formulae. As phenomena, educational environments consist of an array of interdependent individual and contextual variables and, as such, are regarded as highly complex systems. Constructing broad, generalizable and predictive theories of these systems is difficult, to say the least. However, while there may be fewer predictive and generalizable educational theories compared to some areas of the natural sciences (cf. Burkhardt, 2006; Flyvbjerg, 2004), this does not reduce at all the importance of theory in educational research.

Some educational researchers have refined their focus in educational environments to specific components of those environments and the individual learners within them. For example, *dual coding theory* (Paivio, 1971, 1986) or *cognitive load theory* (Sweller, 1988) are theories based on an information-processing model of learning that allow researchers to make some predictions about what happens cognitively – and to learning – when students are faced with different combinations of multimedia representations. Piagetian or Vygotskian conceptions of collaborative learning make similar but distinct predictions about how students gain learning benefits from interacting with peers in educational contexts. Some sociological theories of education and learning seek to make explicit the structural components of learning environments, and propose explanations of how these interact to influence educational processes (e.g. *Activity Theory*, Engeström, 1987; Engeström, Miettinen & Punamäki, 1999).

In addition to established theories of education and learning, there is a proliferation of *models* and *conceptual frameworks* in educational research. These are looser than theory, and are generally not encumbered by the need to offer predictability. Their central purpose is usually to expose, describe, categorize and make order of some phenomenon. Conceptual frameworks will often, by their very construction, highlight the important elements to take into account when considering some phenomenon. One such example is Herrington et al.'s (2009) *authentic learning framework*. It provides order and highlights what is important if you want to adopt authentic approaches to teaching and learning. Similarly, the *LEPO framework* we proposed in Chapter 3 is a conceptual framework that provides a way of viewing learning, but has no predictive capabilities, nor is it backed up by specific evidence, other than a critical synthesis of the literature.

As mentioned above, a key tenet of systematic and disciplined research is having an explicit theoretical position that is accompanied by empirical evidence about what has come before. Typically, before undertaking research, investigators would survey the theoretical or empirical research in an area of interest and come to some conclusion about it that represents their own position, which is often summarized in a literature review. This literature review positions the research being proposed in a context (discipline-based and historical) and shows why the research is warranted and needed (to discover something new, to replicate something found, to verify theory, to back up previous data, etc.).

Unfortunately, one of the consistent criticisms of educational research generally, and e-learning in particular, has been that it is often conducted without a strong theoretical basis. Like a ship without a rudder, such educational research risks drifting aimlessly, occasionally arriving at a destination of interest but more typically finding itself on inconsequential islands or at ports of little value or interest.

5.4 Research Goals and Disciplined Inquiry

Before starting a research endeavour, it is important to consider what exactly will be the focus or topic of the research. The nature of the phenomenon to be studied and the principal outcome sought, which are reflected in the goals of the research, to a large extent determine the type of research questions to be asked and the main research activities undertaken. But, while it is attractive to advise researchers simply to select a phenomenon of interest, specify a research goal and then choose an appropriate question, in reality the process is neither as easy nor as formulaic as this. Because learning, including e-learning, is complex, the phenomenon under investigation represents an ill-defined problem, and it can be difficult to determine exactly what the research problem, goal or question is.

Specification of the research problem is likely to be an iterative process derived from describing and defining the learning environment to be studied, considering how students use this learning environment and engage with learning processes, and specifying what the desired learning outcomes are and how you will know they have been achieved. This analysis needs to be informed by theoretical understandings of learning in similar contexts. Potential research goals and questions should emerge or 'fall out' of this process. Once these initial research goals and questions have been established, they can be broadened or narrowed. This whole process can often be usefully carried out through a process of discussion, questioning and reflection with colleagues.

Once research goals and questions have been clarified, it is appropriate to consider the relationship between them and your epistemological position (reflected by the paradigm of inquiry you adopt) and your views on how the research could be conducted (your methodology) (see sections 5.5 and

5.6, respectively). While some have advocated a relatively lock-step, linear approach to making decisions in this area (Crotty, 1998), others have seen these relationships as more reciprocally determined (Salomon, 1991). We, like others, advocate starting the research process with a clear idea of the goal or question, and from this position critically reflecting on the most appropriate paradigm of inquiry and methodology to employ (Reeves, 2000a; Shavelson, Phillips, Towne & Feuer, 2003).

Shulman (1988) suggested, in his seminal work on research in education, that "We must first understand our problem, and decide what questions we are asking, then select the mode of *disciplined inquiry* most appropriate to these questions" [italics in original] (1988, p. 15). So, in addition to being clear about what we are researching, we need to be rigorous in how we carry out research. Both Robson (2002) and Shulman (1988) viewed disciplined inquiry as having the following characteristics:

systematic	thinking and planning about the what, how and why of the research;
explicit	describing the nature of the observations and the circumstances in which they are made;
sceptical	subjecting the ideas and theories to heavy scrutiny with the aim of disconfirmation;
ethical	conducting the research according to an ethically accepted code of conduct.

In addition, research must also be justifiable, where "its data, arguments and reasoning [are] capable of withstanding careful scrutiny by another member of the scientific community" (Shulman, 1988, p. 5).

We have already questioned the value of educational research that is undertaken without consideration of use, without a strong theoretical foundation and with little acknowledgement of what has come before. In addition, we argue that it is incumbent on researchers to scrutinize their work against these characteristics of disciplined inquiry.

5.5 Paradigms of Inquiry

When researchers undertake an investigation they are often said to do it from within a particular paradigm of inquiry. In recent times the term 'paradigm' is often associated with Thomas Kuhn who, in his book *The Structure of Scientific Revolutions* (1996), explored the ways in which scientific research and discovery evolves – or sees dramatic change – over time. In this book, Kuhn saw paradigms as "accepted examples of actual scientific practice – examples which include law, theory, application, and instrumentation together – [that] provide models from which spring particular coherent traditions of scientific research" (p. 10). Those who adopt the same paradigm "are committed to the same rules and standards for scientific practice" (p. 11). While Kuhn used the term 'paradigm' in a more specific way than we intend here, his definition provides us with a very useful guide and frame of reference.

Paradigms of inquiry are often aligned with particular discipline areas but, as indicated in Chapter 4, education (and, in particular, e-learning) is hard to pin down as a discipline. In fact, Shulman (1988) argued that education is not a discipline, but a field of study in which multiple modes of inquiry are possible. Furthermore, as explained in Chapter 1, e-learning is an emerging, interdisciplinary area, drawing from a range of research traditions. Because paradigms bring with them assumptions and beliefs about research, different educational researchers will favour particular paradigms and will tend to choose particular methodologies when designing their studies. However, there is a need to ensure that the paradigm of inquiry adopted is appropriate to the goals and questions of the educational research being conducted. Considerable comment and consternation has been generated in the fields of education and e-learning by researchers unthinkingly applying their own disciplinary paradigm of inquiry to the enterprise of educational research. As mentioned above, the appropriateness of the paradigm of inquiry needs to be justified and justifiable in order to ensure that the educational research is rigorous (Crotty, 1998; Shulman, 1988).

In the following sections we outline the major paradigms of inquiry that have been employed in educational research with a view to assisting readers in making and justifying their choice of paradigm and methodology given the phenomenon of study and goals of the inquiry. Our argument points towards a pragmatic paradigm of inquiry for most e-learning evaluation research.

The paradigm of inquiry an individual adopts and employs in a particular context is informed by a range of factors including personal beliefs, theoretical and philosophical perspectives, and contextual factors. Creswell (2009) discussed some of these issues and proposed that three independent philosophical considerations together inform an individual's paradigm of inquiry and her choice of methodology. Table 5.1 presents a summary of these philosophical considerations, which are partly derived from Creswell.

Table 5.1 Philosophical considerations when choosing a paradigm of inquiry

Consideration	Question	Characteristics
Ontological	What is the nature of reality?	A theory of the nature of being – a certain way of understanding *what is*.
Epistemological	What is the nature of knowledge?	A theory of the nature of knowledge. What it *means to know*. How we understand and explain how we come to know.
Axiological	What is the role of values?	The study of value or quality. Is the phenomenon value-free or value-laden?

Numerous research paradigms are identified in the educational research literature. Some are distinct, while others use different terminology to describe approaches that are conceptually very similar. We have chosen to present four major paradigms of inquiry here, and, for convenience, have intentionally used simple labels: *positivist*, *interpretivist*, *critical theory* and *pragmatic*. A common difficulty in the social sciences is that any one concept is given many different labels, which often simply represent different geographical or theoretical traditions. Education is no different and, in an attempt to reduce confusion, we have provided alternative terminology for the four paradigms in Table 5.2.

The following sections provide a general overview of the main tenets of each paradigm. The purpose is not to provide a detailed analysis of the philosophical underpinning of each; rather it is to give the reader a sense of the main defining features of each paradigm and what sets them apart from each other (see also Reeves (1997) and Soltis (1992)). The characteristics of the four paradigms are summarized in Tables 5.3–5.6 respectively. The characteristics described in each table correspond to the three theoretical properties described in Table 5.1, as well as methodological considerations, including issues of validity, and reflections on the nature of outcomes associated with the paradigm of inquiry.

5.5.1 The Positivist Paradigm

The *positivist* paradigm is derived from *modern* thinking, arising from the *enlightenment* period in the Renaissance and the rise in scientific thought. It is based on assumptions which arose at that time – that reality exists independently, is governed by cause and effect, and can be measured objectively. It originated through the natural sciences (Guba & Lincoln, 1994) – physics, chemistry, geology, etc. – where the characteristics of natural phenomena could be objectively measured with increasing levels of accuracy. In more complex natural sciences (e.g. biology, medicine), statistical techniques were developed to estimate the probability of an event. The goal of positivistic inquiry is to discover,

Table 5.2 Alternative terminology for the four paradigms of inquiry discussed in this chapter

Paradigm	Equivalent terms
Positivist	scientific, objective, empirical, quantitative, analytic, hypothetical deductive, functionalist
Interpretivist	relativist, constructivist, naturalistic, humanistic, hermeneutic, systemic, qualitative
Critical theory	neo-Marxist, postmodern, inductive, praxis, feminist
Pragmatic	critical realist, eclectic mixed methods, disciplined eclectic

Table 5.3 A summary of the characteristics of the positivist research paradigm

Ontological	• Reality is objective, singular and 'partitionable'. • Problems can be defined a priori. • Phenomena are context-free. • Events can be explained in terms of cause and effect. • There is one right interpretation.
Epistemological	• The researcher is objective, rational and external to the research (has no impact upon the research data) and as a consequence researchers agree, in general, on what was observed. • There is a focus on deductive reasoning.
Axiological	• Research is value-free. • There is no judgement, simply observation of reality.
Methodological	• The complexity of social situations can be reduced to a string of previously studied, known variables which are clearly operationalized, often using standardized measures. • Experimental designs dominate, where there are clearly defined 'treatment' and 'control' groups. • There is a focus on accuracy, reliability, validity and inferential statistical analysis.
Validity	• Validity and accuracy are assured by the use of replicable, empirical data.
Outcomes of inquiry	• Context- and time-independent generalizations, leading to theory refinement or building, and ultimately to laws which enable prediction and control.

document, predict and control 'reality' and the universal laws that govern it. Characteristics of the positivist paradigm are summarized in Table 5.3.

As studies in social science became more formalized in the years following the Second World War, the positivist paradigm became accepted as 'the way to do things', and its method of choice, the randomized controlled trial, was seen as the 'gold standard' in approaches to research. While there is clearly value in this approach and in quantifying phenomena of interest, often people and the complexity of social interactions cannot easily be reduced to clearly defined variables without over-simplifying the phenomenon of study. Recent developments in the USA have attempted to impose the positivist paradigm on researchers for political and ideological reasons, rather than because it is the most appropriate approach in any context (Phillips, 2006; Reeves, 2006a).

The positivist paradigm has been used widely in e-learning research. As we mentioned in Chapter 2, studies often seek to compare one group of learners who are using technology with another 'equivalent' group of learners who are not using technology, in order to see if there are any differences in performance.

However, thoughtless use of the positivist paradigm has also been widely criticized (see section 6.7). The use of experimental designs is problematic in e-learning environments because they represent complex systems in which a number of variables interact to influence learning processes and outcomes. Truly controlling single variables in these environments is generally seen as untenable. Furthermore, experimental designs assume that the artificial phenomenon functions as designed, often without evidence to support this assumption.

In a postmodern era which exposed weaknesses in the positivist paradigm, and in part because of the difficulties encountered applying it in social-science research generally, and in complex educational environments specifically, a new pseudo-positivist paradigm emerged called, unsurprisingly, *postpositivism*. Postpositivism maintains the essence of many of the ideals of positivism but recognizes that some of its fundamental tenets – naïve realism, pure objectivism – require softening (see Guba (1990) for a useful discussion). While postpositivists are not confident that they themselves will ever discover an absolute truth, they nonetheless still contend that a 'reality' is there to be investigated. Using measurement, prediction and control to determine cause-and-effect relationships remains central in postpositivist thinking. But there is greater recognition of researcher subjectivity and bias, and an acknowledgement that more critical circumspection is required in research. In short, postpositivists maintain many of the central beliefs and methods of their positivist forebears but, as Guba (1990) suggested, these beliefs have been modified somewhat in response to their exposed shortcomings.

5.5.2 The Interpretivist Paradigm

Reeves (1993) and Alexander and Hedberg (1994), in critiquing the positivist paradigm, pointed towards the *interpretivist* paradigm as being more appropriate for evaluating the complexity of e-learning environments. The goal of interpretivist research is to understand events and discover how people construct meaning. It allows the researcher to talk directly to learners and ask them about their behaviour and what they think of a situation, event or context. The interpretivist paradigm acknowledges that reality is subjective, and that there may be multiple realities (Guba & Lincoln, 1989; Patton, 1990). Research is conducted in a naturalistic way, usually avoiding manipulation of the environment, with data produced largely through qualitative methods, sacrificing wide generalizability for depth of understanding. The focus of interpretivist research is on rich descriptions of complex phenomena, with little interest in judging these phenomena. Characteristics of the interpretivist paradigm are summarized in Table 5.4.

Social-research approaches associated with this paradigm have a focus on qualitatively describing what is happening in a particular context, often with little concern for generalizability. A characteristic of interpretivist research is

Table 5.4 A summary of the characteristics of the interpretivist research paradigm

Ontological	• The world is a socially constructed reality, involving multiple perspectives. Different participants may have different views of reality.
Epistemological	• Researchers are subjective and their beliefs impact on the directions the research takes. Researchers may perceive data and interpret results differently.
Axiological	• No research is value-free. • There is little attempt at judgement.
Methodological	• The perceptions and values of multiple participants in a situation are described in order to explore the dynamics of interactions and various possible interpretations. • Researchers and participants create emergent data that is context-bound. • Interpretable patterns or themes are developed through rigorous analysis, which can underpin both genuine exploratory research and theory building.
Validity	• Validity and credibility are derived from triangulation and contextual plausibility.
Outcomes of inquiry	• Context- and time-dependent 'working hypotheses', leading to deeper understanding and, ultimately, theory development.

negotiation of the inquiry details with the participants, or even in collaboration with them. In some cases, such as an anthropologist investigating a particular culture for the first time, the researcher may have only the broadest of goals, and their interest is purely in description. While purely descriptive studies may be appropriate when we understand little about the phenomenon being studied, this is increasingly not the case with e-learning. Indeed a criticism of e-learning research is that it is overly descriptive and does not seek to explain phenomena. A related limitation of interpretivist studies is that they focus on describing what is happening, often without any form of judgement, which is at odds with the goals of evaluation, and goals of improving artificial phenomena, such as designed e-learning environments.

5.5.3 Critical-theory Paradigm

Neither of the preceding paradigms is directly concerned with change or improvement. A third paradigm used in social science, the *critical-theory* paradigm, emerging from postmodern thinking, has a focus on changing the 'world', not just describing it. It recognizes that "certain groups in any society are privileged over others and … subordinates accept their social status as natural, necessary or inevitable" (Kincheloe & McLaren, 1994, p. 291). The goal of research that adopts a critical-theory paradigm of inquiry is to critique and transform social relations and to introduce an element of Stokes' 'consideration of use' into the social-science research agenda.

Even more than interpretivist research, critical-theory research values a dialogue between the researcher and the researched with the aim of improving the life of socially disadvantaged groups by using the results of research to empower them (Murphy, Dingwall, Greatbatch, Parker & Watson, 1998). Research that falls within the critical-theory paradigm encompasses a range of approaches from neo-Marxism to feminism, but a characteristic common to these approaches is what Murphy et al. (1998) refer to as the "value determined nature of the inquiry" (p. 79). Research that comes from the critical-theory paradigm aims to move beyond the cause-and-effect relationships sought through positivism and the diverse and rich descriptions provided by interpretivism, by placing the process and outcomes of critical reflection at the centre of the research process. Characteristics of the critical-theory paradigm are summarized in Table 5.5.

The critical-theory paradigm is similar in many ways to the interpretivist paradigm in recognizing the importance of understanding the dynamics and multiple perspectives of those involved (Guba & Lincoln, 1994). Qualitative strategies are also used in both, but the distinction between the two paradigms lies in the purpose to which evaluation research is put. The concept of praxis is important – that is, action which is informed by theoretical ideas and by the

Table 5.5 A summary of the characteristics of the critical-theory research paradigm

Ontological	• Reality is objective but people are often unaware of the scope of reality because of historical and social views of power relations.
Epistemological	• The researcher is objective and action-oriented, able to empower the researched, thus eliminating the division between the researcher and the researched.
Axiological	• Research is value-laden, and should serve moral as well as technical purposes. Judgement is an important part of the research.
Methodological	• Methodological approaches are similar to those of the interpretivist paradigm, with a leaning towards critical review and theoretically-informed argumentation.
Validity	• Validity is measured by the successful empowerment of the researched and associated social change.
Outcomes of inquiry	• Evidence-based change in social practice.

process of reflection on existing practice. Theory and reflection feed into the formulation of new practice.

One criticism of adopting a critical-theory approach to research and evaluation is that, at its heart, it takes a partisan approach to research, often explicitly adopting a particular ideological position. This is seen as problematic by some critics who, while not arguing for complete objectivism, would be more comfortable with a less "ideologically and politically motivated" research approach (Soltis, 1992, p. 621). However, others have seen clear utility in this approach.

For example, Friesen (2009) has argued that underlying assumptions associated with the enterprise of e-learning can be valuably criticized. He provides a reflective critique of a number of e-learning myths including: the 'myth of the knowledge economy'; the 'anyone, anywhere, anytime' myth; and the 'technology drives educational change' myth. Reeves (1997) has also suggested that a basic tenet of the critical-theory paradigm is to question the political assumptions underpinning the phenomenon of study, and that this process can be sensibly applied to e-learning evaluation research. The role of questioning and critiquing has relevance – for example, Eisner's (1985) *educational connoisseurship* evaluation model is a valid and valuable activity in peer and expert review of e-learning environments.

While some of the more radical, social-change aspects of the critical-theory paradigm may have limited applicability in the practical conduct of evaluation research of e-learning, change and improvement are important elements of e-learning development, for example, in formatively improving e-learning environments. The concept of change is largely absent from the positivist and interpretivist paradigms, but underpins two approaches useful in educational research, namely *action inquiry* and *design-based research*. These will be discussed in more detail in Chapter 6.

5.5.4 Pragmatic Paradigm

Previous sections have highlighted strengths, and some of the weaknesses, in each of the three commonly used paradigms of inquiry in social science. The final paradigm of inquiry we outline is called *pragmatic*, as it combines the most appropriate or useful features of the other paradigms with the explicit purpose of developing a coherent understanding of the world and to address real-world problems. This paradigm firmly advocates the use of a mix of methodologies, enabling the researcher to use the full range of available data-collection methods, without being tied to methodologies or methods typically associated with particular inquiry paradigms. Increasingly, the pragmatic paradigm is seen as the most appropriate to use for e-learning research. Instead of solely comparing or describing phenomena in e-learning environments, this paradigm is suitable for discovering *how* things work in a particular learning context, and seeking to identify causal mechanisms (Kozma, 1994), using a

Table 5.6 A summary of the characteristics of the pragmatic research paradigm

Ontological	• There exists a real world separate from our existence and observation of it.
Epistemological	• Knowledge is a social and historical construct. • The researcher is variably objective and subjective, depending upon the research goals, is rational, and influences the research to varying degrees. • There are no facts beyond dispute.
Axiological	• Research is value-laden.
Methodological	• Using an eclectic mix of methods appropriate to the given context.
Validity	• Multiple perspectives, triangulation and bracketing.
Outcomes of inquiry	• Rich descriptions of complex phenomena.

mixture of qualitative and quantitative sources of data. Characteristics of the pragmatic paradigm are summarized in Table 5.6.

The pragmatic paradigm of inquiry, by in effect 'borrowing' from other paradigms, is more capable of handling the complexity inherent in e-learning evaluation research. Its focus is on practical problems rather than on issues of reality and theories of society, and it acknowledges the weakness of current evaluation-research tools. One strength of this approach is that it addresses both the 'consideration of use' and 'quest for understanding' components of Pasteur's Quadrant. The advantages of adopting a pragmatic paradigm are outlined well by Reeves (1997) who suggested that:

Adherents to the [Pragmatic] Paradigm … view modes of inquiry as tools to better understanding and more effective problem-solving, and they do not value one tool over another … They recognize that a tool is only meaningful within the context in which it is to be used. (p. 173)

The task of adopting appropriate research methodologies in investigations of the effectiveness of e-learning has been problematic for many educational researchers. This often stems from researchers finding themselves caught between alternative or 'competing' paradigms of inquiry and, often by implication, research methodologies. By adopting a pragmatic approach, researchers are effectively able to side-step this question.

However, the use of the pragmatic paradigm, in a way because it combines diverse research traditions and approaches, can lead to complex evaluation and research plans. While researchers such as Patton (1990), Salomon (1991) and Shulman (1988) have argued that the paradigm of inquiry adopted does not necessitate a single, inflexible methodological position, the practical reality is that sometimes it is difficult in a single investigation to successfully integrate multiple mixed methods and the data generated by them. So, while Shulman (1988) suggested that "the best research programs will reflect intelligent deployment of a diversity of research methods applied to their appropriate research questions" (p. 16), this is not without challenges. We will cover some of these challenges more fully in Chapters 8 and 9.

5.5.5 Summary of the Paradigm of Inquiry Discussion

This section has considered four paradigms of inquiry which are commonly used in social-science research. The positivist paradigm is closely aligned with pure science approaches. It allows researchers to test theories and generalize results. However, we have argued that theories in education are often less predictive and very specific in focus, making generalizability difficult. Moreover, the methodological approaches often aligned with this paradigm – particularly experimental studies – are difficult to apply in the complex systems that educational environments represent. Postpositivism emerged as a moderated approach to inquiry that, while maintaining many of the core positivist tenets associated with measurement, prediction and control, recognizes the limitations of notions of 'pure' realism and objectivity.

The interpretivist paradigm is exploratory, aiming for rich descriptions of complex phenomena, with little interest in judging these phenomena. However, rich case-study descriptions are hard to generalize beyond the case, and often these studies stop at description rather than attempting to provide deeper explanation of the phenomena under investigation. A final difficulty with this approach is that there is often little interest in improving the learning environment, a much-valued goal of applied educational researchers.

Like the interpretivist paradigm, the critical-theory paradigm has a focus on understanding the complex world, but it is also concerned with changing the world for the better. This resonates with the formative nature of e-learning evaluation research, but the political and ideological underpinnings of research adopted within the critical-theory paradigm have raised concerns in some quarters about the appropriateness and relevance of its application in studies of the effectiveness of e-learning.

We have argued (and will argue further in Chapter 6) that the most appropriate approach for evaluation research about the effectiveness of e-learning is a pragmatic one, which takes the best features of each paradigm and applies them to the research problem being studied. By adopting a pragmatic paradigm of inquiry we are able to, at the same time, make judgements about learning environments, seek deeper understanding of them, and aim to improve them. This would not be possible if one of the three commonly used paradigms of inquiry was used independently.

5.6 Research Methodologies and Methods

Methodology refers to "a way to solve the research problem systematically" (Kothari, 2008, p. 8). Where 'paradigm of inquiry' reflects a philosophical position on the whole research enterprise, methodology reflects a philosophical position on how the research will *actually be carried out*. The methodology associated with the conduct of a piece of research describes and explains the overarching research design, the logic associated with the steps in the research process and the rationale for how each aspect of the research is completed. For example, the methodology may describe and justify the context and the question(s) being investigated, the nature of the population and any sampling that will be done, the overall type of research strategies that are employed and the analytic processes to be used, and how ethical issues were considered and dealt with. In essence, a description of the methodology becomes an outline of and justification for the research plan (see section 7.3).

'Methodology' should also be distinguished from 'method'. Where methodology refers to the principles a researcher adopts, reflecting the overarching position on how to conduct an inquiry, method refers to the specific tools and data-collection techniques used in an inquiry (Kothari, 2008). Methods are the tools employed to obtain the data that we use as evidence in our research. Data are important in research because the process of collection, production and analysis of data distinguishes research from other kinds of inquiry. The data that are used to provide evidence in research can be incredibly diverse. It could include, just to name a few, responses to surveys or questionnaires, entries from students on a blog or wiki, electronic logs of students' activities in a learning-management system, audio or video recordings of interviews, the content of policy documents used by a university, recordings of visitation to a library workstation, observations of classroom practice, or eye movements of students in a lab. In research we collect or produce data for a specific purpose – data are our attempt to capture phenomena for later analysis in response to a research question.

There is a strong, but not exclusive, relationship between paradigms of inquiry and the type of data they are concerned with, and therefore the methods and methodologies used to generate the data. Generally, the positivist paradigm of inquiry is associated with quantitative data and a quantitative methodology in which, broadly speaking, numbers represent phenomena. Alternatively, the interpretivist and critical-theory paradigms are typically associated with qualitative data and a qualitative methodology in which textual or verbal recordings, or descriptions, represent phenomena.

The close relationship of these methodologies – quantitative and qualitative – to alternative paradigms of inquiry is routinely highlighted because quantitative data is often used deductively to determine cause-and-effect relationships (consistent with positivism), while qualitative methodologies are often used inductively to derive rich, contextual descriptions (consistent with interpretivism and critical theory) (Creswell, 1994). This classic distinction between quantitative and qualitative methodologies, methods and data is one of the most enduring in social-science research. But, as mentioned above, the mapping between methodologies and paradigms of inquiry is not one-to-one. Paradigms of inquiry do not determine methodologies. While it is fairly safe to say that positivist studies rarely use qualitative data, interpretivist studies may use quantitative methods and data to aid description, or in techniques such as exploratory modelling (e.g. cluster analysis). On the other hand, pragmatic studies will happily use a combination of qualitative and quantitative (or 'mixed') methodologies and methods. We will return to a more detailed discussion of types of data and their analysis in Chapter 9.

In summary, two dominant methodologies are used to define and describe what social science, and therefore educational, researchers *do* when they undertake research. While paradigms of inquiry don't determine these methodologies, as with paradigms it is critical that researchers think carefully about their methodological approach, their methods and the data they collect and create, given the paradigm of inquiry they are adopting and the e-learning phenomenon being scrutinized. The importance of this is not lost on Oliver, Roberts et al. (2007), who suggested that:

> It is impossible to talk about e-learning in a research context without reference to methodology, since any claim about e-learning rests on data collected and interpreted in accordance with some methodological position. (p. 31)

5.7 Summary

This chapter provided a general theoretical overview of educational research. We started with a discussion of the definition of the research problem (the phenomenon, research goals and overarching research questions), and then discussed various epistemological and paradigmatic aspects of research, before discussing methodological approaches. We briefly unpacked the characteristics of the positivist, interpretivist and critical-theory paradigms of inquiry, identifying the strengths and weaknesses of each. We presented a fourth, pragmatic paradigm, arguing that it is more appropriate to adopt this approach given the difficulties any one paradigm would have responding to the complex questions posed in e-learning evaluation research.

Drawing on the discussion presented in this chapter, we conclude by proposing a set of key guiding principles for educational research (Table 5.7). By presenting these principles, we do not seek to be prescriptive about the way in which educational research should be undertaken – we recognize the constraints under which those interested in educational research often operate. We also recognize that adhering to research principles such as these is not easy, particularly given the multidisciplinary nature of e-learning research

Table 5.7 Key guiding principles of educational research

Principle	Description
Conduct theoretically-based research	While there is no general, unified educational theory, it is beneficial to be guided and to build upon previous research models, traditions and findings. Where theory is relatively weak, research efforts should go towards generating new theory.
Aim for generalizability	Theories gain their strength by predicting phenomena in a range of contexts: generalizability. Although it may not be possible, it is important to have a goal to develop generalizable theories from evaluation-research studies.
Articulate clear goals and research questions	Educational research is fundamentally affected by the phenomenon being studied, the goal of the research and the research questions being asked. These characteristics should inform the paradigm of inquiry, the methodology and the methods chosen.
Conduct research that is systematic and part of a sustained research agenda	A criticism of educational research is that it has been approached in a piecemeal fashion. Various theorists have called for a series of studies concentrating on a single problem area over a period of time in order to make a more sustained and significant contribution to the field.
Articulate a defensible choice of paradigm of inquiry	Think carefully about the questions you want to ask about a phenomenon and choose a paradigm of inquiry which best suits these questions. This may require reflection on 'where you come from' when you approach evaluation research. A pragmatic approach will often prove useful.
Adopt methodologies and methods of data collection which are appropriate to the goals of the research	Researchers should critically reflect on what the question is actually asking, consider alternative research methodologies and notice how the application of a research methodology can subtly change the nature of the question. Once a research methodology has been decided upon, the conclusions which can safely be drawn should be contemplated.

and evaluation. But we feel there is value in promoting and emphasizing a commitment to these principles rather than advocating that a particular *type* of research should be carried out.

6

Evaluation-research Approaches
Suitable for e-Learning

6.1 Introduction

This chapter will draw together issues discussed in earlier chapters to identify evaluation-research approaches that are suitable for e-learning. Chapter 1 presented several definitions of e-learning and introduced the idea of e-learning artefacts that are created through a design process. We established that e-learning artefacts are tools which can facilitate engagement with learning tasks. Furthermore, we established that learning environments are designed for a particular context to include e-learning artefacts and learning tasks to facilitate particular learning processes in learners and the achievement of desired learning outcomes.

As outcomes of a design process, e-learning artefacts and environments do not spring to life fully formed and perfect. Instead, they go through continuing cycles of design, development and evaluation, and appropriate evaluation research is needed at each stage of this e-learning life cycle. Indeed, many Web 2.0 examples of technology-enhanced learning (such as twitter streams, mashups, etc.) are in constant flux and their essentially dynamic character is part of the learning design. We make this point explicitly because much existing e-learning research assumes that the e-learning artefact is an unchanging product like a natural phenomenon.

In Chapter 4, we took the discussion of the e-learning life cycle further, examining the types of evaluation required at different stages of the life cycle. The discussion identified four scenarios at different stages in the e-learning life cycle, and discussed the types of judgements or decisions which should be made at each stage:

A. Exploration of new tools;
B. Design and development of e-learning artefacts;
C. Testing and improving e-learning environments;
D. Evaluating the effectiveness of an e-learning environment.

Analysis of these scenarios, particularly scenario D, but also scenario C, indicated that *evaluation*'s focus on judgements and decisions can be too narrow. There is also a need to understand how and why the e-learning environment works, and this takes us into a research activity. We chose to use the term 'evaluation research' to indicate that, in studying the effectiveness of e-learning, we need a mixture of making judgements about the usability and usefulness of a learning environment, and seeking understanding about how the learning environment works.

Chapter 5 continued to explore the research theme, looking at the philosophical underpinnings of rigorous, theoretically-based research. We argued that the nature of the phenomenon to be studied, and the principal outcome sought (the goal) from any research determines the main research activity and the type of research questions to be asked. Once research goals and questions have been clarified, it is appropriate to consider the relationship between them, the paradigm of inquiry in which you are situated, and the methodology you choose to adopt. We made a case for a pragmatic paradigm of inquiry, which builds on the strengths, and addresses the weaknesses, of the positivist, interpretivist and critical-theory paradigms, which we will draw upon in the remainder of this chapter.

6.2 Defining the e-Learning Research Problem

In this section, we will draw together the arguments of earlier chapters to explore statements of the evaluation-research problem at various stages of the e-learning life cycle, using scenarios A–D (see Table 4.2, p. 51). We will revisit these scenarios to discuss what might be appropriate evaluation and research goals at each stage of the life cycle. The discussion is summarized in Table 6.1.

Scenario A is very much an exploratory one, looking at how learners might use a new technology for learning, or how teachers might use it for teaching. An appropriate activity is to trial the technology, with an initial goal of observation and discovery. This may be followed by a period of experimentation by a teacher. The research carried out in these phases may be quite informal, but it will be more valuable if it is informed by previous theory about the use of related tools for learning, and seen as part of a larger agenda to research the use of the technology throughout its life cycle. There is also an evaluation component – a decision about whether or not to continue using the technology.

Scenario B is related to the conduct of a project to develop an e-learning artefact from scratch. The focus here is predominantly on evaluation – with two aspects: evaluating the conduct of the project itself (B1); and evaluating the usability of the e-learning artefact that was designed (B2). There is, however, a third aspect, a research element (B3) that focuses on explaining what makes an effective e-learning environment. This largely formative stage involves making judgements about improving the conduct of the project, the way the technology is used and how the learning environment is designed. This may include a pilot

Table 6.1 Evaluation and research goals at different stages of the e-learning life cycle

Scenario	Description	Goal
A	*Researching and evaluating* how a new technology can be used in teaching and learning	Discovery Observation Experimentation
B1	*Evaluating* the conduct of a project to develop an e-learning artefact	Improvement Judgement
B2	*Evaluating* the usability of the designed e-learning artefact	Improvement Judgement
B3	*Researching* the characteristics of e-learning environments that effectively facilitate learning processes and learning outcomes	Explanation
C1	*Evaluating* how the learning environment was designed and how it could be improved	Improvement
C2	*Researching* how learners engage with the e-learning environment	Explanation
D1	*Evaluating* whether the e-learning environment works	Judgement
D2	*Researching* how and why the learning environment led to particular outcomes	Understanding

stage with learners, with a goal of observing learners and explaining how they use the technology in different contexts and, in this way, there is some overlap with scenario C.

In scenario C, the learning environment is now sufficiently mature to research real use in classrooms or virtual environments. Both the usability of this environment and its fitness for purpose may be evaluated (C1). The goal is to improve the learning environment through formative evaluation. The research aspect (C2) focuses on explaining how learners use the learning environment, investigating their learning processes and, to some extent, their achievement of learning outcomes.

The final, summative scenario (D) involves studying the effectiveness of a mature e-learning environment that is known to function as it was designed. Once again, there are two components: evaluating (D1) that the e-learning environment can be used by learners to achieve, to a varying extent, a range of learning outcomes, and researching (D2) how and why the learning environment leads to particular outcomes.

This discussion illustrates that the goals of e-learning evaluation research vary according to the stage of the e-learning life cycle being studied (Shavelson, Phillips, Towne & Feuer, 2003). The research activities undertaken should derive from the evaluation-research goals and should, therefore, also be appropriate to the stage of the e-learning life cycle.

What we are arguing here is that evaluation research of e-learning is an ongoing cyclical process which is closely related to the cycle of development of an e-learning environment (Bannan-Ritland, 2003; Nieveen, McKenney & van den Akker, 2006; van den Akker, 1999; Wang & Hannafin, 2005). Moreover, the characteristics of e-learning evaluation research are different at various stages of the e-learning life cycle. This notwithstanding, evaluation research at each stage should be based on a theoretical view of learning and/or contribute to the development of a theoretical view of learning.

It is important to distinguish between the overall paradigm of inquiry and the actual evaluation methods or strategies that are selected in order to gather and analyse data. The paradigm of inquiry that an evaluation researcher adopts is relatively stable and reflects philosophical views about the nature of knowledge and what constitutes defensible evidence for judgements (see section 5.5). However, one's choice of methods can be quite eclectic, especially if a pragmatic paradigm is adopted. In the early cycles of evaluation research into an e-learning environment, results are likely to be context-specific, and unlikely to be generalizable (Design-Based Research Collective, 2003); qualitative strategies may be more appropriate to capture contextual differences. Over time, as the e-learning environment matures and is used in various contexts, our (theoretical) understanding of it may be sufficient to conduct research using quantitative methodologies (Shavelson et al., 2003) in order to establish systematic correlations between aspects of the designed learning environment, to demonstrate its effectiveness and predict how it could be used in the future. This does not mean that the paradigm of inquiry has become positivist but, rather, that the characteristics of the environment are now more stable and quantitative strategies – such as large-scale surveys, or correlations between log data and final assessment grades – can now be sensibly interpreted. It is a question of carefully matching evaluation-research questions for each stage of the e-learning life cycle with appropriate data-collection strategies so that the overall set of evidence enables useful and insightful conclusions to be drawn.

This discussion can be summarized by noting that a holistic study of the entire e-learning life cycle involves a range of evaluation-research strategies which have traditionally been associated with the three commonly used paradigms of inquiry. In our view, this is a persuasive argument for the adoption of a pragmatic mixture of elements of the strengths of each of the three paradigms (Barab & Squire, 2004) – that is, the pragmatic paradigm proposed in Chapter 5.

A second point (made in section 4.3) is that the stages of the e-learning life cycle are not as distinct as presented in Table 6.1. Investigators might be interested in several research goals at the same time. For example, as an e-learning artefact is developed, the designers probably have a good idea of how the e-learning artefact will be used in an e-learning environment, in at least one context. It would therefore be logical that evaluation research would address both scenarios B and C at the same time, perhaps with different levels of emphasis. Similarly, when studying initial trials of an e-learning environment (scenario C), the researchers would also be interested in some evidence of achievement of learning outcomes. Furthermore, as pointed out in section 4.3, summative studies (scenario D) often lead to formative results, so they should address some formative goals.

The argument we have developed here resonates with the approach taken by Reeves and Hedberg (2003). They advocated a linkage between the phases of development of an e-learning product and phases of evaluation research, and a mixed-methods, pragmatic approach. However, the structure of the Reeves and Hedberg book, with a chapter for each phase of evaluation, could give the reader the impression that evaluation mapped to each stage of development is a series of separate tasks. We argue here that the situation is less prescriptive than this, and there will be inevitable overlaps in evaluation-research approaches across the e-learning life cycle.

6.3 Cyclical Research Approaches

The previous discussion has highlighted that e-learning evaluation-research approaches need to be appropriate for studying designed artefacts, and adapted to a cyclical, *continual-improvement*, development process. Systematic, design-based approaches, such as those used in engineering (Burkhardt, 2006; Cobb et al., 2003; Ross & Morrison, 1989; Salomon, 1991) may be more appropriately applied in this area than analytic, scientific approaches.

Scientific approaches tend to be summative, and assume that the object of study has a stable existence, somewhat like a natural phenomenon, at the time it is studied. This implies that there is an endpoint (albeit a distant one) of gaining understanding of the phenomenon under consideration. However, an e-learning artefact is an artificial phenomenon – we need to ensure that it works as well as it can before we commence summative research. Educational environments are constantly changing – not only because the characteristics of learners change from cohort to cohort, but also because of changes in disciplinary understanding, societal views on the attributes of a 'good' education, etc. – and so approaches that allow for change and constant adaptation are likely to be more useful.

What we are seeking here is a cyclical approach that explicitly maps evaluation-research activities to the design-and-development cycle of an e-learning artefact, and applies across many, if not all, of those development phases. Bannan-Ritland's 'integrative learning design framework' is an approach that is similar to that proposed here, derived from approaches that integrate "instructional design, product design, usage-centred design, diffusion of innovations and educational research" (Bannan-Ritland, 2003, p. 21).

Bannan-Ritland's work was developed to support a research approach called *design-based research*, a cyclical approach that originated in engineering and other design fields. It has emerged in recent years as a suitable approach to educational research (van den Akker, Gravemeijer, McKenney & Nieveen, 2006), in particular e-learning research (Herrington et al., 2009; Reeves, 2006a).

A second cyclical research approach which might be considered is *action research*, or more broadly, *action inquiry*. Action inquiry shares similarities with design-based research, but with an emphasis on improvement of personal practice. The following two sections summarize, respectively, the characteristics and applicability of action inquiry and design-based research to e-learning evaluation research. We have chosen to discuss action inquiry first as this methodology has had a long history in educational research.

While this section has placed an emphasis on a sustained, cyclical approach to e-learning evaluation research, this is not to say that 'one-off', stand-alone studies cannot contribute real insights into e-learning. Some attributes and examples of these types of research studies are explored in section 6.6.

6.4 Action Inquiry

"Action inquiry is an umbrella term for the deliberate use of any kind of a *plan, act, describe, review* cycle for inquiry into action in a field of practice" (Phillips et al., 2000, p. 3.1). Action inquiry is practitioner-based, first-person inquiry (Reason & Bradbury, 2006; Schön, 1982) – "it places the 'I' at the centre of the enquiry process" (McNiff et al., 2003, p. 9). It is closely associated with the critical-theory paradigm of inquiry, being concerned with personal and social improvement, collaboration between practitioner and researcher, change in professional practice and the politics of professional practice (McNiff et al., 2003; Peters & Robinson, 1984).

A crucial defining characteristic of all action inquiry is strategic action – action based upon understanding achieved through the rational analysis of deliberately sought information. While a coherent and logical trail of evidence is necessary in all good research, there is an element of action-inquiry studies developing as fit-for-purpose with "research methods tend[ing] to be less systematic, more informal, and quite specific to the [research] problem"(Patton, 1990, p. 157).

With a strong focus on action, theoretical models and the development of new theory have therefore less prominence. Reeves (2000a) noted that "there is little or no effort to construct theory, models, or principles to guide future design initiatives. The major goal is solving a particular problem in a specific place within a relatively short timeframe". van den Akker (1999) is even more direct with his comment that many action-inquiry studies "lack an explicit scholarly orientation on contributions to knowledge that is accessible to others" (van den Akker, 1999, p. 6).

Reflective practice and action research are two kinds of action inquiry which are specifically aimed at seeking and analysing information to learn about our professional practices with a view to improving them. In *reflective practice*, it may simply be ensuring that we consciously look for certain information while engaging in practice (such as observing how actively learners engage in online discussion forums). On the other hand, *action research* involves using a more formal method of data generation, such as a needs analysis, or a survey of user satisfaction.

The important point in both cases, however, is that the planning of subsequent action is based upon appropriate and high-quality information, and it is deliberative: possibilities are created, analysed discussed and chosen in a separate and clearly defined planning stage. Action research can be used in scenario A (researching how a new technology can be used in teaching and learning; see Table 6.1) because this scenario is driven by an individual's quest to improve their own practice. However, the 'first-person' nature of action research arguably makes it inappropriate for the other three scenarios, because these involve 'products' – either an e-learning artefact or an e-learning environment. Action research is appropriate when investigating individual teaching practice, but doesn't apply well to learning activities in an e-learning environment. Design-based research is more appropriate to such a situation.

6.5 Design-based Research

Design-based research is a relatively new approach in e-learning inquiry. It evolved in response to two criticisms of e-learning evaluation and research. The first is that the field has a 'faddish' focus on new technologies and e-learning developments with no solid theoretical base. While much of the e-learning literature is about creatively *doing* something, design-based research also tries to understand what has been done.

The second criticism relates to an inappropriate use of positivistic approaches – for example, attempting summative research into e-learning environments where it has not been established that the e-learning environment functions well as designed. Reeves has been a strident critic of pseudo-scientific approaches to e-learning research and a strong advocate of socially responsible, use-oriented research which is concerned with practical use as well as increased understanding (Reeves, 1993, 2000b, 2005; Reeves, Herrington & Oliver, 2005). These views are described well by Barab and Squire (2004, p. 5): "Design-based research is concerned with using design in the service of developing broad models of how humans think, know, act and learn."

While there are similar terms used in the literature (such as *design research*, *design experiments* and *development research*), a useful concise starting point is that design-based research is:

> … a systematic but flexible methodology aimed to improve educational practices through iterative analysis, design, development, and implementation, based on collaboration among researchers and practitioners in

real-world settings, and leading to contextually sensitive design principles and theories. (Wang & Hannafin, 2005, p. 6)

A further useful distinction is that design-based research should not be described as one possible methodology, but should be considered as an entire and coherent research approach in its own right. We need to be clear that even if design-based research is different in the relationships between participants in the research process – in a manner that is similar to the conduct of participatory action research (Kemmis & McTaggart, 2000) – the types of "underlying questions behind design research are the same as those that drive innovative design: What alternatives are there to current educational practices? How can these alternatives be established and sustained?" (Edelson, 2006, p. 103).

The essence of design-based research can be seen in the distinction between 'predictive' research and design-based research. In predictive research there is a separation between researchers and practitioners, with the application of theory being quite distinct from the generation of theory. In design-based research, practitioners and researchers work together to define problems, develop evaluation-research designs, collect data, consider the findings and then generate design principles for two purposes – to guide further refinements in the e-learning artefact life cycle under consideration, and to make contributions to wider theory on e-learning design principles. This distinction is illustrated in Figure 6.1.

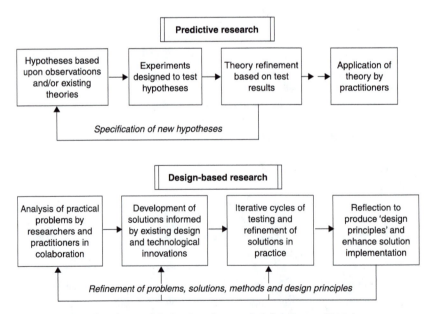

Figure 6.1 Iterative phases of design-based research (after Reeves, 2006a).

Table 6.2 Key characteristics of the phases of design-based research

Phases of design-based research	Key characteristics
Analysis of practical problems	• Using literature • Shared experience of researchers and practitioners • Perhaps a small investigatory pilot study • Articulation of initial theoretical framework
Development of solutions based on existing knowledge	• Detailed design of the artefact with explicit predictions about outcomes
Evaluation research of the solution in practice	• Cycles of formative evaluation research, as summarized in Table 6.1
Reflection to produce design principles (further elaborated in section 6.5.1)	• Design principles are framed to provide both practical solutions to the initial problem(s) and advance theoretical understandings in the field

Reeves (2006a) described the iterative nature of design-based research, illustrated in Figure 6.1, as involving:

- analysis of practical problems;
- development of solutions based on existing knowledge;
- evaluation research of the solution in practice;
- reflection to produce *design principles.*

Each of these phases is discussed in detail in Herrington et al. (2009). Table 6.2 summarizes some key characteristics.

Design-based research as an approach is consistent with the arguments we presented in Chapter 4 about studies of e-learning requiring a mixture of evaluation and research and with Stokes' views on the quest for understanding and consideration of use. "More than most other research approaches, [design] research aims at making both practical and scientific contributions" (van den Akker, 1999, p. 8).

6.5.1 Design Principles

As noted earlier, a criticism of e-learning developments has been the lack of theoretical frameworks to inform design. However, in section 5.3, we pointed out the difficulties in developing meaningful theories of the complexity of human learning. Design-based research has a goal of adding to human knowledge, but addresses this issue by starting 'small', by attempting to develop relatively "humble" theories (Cobb et al., 2003), addressing domain-specific learning processes which are "accountable to the activity of design" (p. 10). This step is one distinction between design-based research and action research.

Theories in design-based research "are not 'grand' theories of learning ... Instead, they tend to emphasize an intermediate theoretical scope" (Cobb et al. 2003, p. 11). They are intimately entwined with the design of learning environments (The Design-Based Research Collective, 2003), with the goal of providing a clear rationale about the suggestions and implications provided to practitioners. We will call these modest theories 'proto-theories'.

Design-based researchers tend to call their proto-theories *design principles*, with an emphasis on producing "heuristic guidelines to help others select and apply the most appropriate knowledge for a specific design task in another setting" (Nieveen et al., 2006, p. 153). With the passage of time, and increasing understanding, design principles can potentially be generalized into theories (Edelson, 2006).

In section 5.3, we distinguished between 'conceptual frameworks' and theories, and noted that our LEPO framework (Chapter 3) is a conceptual framework and does not have the status of theory. One way to validate the LEPO framework would be to use it in a number of iterations of design-based research.

Because proto-theories in design-based research are context-specific, it is very important to specify clearly the context (i.e. the design of the learning environment and any assumptions made) so that the findings of the study can be used in other, similar contexts. Kelly (2006) and The Design Based Research Collective (2003) have provided examples of the use of design-based research in a range of contexts.

The *open-data* initiatives which are currently gaining popularity, and political weight, in some countries (e.g. the UK) can add to the body of data which is available for further analysis and theory-building. However, in line with the previous argument about context, care must be taken that such open data is analysed together with other data from comparable contexts. Alternatively, careful arguments need to be presented as to why a particular analysis is context-independent. For example, standardized survey data is inherently more sharable than in-depth interview data about a particular e-learning environment. Local institutional and ethical issues associated with consent and named researcher access to data collection will also have an impact on the free availability of e-learning research data to the wider research community.

6.5.2 The Rigour of Design-based Research

Now that we have briefly described design-based research as a research approach, we will analyse how it fits the characteristics of high-quality research developed at the end of Chapter 5 (Table 5.7, p. 82). Each principle is discussed in turn.

Conduct theoretically-based research. As discussed in section 6.5.1, design-based research builds on existing theory and attempts to develop design principles (proto-theories). Edelson (2002) noted three types of theories that arise from design-based research: domain theories, design frameworks and design methodologies.

Aim for generalizability. Design-based research recognizes the difficulty in generalizing in theoretically immature fields such as education and e-learning, but seeks to work towards generalizability through its emphasis on relationships between researchers and practitioners. Close working relationships build understanding and facilitate good communication and dissemination of ideas. The notions of 'communities of practice' (e.g. Wenger, 1998) and dissemination (see Chapter 11) are pertinent here. However, the communities in design-based research have the dual intention of sharing and further developing both practical and theoretical ideas.

Articulate clear goals, research questions and/or hypotheses. Analysis of the problem and systematic documentation is a key component of the design-based research approach.

Conduct research that is systematic in its inquiry and part of a sustained research agenda. Iterative and systematic inquiry underpins a design-based research approach, as is clearly shown in Figure 6.1. When a number of cycles of research are appropriately conducted, there is a greater chance that a clear program of research will be developed, where the results and findings from one study are built upon in further cycles. Roblyer (2005) listed "cumulativity" as a "pillar of good educational research". She noted that "technology research suffers from what might be called single-study syndrome" (p. 197), and argued for the need to build on previous work and gather evidence in a cumulative fashion in order to have greater confidence in the ability of research to add genuinely valuable insights to the field of study. Intrinsically cyclical approaches to research, such as design-based research, have in-built cumulativity.

Articulate a defensible choice of paradigm of inquiry. At its heart, design-based research adopts a pragmatic paradigm of inquiry. The substantial, emerging literature, including this chapter, illustrates this principle. A heavy focus in the design-based research literature over the last decade has been on justifying the need to be 'scientific', in response to ideological and political positivist critiques, particularly in the USA. Our view is that this attempt at justification has been overdone, and it is time for design-based research to move forward as a defensible and powerful approach to researching educational innovations of all types. "Design-based research should be considered as a form of scholarly inquiry alongside others" (Bell, 2004, p. 243).

Adopt methodologies and methods of data collection that are appropriate to the goals of the research. The methods for data collection used in design-based research are not different from those used in other research approaches. Situated as it is in a pragmatic paradigm of inquiry, the full suite of both quantitative and qualitative strategies are available for use. The essential requirement for synergy between emerging theory and ongoing design and research acts as an additional check on the appropriateness of each phase of the research. The collaboration between researchers and practitioners provides other opportunities for discussion about selecting the best research strategies to adopt.

Carry out appropriate data analysis and interpretation. This principle will be discussed further in Chapter 9. Data analysis and interpretation is as important as it is in other research approaches, and the desired goals of developing clear design principles provide a focus for careful interpretation.

Arrive at defensible conclusions. Again, the strong internal coherence in design-based research between theory and practice, and between the interests of researchers and practitioners, provides cross-checks on the validity of the research design and the robustness of the conclusions reached at each cycle.

6.6 The Value of Stand-alone Studies

The preceding sections have made a strong argument for iterative cycles of evaluation research that lead to robust findings to inform both practice and theory in e-learning. However, in Chapter 4 and in section 6.2, we have noted that evaluation research can start at any stage of the e-learning life cycle. While inquiry is desirable at all stages of the e-learning life cycle, there are many cases where circumstance and/or the research goal dictate a stand-alone approach to evaluation research – which may subsequently undergo further cycles. For example, there are many relatively mature learning environments that have been designed in the absence of any research activity. Also, we know that many e-learning projects have relatively short time-frames – either because of grant requirements or the need to have a finished product ready for the next term's teaching.

If an opportunity for useful research presents itself, then one should begin the process in the available context. This means adopting a pragmatic and strategic approach to e-learning evaluation research. If the research is worth doing, and opportunities for data collection are available, then stand-alone studies can be very worthwhile. Indeed, with web-based tools, system-recorded data is often readily available to answer particular evaluation-research questions about patterns of access (see section 9.2.7). A useful tip is not to think of projects in one-off terms, but to plan for further cycles of evaluation research as part of a sustained agenda.

Stand-alone studies can be seen as design-based research, albeit with one cycle, and this has been referred to as a reconstructive study (van den Akker, 1999, p. 6), or as Type II development research (Richey, Klein & Nelson, 1996). e-Learning evaluation research does not have to be cyclical, but it should be able to demonstrate the same level of rigour outlined in section 6.5.2.

As evaluation researchers over many years, the authors have all been involved in a wide range of evaluation-research activities, many of which could be described as stand-alone or one-cycle studies. For example, the wiki-based collaborative writing example from section 4.6 was a stand-alone study conducted over 12 weeks, rather than an iterative design-based evaluation-research study.

6.6.1 Meta-analytic Studies

One way in which the field of e-learning can maximize the benefits from stand-alone projects is to draw implications from a number of similar studies. Findings from meta-analytic studies have a higher degree of generalizability than that which component single studies can offer. Meta-analytic studies are often carried out on a large scale – in order to maximize the value of their results – and as a result take time and considerable commitment to conduct. Two recent examples are as follows:

1. The US study of over a thousand pieces of research conducted between 1996 and 2008 (Means, Toyama, Murphy, Bakia & Jones, 2009) concluded that blended learning (combining both face-to-face and online learning experiences) does offer learning advantages; however, the advantages are not due to the technology per se but relate to time spent in learning, curriculum design and pedagogy.
2. A study of 74 distance education studies (Bernard et al., 2009) concluded that learning designs involving learner–learner, learner–teacher or learner–content interactions were more conducive to learning than those with less emphasis on interaction.

Meta-analytic studies of this scale and power are outside the realm of work for most practitioners. However, the emerging 'open data' movement may lead to a wider availability of extensive data sets, which may facilitate wider use of meta-analytic studies. A smaller-scale option is possible and this involves examination across a number of stand-alone cases with similar designs, often coming from one design-and-development group. One example is the study across 70 cases of small projects in Hong Kong where teachers had received assistance from one design, development and evaluation team working in collaboration across three universities (Lam, McNaught & Cheng, 2008). Small-scale meta-analytic studies enable the findings of a number of quite simple stand-alone studies to be considered together. It is a strategy that is much tighter and more rigorous than normal literature reviews, and can result in contributions to theory and practice.

6.7 The Role of Approaches Often Aligned with Positivism

We have argued in section 6.2 that "design research is not, in fact, incompatible with traditional outcomes-based evaluations" (Edelson, 2002, p. 118). In this section we will explore the possibilities that experimental, quasi-experimental or comparison designs offer to e-learning evaluation research.

6.7.1 Experimental or Quasi-experimental Designs

The predominant way that theories have been 'tested' in educational technology and e-learning research has been through *experimental* or *comparison* studies. As we mentioned in Chapter 2, the question is usually couched as 'How does the (new) technology-enhanced environment compare to the old approach?' Researchers typically identify the desired learning outcomes for learners in a particular discipline and compare learning outcomes for two groups, each of which has been presented with different modes of teaching. Thus, one group of learners – termed the control group – receives 'traditional' forms of teaching (lecture, small-group tutorial or laboratory classes) while a second group – termed the experimental group – receives the same content through an e-learning approach. Achievement is measured through a pre-test and post-test, and any differences between groups in terms of changes in pre- and post-tests are attributed to the mode of teaching (e-learning versus traditional forms of teaching). (Readers may like to refer back to section 5.5.1, p. 72, and Table 5.3, p. 73, on the summary of the characteristics of the positivist research paradigm, as this design is common in research within this paradigm of inquiry.)

True experimental designs are conducted through randomized controlled trials where 'subjects' (learners) are randomly assigned to treatment and control groups. This is rarely feasible in educational settings and so often 'matched' groups are sought, for example, in classes of the same size, similar curriculum context, etc., and then comparisons made. This approximation to experimental design is termed a quasi-experimental design.

One premise of the use of experimental or quasi-experimental approaches is the need to have a clear prediction or hypothesis based on some articulated theory. To investigate quantitatively which elements or attributes in the learning environment can accurately predict learning outcomes, researchers need to establish a theoretical model of the learning environment. Once a theoretical model has been established, it can be tested using a data set collected by the researcher(s) and analysed with various statistical tests. However, for three decades, researchers have strongly lamented the lack of theory in educational technology research: "Most experiments in the field of instructional media have not been guided by any *theoretical* framework, yet an experiment without a theoretical base is like a ship without a rudder" [italics in original] (Bates, 1981, p. 219). As we have discussed in Chapter 5, there is no one established theory of learning and teaching, let alone an established theoretical model of e-learning environments (Draper et al., 1996), and this has presented researchers with ongoing challenges.

As noted earlier, in an experimental approach, learning outcomes are usually 'measured' through a pre-test/post-test design. Learners are given a pre-test before they use the e-learning environment to test their 'baseline' or pre-existing knowledge or understanding of the content area. Learners then work their way through the e-learning environment. Sometimes this can occur over an extended period or a number of sessions. When learners have finished their learning tasks, they complete a post-test on the content area. The pre- and post-tests should have close correspondence to ensure that the two scores can be validly compared.

Despite the widespread use of experimental or quasi-experimental designs, numerous authors have, over the years, identified weaknesses in the way they have been applied to e-learning research, and, prior to that, research into educational technology and educational media. Bates (1981) critiqued studies of educational television in the early 1980s, citing several reasons why the experimental method was unsuccessful:

> The first is the failure of researchers to understand or apply sufficiently the basic scientific rationale on which the method depends. The second is that, in many instances, the method, even when properly carried out, is quite inappropriate for many of the situations in which decision-makers find themselves. (p. 218)

These criticisms equally apply to many e-learning studies that adopt an experimental design.

6.7.2 Variables, Results and Interpretation

Many researchers argue that the results gathered from comparative studies tell us very little about the effectiveness of e-learning. A problem with comparative studies is that the experimental design assumes that all other elements in the learning environment are equal when isolating and controlling variables. The learning environment represents a complex series of interrelated variables which, acting together, 'produce' learning. As we indicated in Chapter 3, learner motivation, learners' interactions, teacher involvement, the mode of teaching and classroom culture are interdependent in their effects on learning outcomes. When one variable is changed in this environment, other variables in the environment also change (Salomon, 1991). Any attempt to isolate particular variables and compare them across treatment conditions is not possible in most educational settings. Thus, a fundamental reason why researchers on both sides of the positivist–interpretivist divide have questioned the usefulness of comparative studies is that the 'isolated treatment' variable is potentially confounded by a multitude of other variables in the learning environment (Draper, 1997; Rowe, 1996; Wills & McNaught, 1996).

The difficulty of establishing valid comparison groups has been associated with the plethora of studies that have found 'no significant difference' between treatment and control groups (Russell, 1999).

Given that isolating variables and controlling them across treatment and control conditions in complex learning environments is largely untenable, it can be difficult to attribute any changes in outcomes to any one single factor (such as the 'treatment'). While comparative studies can sometimes establish an effect or a significant difference between two groups, they cannot determine the specific cause of the effect or why it occurred.

Given these considerations, researchers need to be careful about the conclusions they draw from experimental studies. One problem with research studies that seek to determine the 'effectiveness' of e-learning courseware is their over-extension or misinterpretation of research results. Researchers who have used data from comparative studies to champion the use of e-learning as a more effective mode of teaching have seemingly made a surface judgement about the complex nature of learning. Draper (1996) pointed out that:

> ... such [comparative studies] can be taken as establishing that it is now reasonable to take the new intervention seriously having performed well in one real test, but can seldom be taken as proof that it is inherently better or even necessarily effective by itself. (p. 63)

Like others, such as Reeves (1993, 1995) and Alexander and Hedberg (1994), we have identified a range of methodological deficiencies in experimental and quasi-experimental studies. Some suggestions for avoiding these 'traps' are as follows:

- Ensure that there is a robust theoretical framework, firmly grounded in the literature.
- Clearly specify all the variables (dependent and independent) of relevance.
- Ensure a balanced set of measures. Often one finds precise measurement of easy-to-measure variables, while more complex variables, which might be the crucial ones, are ignored.
- Make sure that the treatment time is adequate. Conclusions about learning gains cannot usually be made after learners use materials for less than 30 minutes!
- Keep the focus of the outcome measures on learning.
- Ensure sample sizes are large enough.
- Avoid obscure statistical analysis. Remember that the findings should be interpretable by the e-learning community.

6.7.3 When are Experimental Studies in e-Learning Useful?

While there is ample evidence of poor quality in experimental studies, it may not be necessary to throw the experimental baby out with the bathwater. Just because experimental designs have been poorly and inappropriately applied in the past does not mean the entire e-learning community should forego any attempts to carry out experimental research.

Experimental research can be particularly valuable for investigating fundamental aspects of learning, for example, in areas such as cognition, perception, motivation, communication, collaboration, problem solving, self-efficacy or self-regulation (cf. Mayer, 1999; Mayer & Chandler, 2001; Moreno & Mayer, 2005). Basic research in cognitive psychology underpins many of the popular constructivist teaching and learning models employed to design effective e-learning environments. This is important not only because it shows the scientific lineage of these educational models, but also because it provides e-learning researchers with an opportunity to explore and build on these theoretical models through dedicated research. The practical outcomes of such research may not be immediate – they may take a number of years to be recognized as useful – but this makes them no less critical. We need a balanced mixture of approaches to evaluation research, both to improve educational practice and to understand learning at a fundamental level.

6.8 Summary

We have established in this chapter that e-learning evaluation research is a fundamentally cyclical, design process, even though, in some cases, the evaluation-research cycle may start part-way through the design-and-development process, and may sometimes consist of only one cycle. Two cyclical evaluation-research approaches were explored: action inquiry and design-based research. While both share similarities, action inquiry is concerned with improvement in individual practice, while design-based research is concerned with development of an e-learning artefact or e-learning environment. Design-based research also has a more explicit concern for generating theoretical understandings. We claimed that action inquiry is of limited use in e-learning evaluation research, being primarily applicable in individual exploration of a new technology.

We found that design-based research is well suited to e-learning evaluation research, and we justified its appropriateness against the principles of high-quality research developed in Chapter 5.

However, we stop short of claiming that design-based research is the only approach useful in e-learning evaluation research. There are circumstances where evaluation research does not follow the whole e-learning development life cycle, and a cyclical approach is not warranted. Nevertheless, the theory-generating and methodological characteristics attributed to design-based research in section 6.5.2 (other than the absence of iteration) apply equally well to a range of research approaches.

We feel that proponents of design-based research have spent sufficient time in justifying its rigour and in promoting it as an alternative approach to educational research. Instead, they should be positioning it as a generic research approach for any educational innovation where theory is still developing. On the other hand, in the relatively small number of cases where theory is adequate and predictive, we argue that quantitative, experimental and quasi-experimental approaches – traditionally associated with a positivist paradigm – can be appropriate.

A useful closing comment is to note the criteria for design practice originally set out by Hannafin, Hannafin, Land and Oliver (1997); they are still very relevant today after more than a decade:

- designs must be based on a defensible or widely acknowledged theoretical framework;

- methods must be consistent with the outcomes of research conducted to test, validate, or extend the theories on which they are based;
- designs are generalizable;
- designs and their frameworks are validated iteratively through successive implementation. (Wang & Hannafin, 2005, p. 13)

These design principles are very close to the set of principles of high-quality educational research noted at the end of Chapter 5. The synergy between design and research principles lends weight to the conclusion that designing for e-learning needs to be evidence-based, scholarly and reflective, and, hence, that evaluation research is an essential component of good e-learning practice.

In Part III of this book, we support practitioners and researchers by offering practical guides and advice about how best to plan and conduct evaluation-research studies, and how to make best use of the resulting findings. Chapter 7 breaks down the process of carrying out an e-learning evaluation-research study into components. Chapter 8 explores the stages of the e-learning life cycle and identifies five different evaluation forms that are appropriate at different stages, together with the methods which might be used. Data and methods are discussed in more detail in Chapter 9, as well as analysis and interpretation in evaluation research. Part III concludes with a chapter on project-management evaluation (Chapter 10), and a second on sustainability (Chapter 11).

III
Practical Aspects of
Evaluation Research

7
The Process of Carrying Out Evaluation Research

7.1 Overview

This chapter provides an overview of the process of carrying out evaluation research on an e-learning environment. This practical process draws on previous chapters, and breaks down the activity of evaluation research into a number of factors, as illustrated in a process diagram in Figure 7.1. The development of the process diagram builds on the processes reported by Oliver, Harvey, et al. (2007) and Reeves and Hedberg (2003). By breaking down the evaluation-research process into components, we enable readers to use 'divide-and-conquer' techniques to simplify the process of developing a complex evaluation-research plan. By using a process diagram we hope that readers can retain the sense of the whole process, even while being focused on one aspect.

Figure 7.1 acts as an 'advance organizer' for much of the rest of this chapter, where each element in the diagram will be discussed in some detail. Some elements will be discussed in more detail in Chapters 8 and 9.

7.2 Components of the Evaluation-research Process

7.2.1 Scholarly Positioning of Evaluation Research

As we argued in Chapter 5, scholarship to position evaluation research within the existing knowledge base associated with e-learning involves understanding the problem being studied, through clarifying the phenomenon being studied and generating from this the overall goal of the study. This overall goal then needs to be thought about in terms of the paradigm in which it is situated and the most appropriate methodological approach, which we discussed further in Chapter 6.

We discussed phenomena in an abstract sense early in Chapter 5. In this section we address some practical questions which might be asked about the phenomenon being studied:

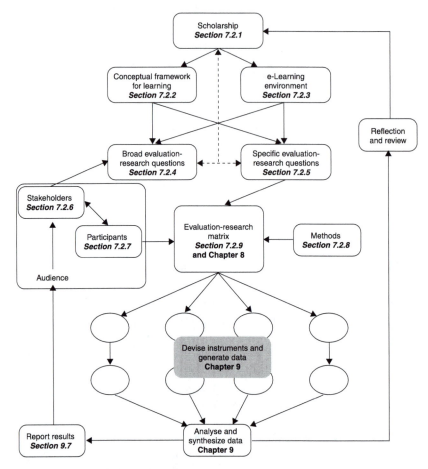

Figure 7.1 The evaluation-research process.

What is the phenomenon in question? What factors influence the situation being evaluated? What is the context? Who are the people? What things are involved? What events? What are the relationships between these?

What is your view of the phenomenon in question? Are you on the outside or inside of the process under investigation, and are you looking inward or looking outward?

Where is your answer situated? Will answering the question involve manipulating the situation or not? Should the data be quantitative or qualitative?

These considerations will assist an evaluator/researcher to understand the paradigm in which the study is situated, and to select an appropriate methodological approach. As we noted in section 5.6, it is important to be able to justify a position on these issues in order to establish the rigour of any evaluation-research study. Chapter 8 will unpack in more detail the nature of the *artificial* phenomenon which is e-learning.

The scholarly positioning of evaluation research also involves building on existing theory, contributing to two other elements of Figure 7.1: *conceptual frameworks for learning* (section 7.2.2), and the *e-learning environment* (section 7.2.3).

7.2.2 Conceptual Frameworks for Learning

A factor contributing to the rigour of e-learning evaluation research is the theoretical grounding of the study – that is, drawing on the existing literature to enunciate what is known conceptually about the aspects of learning that will be studied.

In Chapter 3, we presented a broad conceptual framework (the LEPO framework) that considered learning as an interaction between three components: the learning environment, the learning process and the learning outcome; and two actors: the learner and the teacher. This broad framework is one (of several) which can be used as a conceptual basis for an e-learning study. In Chapter 8, we unpack evaluation-research activities which are appropriate at different stages of the e-learning life cycle and map the LEPO framework against these, in a way which uses a consistent conceptual framework at each stage.

The LEPO framework may well be too broad for detailed investigation of specific learning scenarios. It is perfectly appropriate to use a different framework or adapt the LEPO framework by linking it to another specific conceptual learning framework or theory.

7.2.3 The e-Learning Environment

A second factor contributing to the rigour of e-learning evaluation research is clarity about the phenomenon being investigated – that is, the nature of the e-learning environment. As noted in section 7.2.1, the literature should be drawn on to establish what is known about the effective design of e-learning environments in the particular context proposed.

e-Learning environments are particularly context-specific. Earlier, we established that:

- an e-learning artefact has one of three forms: an interactive learning system, a generic learning tool or a learning object;
- an e-learning environment is built from one or more e-learning artefacts, and placed in context through the desired learning outcomes and the designed learning tasks.

A complicating factor is that the term *e-learning* is often used in a 'one size fits all' fashion, despite its use in a range of contexts (Friesen, 2009). Often the precise way that the term e-learning is used is dependent on the author's particular purposes or specific research agenda. Because the term is often used without explicating the underlying assumptions of the author, or the context of use, understanding of e-learning is hampered. A related issue is that many e-learning researchers simply assume that one e-learning intervention is 'equivalent' to any other e-learning intervention. In other words, e-learning is treated as a natural phenomenon in much e-learning evaluation research. This treatment is at odds with the position that we have argued for in Chapter 6 – that e-learning is an artificial phenomenon, and effort needs to be put into understanding the context of use of the phenomenon, as well as improving the design and implementation of the phenomenon.

This makes it important to establish a baseline description of the e-learning environment and document this clearly (see section 8.4), so that other researchers can understand the context of, and potentially replicate, your work with the aim of generalizing understanding of the impact of e-learning.

Sections 7.2.2 and 7.2.3 draw particularly on Chapters 5 and 6, acknowledging the need to take a scholarly approach to evaluation research and base it on what has previously been published in the literature. These two elements inform the design of both broad and specific evaluation-research questions, which Creswell (2009) calls 'central questions' and 'sub-questions' respectively.

7.2.4 Broad Evaluation-research Questions

In Chapter 5, we discussed specification of the overall research goal and associated questions, and their place in a *theoretical context* of paradigms and methodologies. In this section, we focus on the overall evaluation-research goal as a preparation for *practically* conducting evaluation research on the ground. This goal can be expressed as one or two broad questions, which capture the essence of what the study is about. We will call these evaluation-research questions the "broad question[s] that ask for an exploration of the central phenomenon or concept in a study" (Creswell, 2009, p. 129).

One goal of research is to generate new knowledge, and questions enable us to note a gap in our knowledge, and guide us towards resolving that gap. All research questions are composed of choices from among the following options: What? When? Where? Who? Whom? How? Why? If?

The best evaluation-research questions are open-ended, exploratory questions. For example:

- How effective are the computer-conferencing activities which have been incorporated into this course?
- What is the nature of learning processes used?
- Which factors are important in the design of a learning environment which is intended to foster teamwork?
- How can the course be modified to enable learners to learn more deeply?

The authors have substantial experience in reviewing papers submitted to journals and conferences. A weakness in many of the papers we review for publication is a lack of clarity in specifying broad research questions in order to provide a direction or orientation for the study.

7.2.5 Specific Evaluation-research Questions

A problem with the open-ended nature of broad evaluation-research questions is that they may be too broad to readily obtain evidence to answer them. That is why we recommend the use of a small number of sub-questions, which we will mostly call 'specific evaluation-research questions'. These questions should be *answerable* – we should be able to identify the evidence which is needed to answer each specific evaluation-research question, and we should be able to synthesize the evidence obtained from these specific questions to answer the broad questions. Creswell (2009) claimed that a study should have five to seven specific questions.

Experienced evaluators have acquired the implicit skill to ask these questions and determine methods and techniques to answer them. We suggest that it is worthwhile to articulate explicitly these questions. Creswell (2009) has provided some guidance on how to structure specific research questions: develop open-ended questions using the prepositions *what* or *how*; use words which do not suggest the outcome; and describe the focus and context of the study.

The SMART framework (Doran, 1981) may also be helpful in designing specific research questions. The first four elements of the SMART framework are that questions are Simple, Measurable, Achievable and Realistic. The fifth element, that they are Time-based, is arguably less relevant to question development, but is relevant in developing an evaluation-research plan.

The development of both broad and specific evaluation-research questions is difficult, requiring clarity of thought about what you are trying to achieve. However, as discussed in sections 7.2.2 and 7.2.3, existing scholarly knowledge about e-learning can be used to narrow the range of suitable questions by referring to what we know about the design and development of e-learning environments, and what we know about learning in the context of the proposed e-learning use. Chapter 8 is designed as a scaffold for the development of effective evaluation-research questions at various stages of the e-learning life cycle.

Some examples of specific evaluation-research questions are:

- How does the approach of the lecturer influence the learners' use of the discussion forum?
- What is the nature of the teamwork which occurs?
- How could the online role-play approach be improved?
- How do learners use the online environment in order to learn?

Once sufficient evidence is obtained to answer the specific questions, that evidence can be synthesized to answer the broad evaluation-research questions.

Broad and specific evaluation-research questions are often developed in consultation with stakeholders (see the left-hand side of Figure 7.1). For example, a granting body may want evidence of the effective use of funding, or a Dean may wish to know how widely applicable an innovation is to other contexts.

7.2.6 Stakeholders

The stakeholders are the people who have an interest in the study being undertaken – those for whom the work is being done. When we describe an educational experience as being effective, we need to consider the criteria for effectiveness that the various stakeholders have.

The role of stakeholders is different in the evaluation (judgement) and research (understanding) aspects of an e-learning evaluation-research study, and it will vary according to the mix of evaluation and research, and how the findings are used (Oliver, Harvey et al., 2007). If a study focuses mainly on making decisions for an internal, local audience, then the balance is tipped towards evaluation. If, on the other hand, the study aims at a wider, scholarly audience, then the balance is tipped towards research.

Since the characteristics of the peer-reviewed publication process – what we might call the scholarly quality-assurance process – are well understood, this section restricts itself to considering stakeholders from an evaluation perspective, making judgements and decisions about e-learning effectiveness. There are many stakeholders involved in the conduct of e-learning innovations at universities, and they have a variety of perspectives and vested interests.

In Table 7.1 we have listed a range of possible stakeholders, and some of the interests they might have in an educational activity – whether this is an innovation in the curriculum or the continuation of existing practice. In a study with a strong evaluation component, Table 7.1 can be helpful in understanding the implications that working for these stakeholders has for the information you will seek to gather.

7.2.7 Participants

The participants in an evaluation study are those who actually provide the data. Everybody involved with the educational experience (lecturers, tutors, technical staff, etc.) may be able to provide information to assist in answering the specific evaluation-research questions. Study participants are usually also stakeholders, although not necessarily primary stakeholders.

In line with the pragmatic, mixed-methods paradigm and the characteristics of rigorous evaluation research developed in Chapter 5, in most cases specific questions will indicate the use of data from a range of different participant

Table 7.1 Description of the vested interests of various possible stakeholders

Stakeholder	Examples of the vested interest of each stakeholder
Teachers	• Professional satisfaction • Keeping a job
Learners	• Learning something perceived to have value • Getting qualifications that can lead to employment
Subject and course coordinators	• Ensuring that the learners' learning meets some quality-assurance standards
Faculty deans	• Capacity to provide for increasing numbers of learners • Meeting professional standards of the discipline area
Members of a university's chancellery	• Links to the university's strategic mission • Cost-effectiveness, especially in the provision of technology
Funding bodies	• Assuring that the product is congruent with the grant application
Employers	• A focus on graduate capabilities rather than all the intervening experiences
Professional accrediting bodies	• Standards relating to what skills and knowledge graduates require for the 21st century in particular professions

types. This can contribute to triangulation, confirming the evidence of others (cf. section 9.6).

A further issue concerning participants is the relationship between the researcher and the respondent. Are participants one step removed from the research process, or are they active participants in that process? Different participants can have different participant relations – for example, teachers may be active participants in a study while learners may simply be seen as subjects.

Of course, the role that learners play depends on the methodology that has been adopted. It is quite possible for learners to be active in all phases of the design, development and evaluation of an e-learning environment. One example is the involvement of learners in developing materials – such as e-cases from professional case histories – that then become an ongoing set of learning objects for future learners. Evaluation of these e-learning environments would need data from the learner-developers, peer learners who used the e-cases and the course teacher (e.g. Au Yeung, Lam & McNaught, 2009).

7.2.8 Methods

There is a range of qualitative and quantitative methods which can be chosen pragmatically to obtain evidence to answer the specific evaluation-research questions. Interviews and surveys are the most common.

The 'LTDI evaluation cookbook' (Harvey, 1998) provides an excellent list of available techniques. Beetham's (2007) guide also provides a commentary on commonly-used methods in e-learning research, while Oliver (1999) provides a comparison of various data-collection methods in terms of the effort involved, the type of data obtained and its subjectivity.

In Chapter 8, we will discuss questions which are appropriate at different phases of the e-learning life cycle, and we will cover, in passing, the methods which may provide evidence to answer those questions. These are:

- document review, including peer review, and the use of assessment;
- interviews;
- questionnaires, surveys and checklists;
- observation, including bug tracking;
- think-aloud protocols;
- video-stimulated recall;
- usage logs.

We will discuss methods in depth in Chapter 9, but pre-empt that discussion here in preparation for Chapter 8.

7.2.9 Evaluation-research Matrix

At the centre of Figure 7.1 is an *evaluation-research matrix*. This is a tool to draw together the specific evaluation-research questions, participants and data-collection methods. We derived our approach to evaluation-research matrices from Reeves and Hedberg (2003). A simple example of an evaluation-research matrix is shown in Table 7.2. The development of an evaluation-research matrix is a systematic way to approach the complexity of multiple questions, participants and methods. The matrix provides a condensed overview of the evaluation-research activity, and is an aid to planning the study.

The evaluation-research matrix starts with a consideration of each of the specific evaluation-research questions, listed down the left-hand side of

Table 7.2 Example of a simple evaluation-research matrix

Specific evaluation-research questions	Learner group interview	Learner reflective reports	Forum transcripts	Staff interview	Log data
What sort of team work occurs?	X	X	X		
How do learners use the online environment in order to learn?	X		X	X	X

the matrix. It prompts you to ask, for each question, 'Who can answer this question?', and 'What are the most appropriate method(s) to use to answer this question?' The combination of participant and method indicates a *source of data*; these are listed across the top of the matrix.

The evaluation-research matrix now contains the questions, and the sources of data, on two axes. It remains to work through the matrix to determine which data sources are suitable to answer each question. Typically, there is more than one source of evidence which can provide answers to each question. The development of an evaluation-research matrix is a cyclical, reflective process that can benefit from discussion with colleagues. More abstract representations of evaluation-research matrices are used in Chapter 8 to indicate general ways that questions might be answered at different stages of the e-learning life cycle. These will need to be modified to suit the particular context of a given evaluation-research study.

The divide-and-conquer technique of the evaluation-research matrix can also contribute to the development of the instruments used to generate the data. For example, in Table 7.2, the learner group interview schedule needs to have questions which enquire about both teamwork processes and learning processes.

7.2.10 The Remaining Process Elements

The lower section of Figure 7.1 contains elements for 'devising instruments', 'generating data' and 'analysing and interpreting data', thus recognizing graphically that we are using multiple, mixed methods and drawing them together in a synthesized process. Chapter 9 provides a relatively brief summary of this part of the process. We have chosen simply to provide an overview of this area because there are many 'methods' books and websites available. It is our contention that the challenge with evaluation research occurs most often early on in the process – in deciding on the direction of the study (what questions are to be asked), instantiating the direction into a clear methodology, and then planning the specific details. Once a good evaluation plan exists, most evaluators/researchers can proceed to completion.

Figure 7.1 also shows the need to report the study results to various audiences (some of whom will be stakeholders). This aspect of the process will be briefly discussed at the end of Chapter 9.

7.3 Planning an Evaluation-research Study

Earlier parts of this chapter have broken up the process of evaluation research into its component parts, through a divide-and-conquer strategy. This is a valuable way of coming to grips with the complexity of the task. However, to effectively carry out the 'task' of an evaluation-research activity, it needs to be seen once again as a whole, considering the ways that the components interact, and planning the most efficient and effective way of putting the parts together. In other words, we need an evaluation-research *plan*.

An evaluation-research study is a *project*, just like an e-learning development project. It has a fixed goal, timeline and budget. An evaluation-research plan is a prescriptive account of the what, when, who and how of the evaluation-research process. The sections earlier in this chapter provide an outline of the main issues to be considered in an evaluation-research plan. The evaluation-research matrices provided in Chapter 8 will assist in identifying methods and participants in the study, and the issues discussed in Chapter 9 will provide guidance on the time and costs required to carry out particular evaluation-research activities. This information can be used to 'cut the cloth' of the proposed study to the available time and budget, and a succinct summary of the issues to consider is given in Herrington et al. (2009). We discuss aspects of project planning in Chapter 10, and many of the arguments presented there can also be applied to developing an evaluation-research plan.

In addition, the evaluation-research plan will have to consider issues of ethics, reporting (discussed briefly in Chapter 9) and dissemination (discussed briefly in Chapter 11).

7.4 Summary

This chapter drew upon theoretical material presented in Part II to discuss a very practical approach to carrying out a rigorous, mixed-methods evaluation-research study. The overall process was broken down into its component parts in a divide-and-conquer technique, where the central element was an evaluation-research matrix. We have refined this technique over numerous years in our own work. Novice researchers and research students have found the scaffolded approach to be particularly useful in conceptualizing their studies.

We suggest that readers may wish to refer back to Figure 7.1 when working through Chapters 8 and 9, as they delve deeper into aspects of the evaluation-research process.

8
Evaluation Research Across the e-Learning Life Cycle

8.1 Introduction

The process described in Chapter 7 broke down the complexity of an evaluation-research study into components (Figure 7.1), in a divide-and-conquer strategy. A central component of that process was the development of a number of specific, answerable evaluation-research questions that, together, enable answers to the broader research questions to be synthesized. The development of specific evaluation questions is guided by a conceptual framework, informed by what we know about the design and development of e-learning environments and what we know about *learning* in the context of the proposed e-learning design.

The second part of the divide-and-conquer strategy, introduced in Chapter 7, is the development of an evaluation-research matrix which maps the specific research questions against data sources. We combine these elements in this chapter.

In it, we will discuss the mapping of evaluation-research activities against the various stages of the e-learning life cycle, and then draw in aspects of learning, initially through the LEPO framework. We will use this mapping to unpack the different stages of a cyclical e-learning evaluation-research program in a way which uses a consistent, conceptual framework at each stage.

8.2 Unpacking the e-Learning Life Cycle

In Chapter 1, we commenced discussion of the components of the e-learning life cycle, highlighting that evaluation (with different characteristics) is needed at each stage of the cycle. This discussion was continued in Chapter 4 where, in Table 4.1, we identified different general questions which might be asked at different stages of the e-learning life cycle. We took this further in Chapter 6, where we established the need for cyclical evaluation-research approaches, such as design-based research, which map to the various stages of the e-learning life cycle. We will follow these ideas more practically here.

Figure 6.2 characterized design-based research as having four components: analysis of problems; development of solutions; testing of solutions; and reflection to produce design principles. In this section, we will consider the first three of these components. We will come back to 'reflection to produce design principles' when we discuss 'testing of solutions' in an evaluation-research context in section 8.2. The literature on e-learning development and project management identifies an iterative 'design, develop, evaluate' cycle (Duncan, 1996; England & Finney, 1999; Howell, 1992; Phillips, 1997). We will extend that cycle by adding an implementation phase. For the moment, for simplicity, we use 'evaluate' in a broad sense. We will return to a precise use of the term in the following section.

An e-learning development project, like any software development, starts with an analysis of the problem, identifying needs and defining the requirements of the solution. The second aspect of the design-based research cycle is 'development of solutions'. We see this as including three phases: designing the e-learning artefact, developing it, and then, once the e-learning artefact is mature enough, implementing it on a live system. The third aspect, 'testing of solutions', is further discussed below, but here we use it to specify the types of questions to ask at different stages of the life cycle.

We have mapped these components together across the top of Table 8.1. The rest of Table 8.1 follows the development of an ideal e-learning environment through numerous cycles of development and testing throughout the e-learning life cycle. The cycles are related to three of the scenarios discussed in Tables 4.1 (p. 47), 4.2 (p. 51) and 6.1 (p. 85). Scenario A is not concerned with the development and implementation of an e-learning environment, and so is not relevant. However, scenarios B, C and D logically link to each other as part of an e-learning life cycle. Table 8.1 breaks that life cycle down into individual elements. We recognize that this process is idealized; multiple sub-cycles might occur within each cycle (Gravemeijer & Cobb, 2006), and the cyclical process might be entered at phases other than the first. We will discuss this further in section 8.3.

We classify 'analysis of the problem' as the initial cycle ('zero') – specifying the point at which to start. After analysis of the problem, the first cycle starts with the design of the e-learning artefact and associated documentation. That design should be evaluated to see if it is fit for purpose and how it could be improved. The second cycle begins with a refinement of the design and then the development of the e-learning artefact to a stage where it can be trialled. This initial trial may lead to a revision of the problem analysis – the proposed solution might not work well. Alternatively, if the design was well grounded, it may lead to a process of designing an e-learning environment by embedding the e-learning artefact into a context defined by the designed learning outcomes and designed learning tasks. This e-learning environment is then developed as a pilot (cycle 3) and formatively evaluated. A subsequent cycle of revision and formative evaluation will lead into a full trial, with learners using the e-learning

Table 8.1 Components of an idealized e-learning life cycle

Design-based research phases		Analysis of problem	Development of solutions			Testing of solutions
Cycle	Scenario	Analysis	Design	Develop	Implement	Questions to ask
0		Analysis of problem				What is the problem and how can we solve it?
1	B		Design e-learning artefact	Documentation		How good is the design?
2	B		Refine design	Develop e-learning artefact	Initial trial	Does the e-learning artefact work technically as it should? How can it be improved?
3	C	Refine problem analysis	Design e-learning environment which embeds e-learning artefact	Develop e-learning environment	Pilot	Does the e-learning environment work as its designer(s) intended? How can it be improved?
4	C		Refine design	Revise e-learning environment	Deploy to learners (full trial)	How can the e-learning environment be improved?
5	D	*Refine problem analysis*	*Refine design*	*Revise e-learning environment*	Deploy to learners (live)	How well does the e-learning environment work to support learning?
6	D		*Refine design*	*Revise e-learning environment*	Deploy to learners (live)	How well does the e-learning environment work to support learning?

environment on a live system. Successful completion of cycle 4 indicates that the e-learning environment is ready to be used in a standard teaching situation. Refinement and revision is expected to be minimal at this stage (shown in italics in rows 5 and 6 of Table 8.1). Cycles 5 and 6 correspond to the live use of a mature e-learning environment. While there is still a formative, continual-improvement component, focus turns to the effectiveness of the e-learning environment.

Table 8.1 draws from the work of Richey, Klein and Nelson (2004), and Reeves and Hedberg (2003), but without two extra stages that we consider only in passing in this book, that is, institutionalizing the e-learning innovation and maintaining it in the long term. We will address these issues briefly in Chapter 11, but they are beyond the scope of this work. As we implied in Chapter 1, we aim to evaluate the effectiveness of a single e-learning environment, perhaps in multiple contexts.

8.3 Mapping Evaluation Research to the e-Learning Life Cycle

We have argued in this book that studies of the effectiveness of e-learning involve a variable mixture of evaluation and research, and need to take explicit account of aspects of learning using models, theories and frameworks such as the LEPO framework presented in Chapter 3. Table 8.2 captures these two considerations by expanding on Tables 6.1 and 4.2. As with Table 8.1, the first two columns identify the cycle and relevant scenario from earlier chapters. The third column provides a textual summary of that life-cycle stage, and the fourth column summarizes the main development activity. The remaining columns in Table 8.2 consider the 'testing of solutions' (expanded to consider both research and evaluation activities) and 'design principles' aspects of the design-based research cycle. Table 8.2 explicitly places the learning environment, process and outcomes framework within the cyclical e-learning evaluation-research process.

Elements of the LEPO framework are progressively drawn in as one moves down Table 8.2. The role of the teacher is highlighted in the early cycles in Table 8.2, where the focus is on the design of the e-learning environment itself. Readers will remember from Chapter 3 that we interpret 'teacher' broadly, to include the range of people who may contribute to the design of an e-learning environment – other teachers, educational designers, content experts, etc. Learners are drawn in through initial usability testing. In subsequent cycles, as the e-learning environment is shown to function as designed, the focus shifts from the environment to how learners engage with the environment – their learning processes and outcomes. Consideration of these different characteristics enables us to derive several distinct evaluation-research *forms*, which will be discussed in detail in subsequent sections. In each section we develop questions which might be asked in each 'form', and summarize these in evaluation-research matrices which map questions to methods. The methods used are discussed in more detail in Chapter 9.

Table 8.2 Evaluation-research elements at different stages of the e-learning life cycle

Cycle	Scenario	Life cycle stage	Development of solutions	Evaluate	Research	Role of theory and design principles
0		Analysis of problem	Document the problem	Baseline analysis		Define teaching and learning problem based on scholarship
1	B	Design	Design e-learning artefact	Design evaluation		Design based on principles of e-learning best practice
2	B	Initial trial	Develop e-learning artefact	Project-management evaluation Formative evaluation of the e-learning artefact	Reflecting on the characteristics of the e-learning environment	Refine principles of e-learning best practice
3	C	Pilot	Design e-learning environment	Formative evaluation of the e-learning environment		
4	C	Full trial	Refine e-learning environment	Formative evaluation of the e-learning environment and processes	Effectiveness research into learning processes	Initial learning design principles
5	D	Evaluation research on mature system	Confirm effectiveness of e-learning environment	Summative evaluation	Effectiveness research into learning processes and outcomes	Refined learning design principles
6	D	Evaluation research on mature system	Holistic understanding of how learners engage with the e-learning environment	Summative evaluation	Effectiveness research into learning processes and outcomes	Refined learning design principles

- *Baseline analysis* is analogous to the 'analysis of the problem' aspect in design-based research (section 8.4).
- *Design evaluation* involves making judgements about the documented design of the learning environment (section 8.5).
- *Project-management evaluation* makes judgements about, and suggests improvements to, the conduct of an e-learning development project (Chapter 10).
- *Formative evaluation* is appropriate at various stages of the e-learning life cycle, making judgements about, and suggesting improvements to, the e-learning artefact, the e-learning environment and engagement in learning processes (section 8.6).
- *Effectiveness research* mixes components of evaluation and research, seeking to confirm the effectiveness of the e-learning environment and develop understanding of how learners engage with learning tasks to demonstrate learning outcomes (section 8.7).

Table 8.2 also indicates the role of *design principles* at different stages. Early stages draw from what is already known, while subsequent stages focus on generating and refining design principles, from both an e-learning best practice and a learning theory perspective.

Before we discuss these five research approaches in detail (in sections 8.4 to 8.7 and Chapter 10), we need to caution against taking this section too literally. e-Learning is complex, and studies of e-learning can't be applied in a lock-step, formulaic way. The particular context of the study needs to be taken into account when applying the approaches presented here.

While the questions asked and methods used in each of these approaches will differ, there is a degree of cumulativity among them, as we indicated in section 6.2. That is, while a particular approach (or approaches) will be the focus at each stage of the e-learning life cycle, aspects of the evaluation-research approach for each previous cycle will also have some relevance. We have illustrated this in Figure 8.1, where the e-learning life cycle is represented as a spiral. Baseline analysis and design evaluation clearly have a higher relevance at the start of the cycle, but may need to be revisited as a result of formative evaluation in other cycles. Figure 8.1 indicates that project-management evaluation is an ongoing activity, which stands outside the main e-learning life cycle. For this reason, we treat this evaluation-research form separately in Chapter 10.

On the other hand, formative evaluation occurs throughout the life cycle, starting small and increasing in importance as the design solidifies and is developed. As the e-learning environment matures, formative evaluation diminishes in importance at the same time that effectiveness research increases in importance. However, we argue here that there is a formative element even in effectiveness studies of mature e-learning environments, because there is always an opportunity to improve the e-learning environment further.

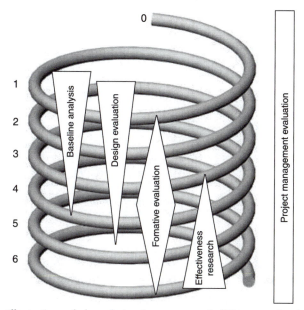

Figure 8.1 Illustration of the relative importance of different evaluation-research activities at different stages of the e-learning life cycle.

This discussion, and Figure 8.1, indicates that any e-learning evaluation-research cycle is likely to use multiple approaches at the same time. They are described separately in this chapter because they have different characteristics, but they should be applied in a mixture which suits the context of the study.

A second contextual issue that arises from this discussion, and the idealized nature of Table 8.1 and Table 8.2, is that e-learning evaluation-research studies can commence at many points in the e-learning life cycle, not just at the beginning of the overall cycle, as implied by this discussion. The ideal process illustrated in Table 8.1 applies to two of the types of e-learning artefacts that we identified in section 1.5: interactive learning systems and learning objects, which are developed from scratch. It doesn't apply directly to the third type of e-learning artefact, generic learning tools, because they involve minimal technical development – the tool is used as it is to develop an e-learning environment. Neither does the entire cycle apply to an existing learning object sourced from a learning-object repository and repurposed for a new context or embedded as is into an e-learning environment. Table 8.1 and Table 8.2 apply even less to a stand-alone study of a mature e-learning environment (cf. section 6.6). Table 8.3 summarizes these scenarios and highlights the elements of the e-learning evaluation-research life cycle which apply to each.

8.4 Baseline Analysis

Baseline analysis has a documentation focus, providing "comprehensive and accurate portrayal of the context" (Nieveen et al., 2006, p. 153) of

Table 8.3 e-Learning evaluation-research scenarios which start at different stages of the e-learning life cycle

Nature of the e-learning environment	Starting cycle*	Characteristics
An interactive learning system or learning object is developed from scratch.	1	Table 8.1 and Table 8.2 apply as they are.
A learning object (or interactive learning system) is sourced and repurposed for the current context.	2	Cycle 0 is still necessary, and some design and development is necessary to refine the learning object for the new context. Some usability work is required (to ensure that the learning object is easy to use). Subsequent cycles apply unchanged.
A learning object (or interactive learning system) is sourced and embedded in a learning environment.	3	Cycle 0 is still necessary, but 'development of solutions' starts with the design of the e-learning environment, and this design needs to be evaluated, asking 'How good is the design of the e-learning environment?' Subsequent cycles apply unchanged.
An e-learning environment is developed from generic learning tools.	3	Cycle 0 is still necessary, but 'development of solutions' starts with the design of the e-learning environment, and this design needs to be evaluated, asking 'How good is the design of the e-learning environment?' Subsequent cycles apply unchanged.
A study is commenced of a mature e-learning environment.	5	Cycle 0 is still necessary, but this is reverse-engineered as a stand-alone study (section 6.6). The focus is very much on effectiveness research, with a small formative component.

* From Tables 8.1 and 8.2

an e-learning design and evaluation-research study. Different aspects of baseline analysis have been called *conceptualizing* by Reeves and Hedberg (2003), *preliminary investigation* by van den Akker (1999), and *informed exploration* by Bannan-Ritland (2003). Bain (1999), on the other hand, conflated the activities of design and analysis into one evaluation-research activity, but our view is that it is more sensible to treat them separately. Baseline analysis shares similarities with Owen's (2006) *clarificative* phase in program evaluation. One approach used in clarificative evaluation is *program logic* (Funnell, 1997), which seeks to determine the underlying assumptions of the design team and other stakeholders. Design-based researchers also promote this view:

> Engaging in design as a research process means taking the elements of design that typically remain implicit in a design and making them explicit. ... Systematic documentation can be used to produce ... a rich

> description of a problem analysis, solution, and design procedure for a
> particular design experience.   (Edelson, 2002, p. 117)

We argue that a baseline analysis is required for all types of e-learning evaluation-research studies, whether they follow a cyclical, design-based research approach, or are stand-alone, reconstructive studies. We contend that a significant omission from many e-learning research studies is a clear description of the context of the study.

A baseline analysis documents teaching and learning practice (Littlejohn & Pegler, 2007). This includes the characteristics of the educational context discussed in section 3.5.6 (for example, the nature of the institution and policy context), the structure of the degree program and any faculty- or department-specific information. It also describes the nature of the teaching and learning problem to be addressed. This includes a literature review and theoretical positioning of the research problem (see sections 7.1 and 7.2). The pedagogical and technological assumptions of the designers should also be clarified in the baseline analysis.

Needs analysis is a core component of the baseline analysis. It should describe the inadequacies/insufficiencies of the current curriculum, with particular attention to any shortfalls in learning. A related consideration is to describe the characteristics of the cohort and identify their learning needs. The baseline analysis should identify the need for an innovation, and its goals, and explore potential solutions, concluding with a broad definition of the proposed solution, including any technical requirements. Questions which might be asked during the baseline analysis are outlined as an evaluation-research matrix in Table 8.4, where data sources are mapped against questions. The interview column contains 'T's to indicate that interviews are with teachers, rather than learners or other stakeholders.

Table 8.4 Evaluation-research matrix for baseline analysis

Question	Data sources	
	Document review	Interviews
What is the teaching and learning context?	•	T
What are the characteristics of the learner cohort?	•	T
What is the teaching and learning problem to be addressed?	•	T
What is the relevant literature?	•	T
What are the pedagogical and technological assumptions of the designers?	•	T
What is the goal of any solution?	•	T
Which solution(s) is appropriate to the teaching and learning problem?	•	T
Is an e-learning approach appropriate to the teaching and learning problem?	•	T

Data for the baseline analysis can come from two scenarios. In projects which start from scratch, the evaluator would typically review project documents produced by the design team. However, in stand-alone, 'reconstructive' studies, project documentation may be lacking, and the evaluator may need to interview the teachers/designers to capture relevant baseline data. Table 8.4 should not be interpreted to mean that *both* document review and teacher interviews are needed for all questions. Interviews are only needed where suitable documentation is deficient.

8.5 Design Evaluation

Within the design–develop–implement process of the e-learning life cycle, the design process requires "decisions about: (a) how the design process will proceed; (b) what needs and opportunities the design will address; and (c) what form the resulting design will take", the outcome of which is a set of documentation (Edelson, 2002, p. 108). The purpose of the design evaluation is to describe and justify the proposed e-learning artefact. In practice, this documentation may overlap with documentation produced as part of the baseline analysis, although there is a chronological distinction between the two. We, perhaps artificially, distinguish them here to maintain a mapping between evaluation-research stages and the e-learning life cycle.

In Chapter 3, we unpacked the characteristics of the learning environment from a design perspective, identifying three distinct components: curriculum design, learning design and the design of the e-learning artefact. It is useful to continue this distinction here, as part of the educational design process, in preparation for discussion of other evaluation-research activities at different stages of the e-learning life cycle. These three characteristics of the learning environment also put the focus clearly on learning, making clear that technology is only one part of the design equation.

The characteristics of these three components, and the questions we ask about them, can inform both the initial design of the e-learning environment, and the evaluative judgements made about that design.

Once an educational design document has been produced, it is sensible to evaluate it, with a formative emphasis, making judgements about its quality and suggesting areas for improvement. In many cases, the most appropriate way to carry out this evaluation is through expert peer review, using a *connoisseurship* model of expert criticism (Eisner, 1991).

In the past, the design phase has been underemphasized in terms of evaluation, because this has been seen as preparation for what is to be developed and evaluated, and hence is not in need of separate evaluation in its own right. However, as a meta-analysis of e-learning projects has demonstrated (Alexander, 1999; Alexander, McKenzie & Geissinger, 1998), many relatively unconvincing projects lack a clear learning rationale and result in products for which few if any benefits can be claimed. This problem has led Alexander to conclude:

A greater emphasis on formative evaluation at the design stage could potentially reduce the wasted time and cost involved in producing these projects which are never likely to realize the intention of improving learning. (1999, p. 181)

On the other hand, as we discussed in section 8.2, not all e-learning evaluation-research studies commence with the initial design of an e-learning environment or e-learning artefact. In such stand-alone studies (cf. Table 8.3), the form of the educational design needs to be reverse-engineered. Existing documentation can be used to describe what has been done, and the design team can be interviewed to clarify details and provide justification for decisions made.

As indicated in Figure 8.1, design evaluation is not a *one-off* activity. While it is clearly a major activity at the beginning of the e-learning life cycle, the design needs to be revisited after each cycle of design, development and implementation. Evaluation data at each stage will inform a revised design for the learning environment. Each new design should be subjected to a design evaluation, which may require a new round of peer review or expert judgement. However, peer-review evaluation approaches can be both formal and informal (see Worthen et al., 1997). Therefore, design evaluation of incremental changes to a design may stay in-house, with the design team reflecting on their design based on observation of the learning environment in use.

A design evaluation is generally concerned with the following overarching questions.

- Is the design consistent with the baseline analysis?
- Should the design achieve the planned outcomes?
- Is the design founded on evidence-based e-learning best practice?
- How can the design be improved?

The multidisciplinary nature of e-learning design may make it difficult to find a single person who has the expertise to perform all aspects of a peer review of an e-learning artefact. It is perfectly appropriate to use a team of peer reviewers, who can each comment on specific aspects of the e-learning design.

The following sections explore specific evaluative questions for each of the three design elements.

8.5.1 Curriculum Design

In Chapter 3 we characterized the curriculum as 'what to learn' – that is, the teaching and learning context, the desired learning outcomes, content and resource, and what will be assessed. However, curriculum design also includes consideration of *why* something is to be learned and why it is to be taught in the way envisaged.

Table 8.5 Evaluation-research matrix for curriculum design evaluation

Question	Data sources	
	Peer review	*Interviews*
How appropriate are the desired learning outcomes?	•	
What should be assessed?	•	
What content should be covered?	•	
Why is this an appropriate solution to the educational problem?	•	
How appropriate is the content for achieving the desired learning outcomes?	•	
How appropriate are the learning resources (electronic or traditional)?	•	

Some questions which might be asked in a curriculum-design evaluation are considered in Table 8.5, as an evaluation-research matrix. We would recommend that the most appropriate method to use would be expert peer review of design documents, although interviews with teachers and designers may be appropriate where documentation is lacking.

8.5.2 Learning Design

Similarly, in Chapter 3 we characterized learning design as 'how to learn', or, more specifically, 'how what is to be learned is planned to be taught'. The learning design includes the learning tasks set by the teacher, and how learners will be assessed. The roles of both the learner and the teacher within these learning and assessment tasks also needs to be specified.

A learning-design evaluation should describe the teaching/learning/assessment process and justify its ability to bring about the desired learning outcomes. It might include questions such as those given in Table 8.6. In this case, a mix of data sources is appropriate, depending on the question being posed.

8.5.3 Design of the e-Learning Artefact

Evaluation of the design of an e-learning artefact will usually vary according to the scale and nature of that e-learning artefact, and the amount of technical development required. Of the three types of e-learning artefacts we identified in section 1.5, interactive learning systems are the most complex. Such systems typically engage learners in numerous activities over multiple weeks in media-rich environments, which can be complex to navigate. Interactive learning systems, such as educational games, are usually developed by teams of professionals – with concomitant expense. There are numerous elements to the design of an interactive learning system, some of which are listed after Table 8.6.

Table 8.6 Evaluation-research matrix for learning design evaluation

Question	Data sources		
	Document review	Interviews	Peer review
To what extent is the learning design appropriate to the proposed curriculum and desired learning outcomes?	•	•	•
Is the learning design consistent with the beliefs of the teacher about teaching and learning?		•	•
Is the learning design grounded in the teaching and learning literature for this discipline?	•		•
How well aligned are the learning and assessment tasks to the desired learning outcomes?			•
To what extent does the learning design enable learners to interact with others, if appropriate?	•		•
To what extent does the learning design enable learners to reflect on their work and develop generic learning outcomes?	•		•

- overall design of the e-learning artefact vis-à-vis the curriculum and learning design (cf. sections 8.5.1 and 8.5.2);
- graphic design look and feel;
- design of navigational mechanisms;
- design of a software architecture;
- design of interactive learning tasks;
- design of any media elements.

Because of the complexity, the design of an interactive learning system can be a large undertaking, resulting in substantial amounts of documentation. Design will usually involve multiple cycles of design and various levels of prototyping, each with an associated cycle of design evaluation.

A second type of e-learning artefact, which we generically call a learning object, also typically has to be developed from scratch; but sometimes an existing learning object can be repurposed for a different context, for example, an 'open educational resource'. As we noted in section 1.5, learning objects are generally small, self-contained artefacts, designed to address a specific learning outcome. Navigational mechanisms and software architecture have arguably less importance than for interactive learning systems, but the other elements of design ('look and feel', media elements and learning tasks) remain important.

The third type of e-learning artefact is represented by generic learning tools, which have usually been through numerous cycles of development prior to being made available to develop e-learning environments. Apart from the newest generation of tools, this type of e-learning artefact is usually mature and stable, e.g. learning-management systems, blogs and e-portfolios. The graphic design, software architecture and navigation are well defined and not usually subject to modification. Generic learning tools typically allow the user to use predefined tools in various ways, and the focus turns to the way these tools are used to facilitate the desired learning processes and outcomes, and the appropriateness of the tools used to facilitate the performance of learning tasks by the target audience of learners.

When considering generic learning tools, our focus turns to the design of the learning environment which uses these tools, rather than the e-learning artefact itself.

Table 8.7 summarizes the considerations discussed above and expresses them as a series of questions which might be asked about different elements of e-learning artefact design. In columns 2–4, it indicates which of these questions might typically be appropriate for the three different types of e-learning artefacts we have identified in this book. Columns 5–7 map these same questions against data sources in an evaluation-research matrix, identifying three relevant data sources: document review, peer review and interviews (with the design team). The most appropriate data source will depend on the scope of the development. In a small-scale development, using a generic learning tool, the educational designer is likely to be involved in the evaluation research, and external peer review is recommended to get an independent view of the design. However, internal peer review of revisions to the design may be appropriate. If the development is a large-scale interactive learning system, the evaluator is likely to have a role removed from the educational design team. In this case, document reviews and interviews serve the same purpose as external peer review.

8.6 Formative Evaluation of the Learning Environment

In section 8.3, we introduced the idea of formative evaluation as an evaluation-research form which is appropriate at various stages of the e-learning life cycle. The focus is on making judgements about, and suggesting improvements to, either an e-learning artefact or an e-learning environment and the learning tasks which are embedded in that environment. The primary interest of formative evaluation is to verify that the e-learning artefact, or e-learning environment, works in the way it was designed, and to identify any areas of improvement.

In Figure 8.1, we illustrated how formative evaluation plays a role throughout the e-learning life cycle, initially as a small component which increases in importance as the design solidifies and is developed. Where the technology needs to be developed from scratch or is new to the practitioners,

Table 8.7 Design evaluation questions relevant to different types of e-learning artefacts, combined with an evaluation-research matrix for design of the e-learning artefact

Question	Type of e-learning artefact			Data sources		
	Interactive learning system	Learning object	Generic learning tool	Document review	Peer review	Interviews
Are there any gaps in the written design specification?	X	X	X	•		
How will the design of the e-learning artefact facilitate the desired learning processes and outcomes?	X	X	X		•	
How appropriate are the interactive learning tasks to the teaching and learning problem?	X	X	X		•	
To what extent is the graphic look and feel appropriate for the subject matter and the target audience?	X	X			•	
To what extent are media elements attractive and suitable for the target audience?	X	X			•	
To what extent will the designed navigational mechanisms allow learners to gain access to materials and perform the requisite tasks?	X				•	
Are the tools used to implement the design appropriate for the functionality and interactivity of the e-learning artefact?	X	X			•	
Does the software architecture facilitate content updating, repurposing and future scalability?	X				•	

a first (possibly repeated) round of formative evaluation will look at a pilot/ prototype of the e-learning artefact. As the e-learning artefact is developed and/or refined, it becomes embedded in a learning environment, and this e-learning environment also needs to be formatively evaluated. There may be multiple phases of this but, as the e-learning environment matures, formative evaluation diminishes in importance as effectiveness research increases in importance. However, there is always an opportunity to improve the e-learning environment further.

We identify two separate aspects of formative evaluation at different stages of the e-learning life cycle, which will each be discussed separately in sections 8.6.1 and 8.6.2.

We have decided, perhaps arbitrarily, not to discuss learning processes in a formative sense in this section (cf. section 8.7), although we recognize an overlap between learning environments and learning processes. In Chapter 3, we made a conceptual distinction between learning tasks designed as part of the learning environment, and the use of those learning tasks by learners, which we called learning activities. We also identified two distinct, but interrelated, aspects of learning processes: learning activities that can be observed in a particular setting and comprise various contextual elements; and 'mental' or cognitive processes that are internal to the learner and reflect cognitive learning strategies such as critical thinking, knowledge building, problem solving and reflection. We call these contextual learning processes and cognitive learning processes respectively.

In this section, we restrict our interest to improving the learning tasks until we can be relatively certain that they work as designed. We do this because observing learning activities for their effectiveness, or lack thereof, will point us to ways to improve learning tasks at the same time.

At this stage, we are interested in observable contextual learning processes because these are things about which we can make judgements, and seek to improve. Because cognitive learning processes are internal to the learner and we cannot see them directly, we can only seek to improve the e-learning environment and learning design in order to support beneficial cognitive learning processes. Evidence of cognitive learning processes is treated in a summative sense in the following section.

8.6.1 Formative Evaluation of an e-Learning Artefact

The formative evaluation of e-learning artefacts is a relatively well-understood activity, with fields such as 'human–computer interaction' and 'human factors' having strong research traditions (cf. Preece et al., 1994). From a more educational perspective, studies of functionality, usability and appeal are well covered by Flagg (1990) and Reeves and Hedberg (2003). The fundamental goal of formative evaluation of an e-learning artefact is to determine whether it is functional in a given context and accessible/attractive to learners, and then to modify it as needed. Common questions to ask are summarized in Table 8.8,

Table 8.8 Evaluation-research matrix for the formative evaluation of an e-learning artefact

Question	Data sources						
	Document review	Interviews	Surveys	Observation	Think-aloud	Stimulated recall	Usage logs
Does the e-learning artefact function as it was designed? What are the bugs?				•	•		
Are interactive learning activities within the e-learning artefact working as designed?		•		•	•	•	
Can learners use the e-learning artefact easily (can they navigate, gain access to materials, etc.)?		•		•	•	•	
Is the graphic design attractive, approachable and accessible?		•			•		
Are response times, screen refresh rates and media download times acceptable?		•		•			
To what extent does the software architecture facilitate ongoing development and modification?	•						
Does the e-learning artefact meet relevant 'accessibility' standards?				•			

together with the methods that we have judged to be most appropriate to answer these questions.

8.6.2 Formative Evaluation of the Learning Environment

We have distinguished in this book, perhaps artificially, between an e-learning artefact and an e-learning environment. We have conceived of an e-learning artefact as being a technological tool divorced from a learning context. An e-learning environment explicitly recognizes that learning context, particularly the learning tasks that a learner is expected to engage with while using an e-learning artefact. This distinction varies according to the type of e-learning artefact, as in section 8.5.

In a 'monolithic' interactive learning system, learning content and learning tasks are embedded within the system, and the interactive learning system provides much of the context. For example, award-winning e-learning products such as 'Investigating Lake Iluka' (Corderoy, Harper & Hedberg, 1993; Harper, Hedberg, Wright & Corderoy, 1995) and 'Exploring the Nardoo' (Harper, Hedberg, Corderoy & Wright, 2000) contain huge amounts of content and numerous tools to interact with this content, in systems which are designed for high-school learners. However, despite this, there is a contextual element to the use of these systems. For effective use, learners need guidance in how to use these complex environments to work towards the desired learning outcomes. In the latter case, this is provided by a detailed workbook (Interactive Multimedia Learning Laboratory, 1996).

With the learning object class of e-learning artefact (e.g. an open educational resource), content is usually embedded in the learning object, and the learning object itself functions as a tool to interact with that content. However, the relatively discrete size of the learning object usually means that it needs to be embedded in a broader learning environment to give meaning to its use. This learning design may include paper-based resources, classroom activities and other learning objects.

Generic learning tools (e.g. a learning-management system) typically do not contain any content, but simply provide a set of tools. In this case, both curriculum content and learning design form part of the e-learning environment.

Given this discussion, in each case, there is an educational context which supersedes the technical dimensions of the e-learning artefact. This is the focus of the formative evaluation of the learning environment. This includes: interaction with the learning environment; engagement with designed learning tasks; how this engagement occurs (e.g. individually, in groups, as directed by the teacher); and self-directed review and reflection activities.

Table 8.9 is an evaluation-research matrix containing some representative questions which might be asked about the learning environment, and methods which might be appropriate for answering them.

Table 8.9 Evaluation-research matrix for the formative evaluation of an e-learning environment

Question	Data sources					
	Interviews	Surveys	Observation	Think-aloud	Stimulated recall	Usage logs
How do learners use the learning environment?	•		•	•	•	•
How can contextual aspects of the learning environment be improved?	•		•	•	•	
To what extent do learners engage with learning tasks as intended?	•		•	•	•	
Are the learning tasks appropriate for the target learners?						
What is the association between elements in the e-learning environment?	•		•	•	•	
Is the e-learning environment used in unintended ways?	•		•	•	•	
Does the manner in which learners use the e-learning environment encourage the desired contextual learning processes?	•		•	•	•	
What forms of collaborative activities are occurring?	•	•	•			
How useful do learners find the e-learning environment?	•	•				
What types and degree of interaction do learners have with each other and with their teachers?	•	•	•			

8.7 Effectiveness Research on the Learning Process and Learning Outcome

Issues arising from formative evaluation can be used to identify key issues/questions for subsequent effectiveness research into learning processes and outcomes. At this stage, the educational innovation should be embedded in a unit of study and any changes to the e-learning environment should be minor. In other words, the e-learning environment is functioning as it was designed. As indicated in Table 8.2, a mixture of evaluation and research occurs at this stage. There is an element of summative evaluation, making judgements about whether the e-learning environment is actually effective. However, the focus can now turn to the research side of the evaluation–research continuum, seeking to understand the learning processes that learners experience and the learning outcomes they achieve. We call this activity 'effectiveness research' to capture both of these activities in one term. This is similar to: Bain's (1999) "summative evaluation of learning outcome"; our previous (Phillips et al., 2000) summative evaluation of learning process and learning outcome; and Reeves and Hedberg's (2003) "impact evaluation".

Effectiveness research is concerned with three aspects of the LEPO framework:

1. evidence and understanding of contextual learning processes (as illustrated in Figure 3.1 – how learners interact with the learning environment, other learners and their teachers);
2. evidence and understanding of internal cognitive learning processes (cognitive and metacognitive strategies);
3. evidence and understanding of demonstrated learning outcomes.

In the same way that we excluded learning processes and learning outcomes from the formative evaluation form, we exclude the learning environment from the effectiveness research form. We do this because evidence of learning processes and outcomes provides, ipso facto, evidence of the effectiveness of the learning environment.

Because we are interested in research into learning in this evaluation-research form, we should base our investigation around some theoretical or proto-theoretical framework – the design principles we discussed in section 6.5.1. These design principles should be relevant to the particular research goal being investigated. The LEPO *conceptual* framework is too broad to be of assistance here. We have used the LEPO framework to deconstruct the elements of e-learning evaluation research into manageable parts, but we need more specific guidance to probe a particular aspect of learning, and to develop specific, answerable questions.

In some cases, such as conceptual understanding in physics and mathematics, the domain is well understood, and validated surveys and conceptual tests are available to provide evidence of learning processes and outcomes (Hestenes,

Wells & Swackhammer, 1992; Hestenes & Wells, 1992). In other cases, the goals are more diffuse – e.g. improving learning through discussion forums – and broader theoretical perspectives are used, such as deep and surface approaches to learning (Ellis & Goodyear, 2009). These theories and/or design principles should guide our effectiveness research of the learning process and learning outcomes.

8.7.1 Effectiveness Research of Contextual Learning Processes

There are similarities between some aspects of *formative* evaluation of the learning environment and effectiveness research of the learning process. The same broad question 'How do learners use the learning environment?' might be asked in both cases, but there is a subtle difference. In the former case, the focus of the question is exploratory – because we don't necessarily know how learners will engage with the learning environment, and we want to find out. In the latter case, we are interested in how learners use the learning environment *in order to learn* and would typically have a concrete model or theory to guide our investigation of specific research questions about learners' interactions in the learning environment.

Effectiveness research of contextual learning processes is concerned with questions like those shown in Table 8.10. Evidence of observable learning processes can be obtained by overt or covert (e.g. computer usage logs) observation, and by interviews and surveys, among other methods.

8.7.2 Effectiveness Research of Cognitive Learning Processes

Evidence of learners' internal cognitive learning processes is more difficult to obtain, for the obvious reason that they are hidden to the researcher. Despite this, education researchers have developed a range of methods and measures to obtain proxies for what is going on inside learners' heads when they learn. Standardized questionnaires, think-aloud protocols and video-stimulated recall can all be used to delve into learners' cognitive processes. However, these measures are based on asking learners for perceptions of their own learning, which may be incomplete or inaccurate. While emerging techniques, such as brain scanning, attempt to resolve some of these issues, they represent an expensive approach that is typically appropriate only in particular circumstances.

Indirect evidence about learners' cognitive processes can be gained from their assessed work. In this case we are interested as much in how well a learner demonstrates learning outcomes as we are with *how* they go about demonstrating it. As well as the marks learners are awarded for their assignments, we can gain a deeper insight into their thought processes by analysing the content of any reflective journals or forum posts they have contributed, through document review.

Questions and methods related to cognitive learning processes include those in Table 8.11.

Table 8.10 Evaluation-research matrix for effectiveness research of contextual learning processes

Question	Data sources						
	Document review*	Interviews	Surveys	Observation	Think-aloud	Stimulated recall	Usage logs
How do learners engage with learning tasks in order to learn?	•	•	•	•	•	•	•
What evidence is there that learning is occurring?	•	•		•	•	•	•
What is the influence of contextual factors on learners' engagement? E.g.: • Are learners using the e-learning environment in self-formed groups when it was conceived as a single-user system? • Are learners using the e-learning environment minimally or erratically when you thought it would be highly engaging?		•		•	•	•	
Are there unexpected cognitive benefits deriving from the ways in which learners engage in learning tasks (e.g. do learners pose questions or connect ideas or create repetitive practice in ways that were not anticipated)?	•	•		•			•

* Review of learner work, assignments, examinations, etc.

Table 8.11 Evaluation-research matrix for effectiveness research of cognitive learning processes

Question	Data sources				
	Document review*	Interviews	Surveys	Observation	Usage logs
To what extent does the e-learning environment influence cognitive learning processes?	•	•	•	•	•
What evidence is there that the desired cognitive processes are occurring as the e-learning environment is used?	•	•	•		
Do the e-learning environment and its learning design encourage the desired cognitive learning processes?	•	•			•
Can improvements in assessment results be linked to the cognitive learning process fostered by the e-learning environment?	•	•			
Are learners demonstrating metacognitive and self-regulatory behaviours?	•	•			
What evidence is apparent of changed thinking behaviour among learners?	•	•	•		

* Review of learner work, assignments, examinations, etc.

8.7.3 Effectiveness Research of Learning Outcomes

This part of an evaluation-research study seeks to determine the extent to which the learning outcomes specified in the design evaluation phase of the study are achieved. In section 3.5.3, we provided an overview of different types of learning outcomes, and suggested that the Bloom and SOLO taxonomies, among others, could be appropriate to assess the achievement of learning outcomes. An evaluation-research matrix for effectiveness research of learning outcomes is presented in Table 8.12.

Evidence of students' learning outcomes can often be obtained from course or subject assessment that targets stated learning objectives, which students complete as part of their course requirements (e.g. lab assignments, exams, online discussions). In addition, when e-learning programs target particular

Table 8.12 Evaluation-research matrix for effectiveness research of learning outcomes

Question	Data sources		
	Document review	Interviews	Surveys
What knowledge, skills or conceptual understanding have learners developed?	•	•	•
To what extent have learners achieved the expected learning outcomes after engaging with the e-learning environment?	•	•	•
Are improvements apparent in those assessment(s) that are directly based on the desired learning outcomes?	•		
What unintended learning outcomes have occurred?	•	•	
Are any observed benefits widespread or limited to some learners?			•

content areas, researchers can employ custom-designed tests specifically developed to assess students' understanding in a particular area. The investigator may carefully design these tests or use standardized tests already developed for the content area (see, for example, Hestenes et al. (1992) and Hestenes & Wells (1992) in the area of physics education). Such 'custom' assessments have the advantage of targeting specific learning outcomes in a research project and often free the researcher from any potential course or institutional constraints (e.g. the timing or scope of the test).

8.8 Summary

This chapter used the LEPO framework and the e-learning life cycle to deconstruct the conduct of an e-learning evaluation-research study into five general forms: *baseline analysis*, *design evaluation*, *project-management evaluation*, *formative evaluation* and *effectiveness research*. Apart from project-management evaluation, which applies equally over the duration of a project and is discussed in Chapter 10, there is a logical chronological progression across the evaluation-research forms.

Baseline analysis is what the name implies – a preliminary analysis of the educational need and learner characteristics. We argued that this form is essential in all evaluation-research studies, to set the context in which to judge subsequent cycles of design, development, implementation and evaluation research.

Design evaluation involves making judgements about: whether the documented design of the learning environment is consistent with the baseline analysis; whether it is likely to achieve what is intended; and how the design can be improved. We drilled down into the conduct of design evaluation by considering three distinct components of the LEPO framework: curriculum design, learning design and the design of the e-learning artefact.

The third evaluation-research form that we discussed here, formative evaluation, is appropriate with various levels of importance across the e-learning life cycle. We distinguished between formative evaluation of the e-learning artefact, and of the e-learning environment, seeking to verify that each works in the way it was designed, and to identify any areas of improvement.

Effectiveness research focuses on the learning process and learning outcome elements of the LEPO framework. This evaluation-research form mixes components of evaluation and research by attempting to confirm the effectiveness of the e-learning environment and to increase understanding of how learners engage with the learning environment. We discussed effectiveness research in terms of three aspects of learning: contextual learning processes, cognitive learning processes and demonstrated learning outcomes.

In conclusion, we would like to reiterate the role of *design principles* in framing the evaluation-research activities. No matter at which stage of the e-learning life cycle evaluation-research activities are undertaken, these activities should draw from what is already known, refine existing knowledge and generate new design principles. This should occur both in the context of e-learning best practice and in extending learning theory.

9
Conducting an Evaluation-research Study

9.1 Introduction

This chapter builds on Chapter 8 to detail some of the practical considerations associated with conducting an evaluation-research study. The first part of the chapter provides practical advice about data-collection instruments, while the second half explores issues associated with managing evaluation studies, and generating and analysing data.

In this chapter we are purposely less explicit in some of the terms we use. Recognizing the overlap between evaluation and research, we will use the terms evaluation, research and evaluation research interchangeably. We similarly use practitioner, investigator, evaluator and researcher as best fits the context, recognizing the overlap between these roles.

9.2 Data Collection – Evaluation and Research Methods

A critical component of any e-learning investigation is choosing appropriate data-collection techniques or methods. Like any work, sourcing the 'right' tool for the job is a key factor in a successful outcome. When that work is evaluation research, practitioners are spoilt for choice. In this section we describe some of the main evaluation methods available to practitioners, while in the following section we consider some of the advantages and disadvantages of each of these methods.

The methods we will discuss here are:

- document review
- interviews
- questionnaires, surveys and checklists
- observation
- think-aloud protocols
- video-stimulated recall
- usage logs.

9.2.1 Document Review

We take a broad view of documents – they may be design documents, or they may be documents produced by learners as they use an e-learning environment. While the documents may be different, similar approaches are taken to reviewing and analysing them

Most e-learning environments will be accompanied by some sort of documentation, developed through a baseline analysis or design evaluation. This need not be documentation in the traditional sense of documents that explain and support the set-up, running and functions of a computer program. As discussed in sections 8.4 and 8.5, documentation in this context can refer to all manner of documents associated with an e-learning environment, including curriculum outlines, learner work books, lecture synopses or laboratory notes. These documents can be a valuable source of data in evaluation research – providing background or context to a study. Design documents can be reviewed by the evaluator, or by an expert peer review using a connoisseurship approach (see section 8.5).

Other documents may be produced by learners and used as evidence of the effectiveness of the e-learning environment, e.g. essays, assignments, reflective journals, blog posts and forum discussions. The data in these documents can be treated through a content or thematic analysis in response to specific questions about an e-learning environment (see section 9.5.2.7).

9.2.2 Interviews

Interviews are a popular way for evaluators and researchers to elicit a range of detailed responses from participants in an investigation. They are essentially a conversation between an investigator and a carefully chosen participant (e.g. a learner, tutor or technical designer) that can vary in its degree of structure. With structured interviews, the interviewer essentially controls the flow of the interview with a series of scripted questions that require responses. Semi-structured interviews are more common and allow more flexibility for both the interviewer and interviewee, and they often result in more detailed data. In semi-structured interviews, the interviewer has a series of themes that she uses to guide the interview. These are reflected in specific questions, and possibly follow-up or sub-questions. Interviewees are given some latitude in the conversation, being encouraged to talk about experiences not originally foreseen by the interviewer. The interviewer uses a 'running sheet' to focus the conversation when necessary.

Interviews can be conducted with individuals or with small groups. The latter are loosely referred to as focus-group interviews and they allow a researcher to capture efficiently a variety of perspectives of one or more issues related to the investigation.

9.2.3 Questionnaires, Surveys and Checklists

One of the most common forms of data collection is through questionnaires, surveys or checklists. The terms 'questionnaire' and 'survey' are typically used interchangeably (though 'survey' can also mean the process of administering a questionnaire) and simply describe a structured series of open and closed questions that are used to elicit information on specific topics. A checklist is a structured form that is used to indicate the presence or absence of certain characteristics. Regardless, questionnaires, surveys and checklists are a relatively inexpensive way of gathering information from numerous participants in an e-learning evaluation-research study.

Questionnaires are made up of a series of items that are typically grouped into themes. For example, demographic characteristics such as age, gender or year of study are often used at the start of a questionnaire before more specific questions aligned with the focus of the evaluation are introduced (e.g. usability, time spent on an aspect of an e-learning environment, usefulness of an e-learning artefact). The items on a questionnaire can be either open or closed. Open questions allow the responder to enter a text-based response while closed questions ask the responder to answer using a rating scale or by making one or more selections.

The range or type of questions that can be asked in a questionnaire is driven by the evaluation or research question of interest. If usability is the focus, learners may be asked about the clarity of the interface, navigation and usefulness; if communication between learners is the focus, a questionnaire might ask about whom learners corresponded with online, how often and for what purpose; if learners' engagement with a new learning task is the focus, learners might be asked to complete a standardized questionnaire on learner engagement or motivation with learning (e.g. Pintrich, Smith, Garcia and McKeachie (1991), *Motivated Strategies for Learning Questionnaire*).

9.2.4 Observation

There is nothing like seeing with your own eyes how learners are – or are not! – engaging with an e-learning environment that you have introduced into a unit of study. Observational data collection involves investigators systematically observing learners in order to gain a detailed understanding of the ways in which they use an e-learning environment and the problems they encounter with it. The observational focus is typically concerned with how learners are going about their learning tasks and how they interact with the e-learning environment.

Like interviews, observation can be carried out with either individuals or a group. A classic usability technique, individual observation can be used to gather a great deal of information about how a learner uses an e-learning environment – in ways that are both expected and unexpected by the researcher.

Individual observations are often video-recorded and are sometimes used with other data-collection techniques such as think-aloud protocols and usage logs (see below). Group-based observation is carried out with a class or learner group using an e-learning environment. Due to their physical scale – typically a tutorial room or a computer lab – these observations are more difficult to record using audio-visual equipment, unless specific individuals or areas are focused upon. Investigators may choose to use a video camera to record the context of the observation (effectively videoing the whole room) and use this to provide context for their own detailed field notes. Field notes are typically the hand-written record a researcher makes of the behaviour and activities of participants in an evaluation setting of interest. These are sometimes supported by a checklist or photos. As Creswell (2009) observed, like interviews, field notes can be either unstructured or semi-structured, with the observation and recording of specific aspects of the setting being the focus in the latter. Field notes can be used as the stimulus for other data-collection activities such as interviews or focus groups.

Sometimes, rather than extensive and detailed field notes, investigators take a more structured approach to data collection through observation. Checklists or proformas can be used to record the number and timing of predefined events that occur in a classroom. For example, an electronic-response (clicker) system might be introduced into a classroom to encourage learners to interact with each other and to reduce the amount of time teachers spend lecturing. Through a structured observational checklist, an investigator can record the number of questions being asked by the teacher, the amount of time spent lecturing or the amount of class time spent on discussion.

A further approach to structured data collection through observation is in identifying bugs in early iterations of e-learning artefact development. A structured form can be used to record when and where bugs occur. Bug reporting can arise from observation of learners using the e-learning artefact, or from project staff using the e-learning artefact.

9.2.5 Think-aloud Protocols

Think-aloud protocols are a less-frequently-used technique to collect data, but are particularly valuable in determining exactly how an e-learning environment is used by learners. Learners are given a learning task, perhaps a series of constructed exercises that require the use of an e-learning environment. While learners are performing the learning task, they are asked to say what they are thinking. The researcher can simply observe and take notes on what the learner is saying and doing, although often the learners' statements will be audio-recorded. Depending on the degree of structure planned in the think-aloud activity, researchers may also use a protocol to prompt both learners' activity (e.g. direct them to go to particular sections of the e-learning environment) and verbalizings (e.g. 'What were you looking for when you accessed that section?').

Think-aloud protocols are useful for tapping into learners' 'thought processes' while using an e-learning environment: the logic that underpins their actual use of a system, or how they are thinking about the learning tasks presented to them. The most commonly-recognized difficulty with think-aloud protocols is that, when the tasks learners are undertaking become taxing, whether because of the content of the activities or because of how it is presented to learners on-screen, learners tend to stop verbalizing. This can present methodological problems for evaluation research that is particularly involved with learners' cognitive or learning processes.

9.2.6 Video-stimulated Recall

A technique related to think-aloud protocols is video-stimulated recall. With this method, learners are again asked to complete a learning task or exercise using an e-learning environment. Learners' interactions with the environment are video-recorded, typically with a digital video camera or with screen-capture technology that provides an animation of learners' screen-based activity (e.g. Camtasia). When they have finished the learning task, learners are shown the video of themselves interacting with the e-learning environment, and are asked to say what they were thinking and why. Like think-aloud protocols, the goal is to have learners describe their actions with the view of reconstructing their understanding of the interactions and their thinking as they used the e-learning environment. While video-stimulated recall is less prone to the verbal 'drop out' sometimes seen in think-aloud protocols, it is reliant on learners recalling what they were thinking, based on a video to cue them, and as such it is advisable to use this method soon after learners have completed the e-learning activity.

9.2.7 Usage Logs

Many e-learning artefacts automatically record electronic measures of learner activity within the system. Unlike other areas of educational innovation, this gives investigators the opportunity to access direct evidence of learner behaviour, in contrast with other approaches (e.g. surveys and interviews) which provide indirect evidence, filtered by the perceptions of the learner (Salomon, 1991). When learners are asked to contribute to a wiki, blog or discussion list, a digital recording of their activity and contributions is available as data for an evaluation-research study. For example, the ways in which learners have used discussion boards in learning-management systems has been the topic of much research and is often based on learners' electronic contributions in these systems (e.g. Luca & McLoughlin, 2004). Alternatively, in one of our projects we recorded the comments learners made to each other on a wiki-based learning task (i.e. not the learners' actual wiki contributions) and analysed these comments in an investigation of how a wiki-based writing task supported collaboration (Judd et al., 2010).

A less explicit way in which e-learning environments can be used for data collection is through automatically captured system-based records of users' activities within electronic learning environments – termed usage logs, audit trails or academic analytics – which record who accessed what, and when (Goldstein & Katz, 2005; Judd & Kennedy, 2001; Kennedy & Judd, 2004; Misanchuk & Schwier, 1993; Oblinger & Campbell, 2007). Usage log data can be used to track how students use web-based learning management systems (see, for example, Phillips & Baudains, 2002; Phillips, Baudains & van Keulen, 2002; Dawson, McWilliam & Tan, 2008; Phillips, 2006), including how social networks form during online discussion forums (Dawson, 2006a, 2006b; Dawson, Bakharia & Heathcote, 2010). Similarly, Google Analytics can be used to examine learners' collaborative use of Google Docs.

It is important to recognize that usage logs simply record users' behaviour in an e-learning environment, but they do not explain why that behaviour occurs. As Kennedy and Judd (2004) suggested, "at their most basic level audit trails measure the behavioural responses and activities of users" without explaining why they do what they do. So, while usage logs of learners' activities in e-learning environments are often easy to access and data is often relatively simple to generate, care should be taken in analysing and interpreting this data. This is another argument in favour of the adoption of a mixed-methods approach to e-learning evaluation research.

9.3 Issues with Mixing Methods

The previous section has provided a descriptive overview of the main data-collection methods available to those interested in e-learning evaluation research. Consistent with Chapters 5, 6 and 8, where we advocated a pragmatic approach to evaluation research, it should be clear that these methods can effectively be mixed together in a single evaluation-research study. Whatever combination of methods we use in our investigation, first and foremost they need to generate data that can appropriately respond to our evaluation and research questions. Questionnaires can be used alongside focus groups; audit trails can complement interviews; and observation can be used in concert with think-aloud protocols.

Due to space constraints, we have not referred to a number of other data-collection methods here, including teach-back, concept maps, reflective journals, eye tracking and brain imaging. Some of these techniques (e.g. concept maps) are useful in that they involve learners or teachers creating a visual representation that offers a different quality of data when compared with text. Other techniques, such as eye tracking or brain imaging, have a more recent history in e-learning and educational research, and are underpinned by sophisticated techniques for gathering data on cognitive and physiological function. We have also neglected broader methodological approaches (e.g. ethnography, experience sampling methodology), as these typically employ the fundamental techniques described above but extend them with a particular emphasis.

With such an array of tools at our fingertips, it might be difficult to choose particular methods to employ. The trick is to foreshadow the type of data the method will produce and imagine how this data could be used as evidence in response to the evaluation-research questions. Given this, it is useful to consider some of the inherent and practical advantages and disadvantages of each of the tools we have described above, for example:

- the amount of time and effort to prepare and set up data collection;
- whether or not specialist equipment (e.g. cameras) or tools (e.g. software applications) are required;
- the financial and personnel costs associated with collecting data;
- the volume and form of data that is returned after collection;
- the time and effort required to prepare and analyse the data.

We consider here two examples that, to a certain extent, fall at opposite ends of the spectrum of practicality: questionnaires and video-stimulated recall. Questionnaires are relatively cheap and easy to prepare and set up, particularly if an existing questionnaire is used as a template. The volume of data returned is dependent on the sample size and the length of the questionnaire, and can therefore be limited by the researcher. Data collection can take place quickly and a relatively large number of individuals can take part in a short amount of time. Quantitative rather than open-ended questions can be used to minimize the time required to collate and analyse the data.

Conversely, video-stimulated recall requires a video camera or screen-capture technology to be acquired and set up in a dedicated place. Learners will need to be recruited and organized into a scheduled series of trials, which could last for a relatively long period of time (days or weeks), and this may require the researcher to be 'on-call' for the entire data-collection period. The data returned will inevitably be rich and detailed – full of great potential. And, while the time and effort required to prepare and analyse the data will depend on the number of participants in the investigation, it will typically be a long process.

The purpose of this comparison is not to laud questionnaires over video-stimulated recall as a method; this is neither appropriate, nor to the point. The point is that, depending on the combination of data-collection techniques used, there will be practical advantages and disadvantages, which need to be weighed up carefully in an overall evaluation-research strategy. At the end of the day, there is no point in collecting 'cheap' questionnaire data if it fails to respond to the research question of interest, particularly if that question would be greatly illuminated by having three or four learners engage in a video-stimulated recall activity.

9.4 Sampling

Once data-collection tools are ready to be used, an optimal sample of participants needs to be determined for the study. Sampling involves the careful selection of study participants so that, to a greater or lesser extent, they reflect the broader population of interest. If an evaluation-research study aims to shed light on undergraduate learner experiences, then a sample of undergraduate learners will be appropriate. If a study is particularly interested in creative arts learners' experience with technology, then this would direct the type of sample used. Sometimes a researcher will decide to stratify her sampling of participants, which means that subsections of a population (e.g. undergraduate and postgraduate learners, international and local learners, arts and science learners) are intentionally targeted in predefined numbers to ensure that the sample appropriately reflects the population when it comes to these characteristics. While random sampling has historically been seen as a type of 'gold standard' in academic research, this need not be applied for many evaluation-research approaches (see Chapter 5) and targeted convenience sampling is commonly employed by educational researchers. In this approach, a sample of participants that is convenient, available and judged appropriate in the context of the evaluation research is used.

If quantitative analyses and inferential statistics are planned, then the *size* of the sample is an important consideration. There are no fixed rules here but basically the larger the sample the better, as this will increase the statistical power of the tests (giving greater confidence in the validity of the observed results). However, there are typically practical constraints when seeking evaluation-research samples and these will often factor heavily in decisions in this area.

With qualitative data collection and analyses, the researcher needs to balance the number of individuals or groups sampled and the reliability and validity of the themes that emerge from the analysis. Conceptually, it is suggested that sampling needs to continue to the point of 'saturation' or "the point at which no new information or themes are observed in the data" (Guest, Bunce & Johnson, 2006, p. 59).While this is difficult to determine at the outset of data collection, by carefully considering the scope and structure of the study, as well as the homogeneity of the potential samples and variations in their demographic make-up, researchers can arrive at appropriate people and settings to sample (cf. Guest et al., 2006; Miles & Huberman, 1994).

9.5 Analysing and Interpreting Data

As we argued in Chapter 5, it is critical that researchers think carefully about their methods and the data they collect and create, in terms of the e-learning phenomenon being scrutinized, the paradigm of inquiry they are adopting and their methodological approach.

This section provides practical advice about how to analyse and interpret data that have been collected as part of an evaluation-research study. As with the selection of data-collection techniques, the analysis and interpretation of data will be aligned with the evaluator's paradigm of inquiry and will respond to the evaluation plan (see Chapter 7). We will discuss the differences between qualitative and quantitative data, and a variety of analysis and interpretation techniques, including descriptive and inferential statistical techniques, and thematic or content analysis.

Once evaluation-research data have been collected, strategies must be established to analyse, interpret and report them, with the overarching purpose of providing information about the evaluation-research questions set out in our evaluation plan. Data analysis is about a systematic approach to gather evidence that responds to evaluation or research questions.

When faced with the data collected in an evaluation, it is easy to feel overwhelmed. This is especially the case if data have been collected using a number of methods, and from a number of different sources. So, the first aim of data analysis is to reduce the size of the data set. Typically raw data, whether quantitative or qualitative, require some sort of systematic reduction, as they are not practical to use in their raw form. For example, it would be impractical to report in their raw form all learners' contributions to a discussion list over a semester. Raw data are also more difficult to interpret. For example, it is easier to interpret a summary of learners' responses to items on a questionnaire than every learner's response to each item. The challenge for evaluators in reducing the volume of data is to complete this task without distorting the essence of the message contained within the original data.

Quantitative data typically come from two of the data-collection techniques described above: questionnaires and usage logs. Qualitative data can be generated by most commonly-used data-collection techniques. Despite the overlap in collection methods, in the following sections we will discuss the analysis and interpretation of quantitative and qualitative data separately. This is done primarily for convenience, as we regard the boundary between quantitative and qualitative data analysis as a blurry one, given that data collected qualitatively (e.g. recordings and text transcripts of focus groups) can be analysed in a relatively quantitative way (e.g. through frequency counts), just as numerical quantitative data (e.g. from a questionnaire or audit trail) can be used in a wholly descriptive fashion.

9.5.1 Quantitative Analyses

Generally two types of quantitative data exist: categorical and continuous. Categorical data classify individuals in terms of some sort of category. An obvious example of this data results from asking learners to classify themselves as either 'male' or 'female'. Continuous data are usually derived from learners' responses to scaled items on a questionnaire. Likert scales are most commonly used to gather continuous data. They present the questionnaire respondents with a question (e.g. 'How much do you agree or disagree with the following statements?'), which is accompanied by a linear scale that contains a number of points with numerical or textual labels (e.g. 'strongly agree', 'agree', 'neutral', 'disagree', 'strongly disagree'). Respondents record their subjective perceptions, attitudes or beliefs by marking a rating on the scale. Continuous quantitative data can also include assessment test scores and data from academic analytics such as time on task.

Once the quantitative data from questionnaires have been collected, the process of analysis will start. The first steps in an analysis will involve collating the questionnaires and ordering them. If an online survey tool (e.g. Survey Monkey) has been used, then this process may have been done already. If data have been collected using paper questionnaires, these should be ordered, checked for completeness, numbered and then entered into an analysis tool (e.g. Excel or SPSS).

Quantitative analysis starts with the process of descriptive analysis. The data are first reviewed or 'screened' to see whether there are missing values for variables and for continuous data whether outliers exist (variables where one or two data points clearly sit outside the distribution of all other data points) (cf. Tabachnick & Fidell, 1996). Data points that have been incorrectly entered into the analysis tool are typically identified in this process.

Researchers typically present the key variables of descriptive analysis using summary statistics such as frequency counts and percentages, mean scores and standard deviations, and representations such as tables, bar charts and histograms. These are most usefully accompanied by a text-based description. For some evaluation-research projects, the quantitative analysis will end here with a comprehensive descriptive analysis. This will depend on the nature of the broad question being considered and the evaluation research being undertaken. While not exclusively the case, in early stages of the e-learning life cycle, where exploratory or pilot studies are being undertaken, descriptive analyses are very common (see Table 8.2, p. 117). In addition, descriptive analyses are common when the focus of the inquiry is geared toward evaluation rather than research.

However, many studies that employ quantitative data use inferential statistical analyses in addition to descriptive analyses. These are used to determine association (how strongly associated two or more variables are to each other), or group-based differentiation (how different two or more groups – of learners, courses, universities – are on a particular variable or set of variables). Inferential analyses or tests are sometimes referred to as 'significance' tests because one outcome from such tests is a statistic that enables researchers to say whether the *strength of association* between two variables is significant (they are more closely related than what would be expected by chance) or the *numerical difference observed between groups* is significant (more different to that which would be expected by chance).

Inferential tests are most robust when underpinned by a strong theory, research question or hypotheses, as these direct the researcher to consider particular tests or comparisons. Common tests of association include correlation, chi-squared tests and regression, while common tests for comparing groups are t-tests, and analyses of variance. Creswell (2009, p. 153) provides a useful table that can assist researchers to select statistical tests for common evaluation-research scenarios. Each of these inferential tests typically has a number of sample-based distribution and/or statistical assumptions that need to be satisfied before they can be undertaken.

9.5.2 Qualitative Analyses

Where quantitative analyses deal with numbers, qualitative analyses deal in text, sounds and images. The statistical techniques used with quantitative data do not apply here, and there are fewer rules and standardized procedures when dealing with qualitative data. Qualitative data analysis is marked by an iterative set of processes, characterized as a data-analysis spiral (Creswell, 2009). Data are revisited again and again, and, as meaning is refined, new connections are made and additional questions emerge, along with a deepening understanding of the material. While this iterative process can occur in quantitative data analysis (cf. Kennedy & Judd, 2004), it is more often associated with qualitative analysis and is typically seen as central to this approach. While there are a number of specific approaches to qualitative data analysis, the iterative process can be described in generalized terms. The description below is based on Creswell (2009), who outlined a generalized approach that included six steps.

9.5.2.1 Organizing and Preparing Raw Data

The first step is to gather the audio, video, text and images that form the base data for the study and organize them in a coherent way. This will often involve transcribing (and perhaps translating) interview or focus-group recordings, collating field notes and ordering these data into folders in a common-sense way (e.g. by all data collected from one individual or by focus group). If the data are digital (e.g. text transcriptions) and a qualitative-analysis software tool is being used to support the analysis (e.g. NVivo), then they can be uploaded, integrated and organized within the tool.

9.5.2.2 Reading Through All Data

Experienced qualitative researchers often tell a novice qualitative practitioner to 'immerse yourself in the data'. Novice researchers, perhaps unsurprisingly, are sometimes confused when their mentors are seemingly asking them to treat their collated text and images as a swimming pool. What is being advocated through this immersive process is reading the data over a number of times and gradually becoming intimate with their detail. This includes not only the actual content, but how it is said, how parts of it are the same and how other parts are different. Often researchers make brief notes or comments to assist with this process and to help them 'hear' what participants are saying.

9.5.2.3 Coding the Data

Once the data have been reviewed as a whole, it is time to start more formal coding. Coding refers to the process by which a researcher systematically reviews and annotates qualitative data (often text) in order to classify and establish themes or generic meaning (Creswell, 2009; Miles & Huberman, 1994). Creswell suggested that the coding process can be usefully started by selecting a manageable chunk of the data: a single case, a short transcript or a sub-section.

A key consideration at this point is whether the coding is based on a pre-existing framework based on established theory and reflected in the evaluation-research questions of interest, or whether codes are developed and emerge based on what is represented in the actual data. We, like others, advocate that both approaches can be adopted (Berg, 2009; Creswell, 2009). Often what is coded by a researcher will reflect the existing theory and the research that has led to the study in the first place. But it is also very common for unanticipated attitudes, behaviour or perceptions to emerge in qualitative research data and these should be coded as well (see below).

Regardless of the balance in the approach, coding begins with the researcher reading through the data and developing or ascribing terms or phrases that describe what the data are saying – what they are about, what they are telling you. A term or phrase may be represented by a particular quote from a learner in a focus group or a comment made in field notes. As coding progresses and more data (e.g. transcripts) are used, these terms and phrases will typically expand and overlap. At some stage the researcher will stop coding and review all the terms and phrases she has come up with and refine them into more distinct categories or themes that describe the data. If a pre-existing framework or clear research questions are being used to guide the coding, this will be used as a point of reference in this review. Terms that overlap can be included under the umbrella of a single category or theme. Coding then continues in a cyclical, iterative process of reading the data, developing categories and themes, reflecting, refining and consolidating. In section 9.6.3, we will discuss how coding by multiple researchers can improve reliability.

It is important that coding of qualitative data is systematic. Categories cannot be fabricated to fit the evaluation questions being considered and data that doesn't suit the evaluator's purposes cannot simply be ignored. The inclusion or exclusion of transcript content under particular categories follows the same criteria. In this context, Guba and Lincoln (1981) described content analysis as *rule-based* – "rules must be derived, procedures delineated, and selection criteria defined" (pp. 240–241).

9.5.2.4 Describing and Interrelating Themes

Creswell's (2009) fourth stage involves building on the codes and themes that have been created. Through the process of coding, typically a large number of themes will emerge. This stage is about drawing the themes together in a manageable way and, where possible, identifying ways in which they relate to each other. The overarching purpose is to find a narrative in the data about their overall meaning. As Creswell suggested, perhaps five or six key themes will emerge, and their description and interrelationships will represent the key findings from the research.

9.5.2.5 REPRESENTING

Once the main ideas have been identified in the qualitative data, it is time to determine the most appropriate way to present these ideas. In qualitative research, a common approach is to create a description or narrative that provides the details of the analysis to a reader. This 'story' would typically be structured into sections and, through detailed description, would show the reader the most important or dominant themes to emerge from the data analysis, and nuances within these themes, highlighted with direct quotations from the evaluation participants which typify or embody the meaning of a theme (e.g. Waycott, Bennett, Kennedy, Dalgarno & Gray, 2010). Consistent with a mixed-methods approach, other researchers may also choose to employ quantitative techniques to represent their data. Frequency counts of themes that emerged in addition to a rich description of how those same themes were manifest in learners' responses could be used as a way of representing the qualitative data analysis (e.g. Liaw, Kennedy, Keppell, Marty & McNair, 2000).

9.5.2.6 INTERPRETING

The sixth of Creswell's (2009) 'steps' is interpreting the data, which may have begun in the previous stage. As data analysis draws to a close the researcher is required to respond to the overarching question of 'What does it all mean?' or more bluntly 'So what?' In responding, the researcher is challenged to draw together the main messages from the coded data and relate these back to theory or research that has gone before. The contribution of the analysis – and the investigation – will often become apparent here, as will ways in which further work can be contributed in the area.

Given that we are advocating a mixed-methods approach to evaluation research, it is worth noting that, in addition to the interpretation of data gathered from one source, it is often the case that a more generalized interpretation will be needed which integrates data collected using a range of methods. As suggested in Figure 7.1, in a comprehensive evaluation-research study, data from multiple sources will need to be pooled and an over-arching message or interpretation will need to be synthesized based on evidence from multiple sources. The ultimate goal here is to develop a coherent message from the data that responds to the research goals, aims and questions developed to guide the study in the first instance.

9.5.2.7 CONTENT ANALYSIS AND OTHER APPROACHES

Broadly speaking, the set of generalized steps described above are the hallmark of *content analysis*, one of the most common qualitative analysis techniques. Content analysis refers to the process by which researchers and evaluators take a set of raw data and systematically and objectively set about coding and categorizing it into major patterns or themes (Lincoln & Guba, 1985; Miles & Huberman, 1994; Patton, 1990; Berg, 2009). Content analysis is also referred to as thematic analysis and, while there are nuanced differences, it is broadly akin to a grounded approach to qualitative data analysis. As mentioned above, some researchers advocate using a 'grounded approach' to content analysis, where the codes and themes emerge unfettered as part of the analysis process. Others point out that solid research is supported by good theory, research aims and questions, and in many cases these can be used to guide the analysis of qualitative data. Berg (2009) suggested that content analysis can be carried out inductively or deductively. The inductive approach would see the evaluator poring over the transcript in order to determine what primary themes or categories emerged from the data. The deductive approach would see the evaluator come to the transcript with a predetermined framework derived from past research or theory. She would systematically go through the transcript and apply the categories where she sees them in the transcript.

In addition to content analysis, there is an array of alternative approaches to the qualitative research and the analysis of qualitative data (cf. Tesch, 1990). Some of these approaches – such as discourse analysis – take as their primary focus the process of interaction, rather than considering their content per se. Discourse analysis is predicated on the notion that the structure of interaction is imbued with meaning, and elements of discourse, such as turn-taking, conversational openings, listening, interruptions and use of minimal encouragers, are often the focus of the analysis. With this type of qualitative analysis, the way in which language is used, and the way in which dialogue takes place, is seen as a critical lens for understanding how individuals negotiate meaning in complex socio-cultural contexts.

Discourse analysis is an appropriate technique to use when seeking evidence of cognitive learning processes or outcomes. Learners' assessed work (exam responses, essays, etc.) and reflective contributions (forums, journals) provide an insight into learners' understanding, which can be uncovered through discourse analysis.

9.5.3 Summary

This section has provided an overview of some of the options practitioners have once they have collected data in front of them. The evaluator's perspective and the decisions she has made to this point – paradigm, questions, methodology, methods – will have a profound influence on how the data analysis will proceed. What we have hopefully made clear is that, regardless of the data collected, the researcher's philosophy and previous decisions will guide the type of analysis she completes. In many circumstances data are 'agnostic'. For example, if a researcher has transcripts of learners' online discussion as her raw data, she could analyse them quantitatively looking at the number of contributions, the length of contribution, the network of contributions (who speaks to whom) and perform statistical tests looking at how key demographic factors (international versus local learners) are able to discriminate learners' level of contribution. Alternatively, she could take the same raw data and analyse them qualitatively to determine either the key content of the interactions (e.g. were they about social matters or course-related material, and if so, what specifically?), or the nature of interactions between participants (e.g. how they were able to support each other in knowledge construction).

9.6 Validity and Reliability

9.6.1 Overview

After collecting, analysing and interpreting data, researchers are often keen to know that the conclusions they draw from that data are valid and reliable. That is, researchers and the readers of their evaluation or research reports want to be confident that there is a sound basis for the conclusions, that they are not reporting just a single instance of a phenomenon or a figment of a researcher's imagination. These issues are concerned with assessing the reliability and validity of data and their analysis. Given the inherent differences between quantitative and qualitative data, it will come as no surprise that the concepts of validity and reliability are treated differently with each.

9.6.2 Validity

In the context of quantitative evaluation research, validity is concerned with the inferences we make about the meaning of the data we collect and analyse, and the extent to which these interpretations can be generalized to a broader context beyond the study (Ray & Ravizza, 1985; Shavelson, 1988). There is a range of different types of validity that can be considered in evaluation-research contexts, but a broad distinction is between internal validity (which considers whether the explanation of the data in a study being offered is the only possible one) and external validity (which considers whether the findings of the study can be applied more broadly to other contexts) (Ray & Ravizza, 1985; Watson, Pattison & Finch, 1993).

Validity has a broader connotation in the context of qualitative evaluation research, but it is still concerned with whether the conclusions being drawn from the data are credible, defensible, warranted and able to withstand alternative explanations. While the qualitative data-analysis process described above allows alternative meanings to emerge in the analysis and interpretation of data, we still want to know whether the responses to our evaluation questions and our conclusions are plausible and hold up to scrutiny. It is essential that meanings and conclusions are revisited, cross-checked and verified throughout the iterative process of data analysis. As Miles and Huberman (1994) suggested: "The meanings emerging from the data have to be tested for their plausibility, their sturdiness, their 'confirmability' – that is, their validity" (p. 22).

Techniques such as triangulation are a way of strengthening the validity of conclusions. Triangulation is a process that aims at gathering more than one perspective or piece of information on a particular issue. Just as a police officer may ask the opinion of a number of witnesses to a car accident in an attempt to build up an accurate picture of the incident, evaluators are encouraged to investigate an issue using more than one technique or source. As Patton (1990) suggested, "multiple sources of information are sought and used because no single source of information can be trusted to provide a comprehensive perspective on the program" (p. 244). Generally, triangulation can refer to either the use of a variety of data-collection techniques (that is, mixed methods using techniques such as observation, focus groups and questionnaires) or to a combination of different perspectives or sources of information on an issue (e.g. teachers, learners and developers). The first is called methods triangulation while the second is called sources triangulation. The process can be seen as one of cross-checking our findings using different sources or methods.

9.6.3 Reliability

Reliability refers to the degree of consistency, dependency or stability in the result of analysis (Ray & Ravizza, 1985; Shavelson, 1988). As social-science researchers and evaluators, it is important to try to maximize the reliability of our results, because results are more credible if they are more reliable. For quantitative data, such as learners' responses on Likert scales, one measure of reliability would be the degree to which the same scores would be obtained if the same learners were asked to complete the questionnaire again under similar circumstances. This is called test-retest reliability. If a number of questionnaire items are used to make up a scale, then a measure of the degree to which the items are consistent can be calculated (internal reliability, often using an 'alpha' statistic).

For qualitative data, say the coding of a transcript, reliability can be assessed by asking two independent 'raters' (or researchers) to code the transcript using the same rules or criteria. The higher the correspondence between the coding of the two raters, the greater the reliability. This is called inter-rater reliability and can be calculated numerically using statistics such as the intra-class correlation or Kappa co-efficient (Viera & Garrett, 2005). Not only should this procedure give an indication of how reliable the analysis is, but it should also highlight areas for discussion and reflection. That is, if the inter-rater reliability was low, this would highlight that either the coding scheme, the criteria or the perspective of the raters might need to be reconsidered and recalibrated or adjusted given the transcript (data) in question.

Within the generalized approach to qualitative data analysis outlined in section 9.5.2, typically the activities of coding, describing and interrelating are repeated more frequently than the other tasks. Just as this process enhances the validity of the outcomes of qualitative data analysis, when data are revisited on a number of occasions to interrogate and review codes, themes and categories, the reliability of the findings is increased. As researchers conclude their final iterations in their analysis, they should regularly reflect on: how valid their interpretations are; how well they would be able to defend their interpretations (what would they point to in the data as the basis or evidence for a code, theme or category?); and how well their interpretations could withstand alternative explanation.

9.7 Reporting and Presentation

Once the results of an evaluation-research study have been analysed, it is time to report them to an audience. Given there may be more than one audience for a single study, thought should be given to this at the outset and it is useful to acknowledge that different audiences may require different reports or types of reports (Reeves & Hedberg, 2003). For example, a report to senior administrators at a university may be shorter and more policy-oriented, compared to a paper presented as a journal article to academic peers, even if both broadly rely on the same data. Moreover, senior administrators at a university may be more accustomed to a personal presentation of the results and an executive summary rather than a full written report.

While it may seem relatively straightforward, novice practitioners often find it difficult to create a coherent report from an evaluation-research study. In part, this may be because typically there are competing considerations in how to 'set up' or structure a report of results. The way in which the results are reported will be determined to a great extent by the results themselves: decisions need to be made about: what results are the most important to report to a given audience; how the results should be reported – in what format and style; and, importantly, what is not reported. In a single report, it will often not be possible to cover everything that has been found in one evaluation-research study, and decisions need to be made about what not to report, which is often quite difficult. In addition to the data, the evaluation-research questions which have guided the investigation, and the data-collection techniques, particularly in mixed-methods research, can also influence how the results are presented. Sometimes, it can be difficult to decide whether the results should be reported so that they align with the research questions that drove the study, or the themes and categories that emerged from the data, or whether they should follow groups of participants or sites of data collection. There is no correct answer here, and each report needs to be generated and tailored on a case-by-case basis.

Despite all of this, in our experience, a clear structure and narrative to the results is essential in all effective evaluation-research presentations, whether journal articles, boardroom talks or internal reports. Presentations of results need to have a clear story of what the purpose of the study was, on the contribution of previous literature, what was done in the study, what was found and what the implications of these findings are. Ultimately it does not matter greatly how the detail of the evaluation-research report is organized – if these key elements are covered, then there is a strong probability that your results will be well communicated.

9.8 Summary

This chapter has provided an overview of the issues associated with collecting, analysing and interpreting data from an e-learning evaluation-research study. As this is not a research methods text, we have only 'scratched the surface' of these issues, pointing readers to the broader literature as necessary. Nevertheless, the information we have provided in Chapters 7, 8 and 9 should provide sufficient detail for practitioners to develop a plan to investigate an e-learning innovation. The following chapter deals with the final evaluation form introduced in Chapter 8 – project-management evaluation.

10

Project-management Evaluation

10.1 Introduction

In Chapter 4, we pointed out that most e-learning developments are *projects* – that is, temporary activities with fixed end-dates and budgets, with the specific goal of producing a deliverable product. We also made a distinction between the conduct of a project (How good were project-management processes, communication channels, etc.?), and the quality of its deliverables (Does the designed e-learning artefact function as designed? Can students navigate as they need?). As Kirschner (2005, p. 78) stated: "Project success is not the same as innovation success: There are two types of 'success', namely the success of the project itself and the success of the innovation (its ultimate implementation)." Chapter 8 looked at the latter element while, in this chapter, we are concerned with the former, the success of the project itself. This chapter diverges from the main thread we have been following throughout this book, but we present it here because we recognize it as a gap in e-learning scholarship.

It focuses on substantial, funded e-learning development projects where a formal project-management process is required. We recognize that the 'message' of this chapter may not be particularly relevant to an unfunded e-learning development conducted by an individual practitioner using a generic learning tool such as a learning-management system. We contend that these are still projects, with a fixed end-date and budget (of in-kind work), although the project-management component may be quite informal. Nevertheless, we claim that the considerations of this chapter can assist in the successful completion of even such informal projects, and can be helpful to novices in preparing funding proposals and setting up funded projects into the future.

Project-management evaluation leans towards the evaluation end of the evaluation–research continuum. We are much more interested in making judgements about processes than we are in understanding what is happening. Project-management evaluation is also, arguably, broader than other types of evaluation discussed in the previous chapter, because it applies to any teaching and learning innovation project, which may or may not involve technology. Numerous teaching and learning development projects are funded annually throughout the world and there is a need for increased expertise in evaluating their effectiveness, value for money and sustainability. This chapter briefly addresses this need.

As in Chapter 8, we seek to identify the component parts of the activity of project management, before discussing how each element might be evaluated.

10.2 General Elements of Project Management

This section synthesizes the experiences of the authors, together with some of the core references on e-learning project management (Bates, 2000; Baume & Martin, 2002; Chesterton & Cummings, 2007; England & Finney, 1999; Heerkens, 2002; Herrington et al., 2009; Jackson, 2005; Joint Information Systems Committee (JISC), 2008; Kirschner, 2005; Phillips, 1997).

Project management can proceed with varying levels of formality. For large and complex undertakings, such as building a bridge or holding an international sporting event like the Olympics, project management needs to be comprehensive, detailed and rigorous. e-Learning developments are neither as critical, nor as complex, and project management can be less rigorous, although no less important.

> Learning and teaching projects tend to be journeys of exploration: the operational plan is a rough map but it does not necessarily take account of road conditions and travelling companions!   (Varnava, 2002, p. 70)

Off-the-shelf project-management methodologies, such as the 'Project Management Body of Knowledge' (Duncan, 1996), can be used for complex software developments, but more flexible approaches can be used for many e-learning developments (cf. agile software development and flexible product development (JISC, 2008)).

In Table 8.1, we characterized the 'development of an e-learning solution' as having three activities: design, development and implementation. A project designed to achieve this solution also has three components: planning the activities; carrying out the activities in a timely manner; and managing these activities. The first and last of these are largely the responsibility of the project manager, while various professionals perform most of the second activity.

10.3 Planning a Project

Planning a project is essentially an imaginative process. While experience with similar projects is clearly valuable, project planning involves informed speculations about the various activities which are required, and how they interact with each other.

The project plan starts with a consideration of the overall approach to be taken. It is a "simple, clear picture of what you will do and how" (JISC, 2008, p. 28), broadly looking at what will be produced and who is expected to use it in what contexts. This process results in agreement on project objectives and outcomes, which should be clear and realistic. The project plan, therefore, draws strongly from the *baseline analysis* (see section 8.4, p. 119).

The project plan should also specify the scope and boundaries of the project, using a *who, what, where, how, why* approach. It should clarify the assumptions that have been made about the project, and the institutional constraints which are present. Critical success factors, on which the success of the project depends, also need to be considered in the project plan, as does an exit strategy. It should also identify any stakeholders who may be interested in the outcomes of the project (cf. section 7.2.6, p. 108).

However, once these global considerations have been resolved, the focus turns to the actual *activities* of the project. In other words, what has to be done, when does it have to be done by and who will do it? The project plan also ensures that members of the project team have well-defined roles and responsibilities.

At first, a project may seem too large and complex, and the development of a project plan may seem daunting. However, a *divide-and-conquer* technique can simplify the task. This involves breaking down a complex task into smaller and smaller sub-tasks, which become more manageable. In section 8.5.3, we started this process when we looked at the design of an interactive learning system. We identified several elements which needed to be designed:

- the overall learning design;
- the graphic design;
- the navigational mechanisms;
- the software architecture;
- the interactive learning tasks;
- the media elements.

Different professional skills are required to actualize these elements, and these tasks can be carried out in parallel. For example, a graphic designer would logically develop the graphic design, while, at the same time, a programmer might develop the software architecture. Media elements might be developed by various professionals: graphic designers, animators, video producers. However, other tasks might require a team approach: the overall learning design might require collaboration between an educational designer and a content expert. Interactive learning tasks involve input from all team members.

Nevertheless, each of these activities can be broken down into smaller, well-defined sub-tasks. To look at one element, the graphic designer might respond to a design brief by developing a prototype with wireframe graphics (showing, by the use of line graphics and sketches, where screen elements will be). They might also develop a colour palette and suggest suitable fonts. On approval, these elements would be drawn together into increasingly sophisticated prototypes, until the design is agreed and 'signed off'. Particular graphic elements will then be developed for each screen, and, as software elements are completed, integrated into the interactive learning system.

This description indicates a time sequence of elements which need to be completed in order (a *timeline* in project-management terms). Discussion with the graphic designer (and *metrics* from previous projects) can lead to estimates of the time required to complete each sub-task. There are, therefore, three core elements in the development of a project plan: the activities (tasks and sub-tasks); the expected completion time of each task; and the people who will do the work (expressed in project-management jargon as *resources*). These components, together, are often expressed as a Gantt chart (see Figure 10.1), after Henri Gantt, who designed the chart in the early years of the 20th century.

The description of the graphic designer's tasks above reveals another element of project planning and management. At various points, the graphic designer's work is dependent on work from others. The prototypes need to be approved by other members of the project team, and graphic elements cannot be integrated into the interactive learning system until programming work is completed. These are called *dependencies*. The project manager needs to plan other work for the graphic designer while they are waiting for dependent tasks to be completed.

A further element of project planning recognizes that projects proceed through stages. So, while several people may be working independently, the 'threads' of this work come together at *milestones*. In Table 8.1, we distinguished between design, development and implementation of an e-learning project. Before development can start, the project team needs to be convinced that the design works, and so consideration of the outcomes of the design evaluation forms a logical milestone.

The final element of developing the project plan involves estimating a budget for the project. This is the second area where the divide-and-conquer technique is useful. Costs can be estimated relatively easily for the individual sub-tasks identified through this technique. While data from similar projects (metrics) can assist this estimation, they are still estimates. However, because there are numerous sub-tasks, any over-estimates of some tasks are likely to be compensated for by under-estimates on other tasks.

The preceding discussion applies for complex, technical developments, such as interactive learning systems, and to a lesser extent, learning objects. When developing an e-learning environment with a generic learning tool, such as a learning-management system, technical and graphical issues take a back seat. The technical functionality already exists, and 'look and feel' issues are often resolved by choosing from a set of predefined templates. In such a case,

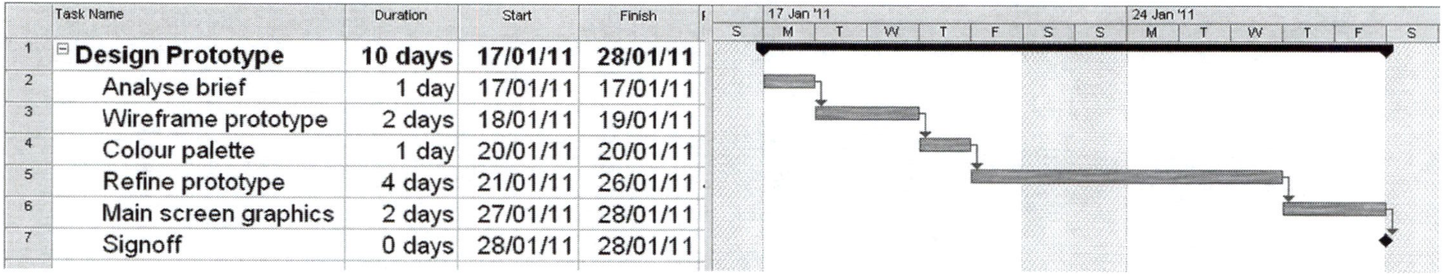

	Task Name	Duration	Start	Finish	
1	⊟ **Design Prototype**	**10 days**	**17/01/11**	**28/01/11**	
2	Analyse brief	1 day	17/01/11	17/01/11	
3	Wireframe prototype	2 days	18/01/11	19/01/11	
4	Colour palette	1 day	20/01/11	20/01/11	
5	Refine prototype	4 days	21/01/11	26/01/11	
6	Main screen graphics	2 days	27/01/11	28/01/11	
7	Signoff	0 days	28/01/11	28/01/11	

Figure 10.1 A representative Gantt chart showing the interrelations between tasks and timelines.

the project is mainly concerned with the *curriculum* and *learning design*, and development is carried out by small teams of academics and educational (or learning) designers, or perhaps individuals. Because the project is simpler, with fewer tasks and dependencies, project planning and management does not have to be so rigorous. However, it is still necessary to ensure that projects achieve their aims on time, and within budget if there is one.

Alexander et al. (1998) reviewed 104 out of a total of 173 teaching development projects funded by the Australian government in 1994 or 1995, which made significant use of a range of information technologies to develop student learning materials. They concluded that many of these projects were ineffective, and one of the contributing factors was ineffective project management. An analysis of 20, more successful, projects revealed the following project-management elements:

- the development team included a skilled project manager;
- software development was adequately analysed, planned, scoped and designed prior to commencing the development;
- the anticipated outcome was realistic, in the context of the time and budget available;
- the project's context of implementation was planned;
- the project team had shared goals and could resolve conflict;
- members of the project team were committed;
- academic team members realized that they could not perform all the technical functions;
- staff on the project team valued the different skills required for successful project completion.

Once the project activities and timelines have been documented in the project plan, some final important elements need to be addressed. These include the development of a dissemination plan, clarification of any intellectual-property issues and identification of any contractual arrangements which need to be made. The project plan is rounded off by a *risk analysis*, which identifies any risks to the project success, with an assessment of the likelihood and impact of each risk. Plans are made to mitigate against any occurrences of perceived high risk.

The resultant project plan will provide a detailed set of documentation, providing "consistent information about the project and the roles and responsibilities of each team member" (Kenny, 2004, p. 398), so that all team members know what is to be done, and when.

A final point to make about project plans and timelines is that they are not set in stone. It is impossible to predict correctly all aspects of e-learning developments, and projects continually evolve, and the project plan has to reflect this evolution.

10.4 Managing a Project

Once a project plan has been made, and team members have commenced work on the project, the emphasis of project management turns to managing the project. There are two aspects of project management – the soft and the hard.

10.4.1 Hard Elements of Project Management

Hard elements of project management are related to ensuring that project aims and objectives are achieved and that project work is performed on schedule and within the allocated budget. This involves ongoing monitoring and coordination of project activities. The project manager needs to be continually aware of which tasks are being done at which time, and which are on schedule or behind schedule. Team members may need to be allocated to other tasks if they are waiting on another team member to complete a dependent task. At the same time, budget expenditure needs to be monitored. A further role is to identify risks, problems and issues, and escalate them as appropriate to the project leader.

The project manager also needs to ensure that all decisions made by the project team are recorded through updating design specifications, and keeping minutes of project meetings, with action items and notes of their subsequent resolution. The preparation of progress, final and other project reports is also the responsibility of the project manager, as are contractual and legal arrangements.

10.4.2 Soft Elements of Project Management

Remaining on top of the hard elements of project management involves communicating with other members of the project, facilitating the development of a team approach and communicating with stakeholders – all of which are *soft* skills.

A synthesis of findings from Kenny (2004), JISC (2008) and Kirschner (2005) indicates that the soft skills that contribute to successful projects include:

- creation of a team with shared ownership of the project and clearly defined roles;
- creation of effective communication within the team, with agreed methods for planning and making decisions;
- creation of formal feedback channels so that the project team has a mechanism to reflect on its work and take a positive and flexible approach to updating plans.

However, the soft skills of project management do not apply only *within* the project team. They also apply to the perception of the project by stakeholders. A role of the project manager is to facilitate communication of project plans and progress to stakeholders through a dissemination plan. This may include organizing workshops and networking events to disseminate project outcomes to the wider stakeholder community and encourage wider uptake of the project deliverables.

A project cannot be regarded as successful if its outcomes are not disseminated widely. We will discuss this further in Chapter 11.

10.5 Characteristics of a Project Manager

To be effective, project managers need to have a particular set of skills, some of which have been mentioned in preceding sub-sections. They clearly need to be "technically competent to help design and execute a total project" (Kirschner, 2005, p. 86).

Many of the 'hard' aspects of project management require fine-grained attention to detail on the part of the project manager. However, at the same time, a project manager needs to "keep the 'big picture' in mind . . . understanding the interrelationships among the various parts of the program and the implications of any proposed changes to the design" (Phillips, 2001, pp. 236–237). They have to be "strategically capable of envisioning and conceptualizing the entire project process though all its phases" (Kirschner, 2005, p. 86).

At the same time, project managers need to have excellent soft skills, including the ability:

- "to inspire, motivate, discipline, resolve conflicts, negotiate competing interests, and sell the project" (Kirschner, 2005);
- "to communicate the big picture to the rest of the team" (Garstang, 1994), and build a shared understanding of the complexity of the project (Phillips, 2001);
- "to speak the 'language' of the experts on the team" (McDaniel & Liu, 1996), and "to translate what one team member says into words which another team member can understand" (Phillips, 1997, p. 44);
- to establish a common language with clients (Phillips, 2001).

However, there is also an overlap between the soft and hard aspects of project management. For example, when tasks are clearly defined, this can give team members a sense of ownership and value in their work (Canby Mugg, 1996).

10.6 Evaluating Project-Management Elements

As a project progresses, project managers, as part of their normal duties, will monitor the conduct of the project and reflect on and report the general 'health' of the project. Project managers will typically monitor projects through various documents, including: a project diary, and personal notes and anecdotal records from meetings; project-meeting minutes and status reports; timelines and Gantt charts, and documentation of schedule changes; and financial records, including printouts of budgeting spreadsheets, receipts, invoices and so on.

All of the above are evaluative activities, as well as being part and parcel of normal project-management activities. However, funding bodies in the UK and Australia (the Joint Information Systems Committee and the Australian Learning and Teaching Council (ALTC) respectively) require funded projects to have external evaluators. Such an evaluator provides an external viewpoint to 'keep the project team honest'. Having someone 'looking over your shoulder' can maintain a focus on the 'big picture' of a project when there might be a tendency for the project team to focus on the immediate tasks at hand. This said, there is still a close link between good project management and project evaluation – it is simply that one has an internal focus, while the other is one step removed from the project. At the same time, the data produced by a project manager as part of monitoring a project forms a valuable source of data for the project evaluator.

In section 8.3, we claimed that project-management evaluation has two elements: making judgements about the conduct of an e-learning development project, and suggesting improvements to it (Jackson, 2005). There are, therefore, both summative and formative aspects to project-management evaluation. In the previous section, we also identified two separate aspects of project management: creation of a project plan; and the actual management of a project, with both hard and soft aspects. We should evaluate each of these elements.

Project-management evaluation is primarily interested in processes, rather than outcomes. Project outcomes are, largely, addressed by other evaluation-research activities. Because project management is process-oriented, project-management evaluation is primarily concerned with formative evaluation. It is not particularly helpful to discover after a project's budget and deadline are reached that project processes have not been effective. It is far more appropriate to identify issues and problems as they occur (Jackson, 2005), and to address them so that the project deliverables can be achieved on time and under budget.

The project team needs to be open to review and feedback, and have a willingness and ability to re-plan and revise where necessary. Project-management evaluation should lead to continual modification of the project plan based on reflections on progress, as well as reflecting on processes at the completion of a project.

10.6.1 Formative Process Evaluation

Process evaluation, as conceived here, shares many similarities with Owen's (2006) *monitoring* evaluation form. The broad question to be asked is: 'To what extent was the project implemented as planned and funded, and how can the process be improved?' Answering this question involves monitoring details of the project's implementation and the timely and accurate collection of data. Process questions can be asked about both the project plan and the project management. The questions below are derived from lists published by Chesterton and Cummings (2007) and the JISC (2008).

10.6.1.1 FORMATIVE – PROJECT PLAN
The following questions might be asked when trying to evaluate and improve a project plan.

- Why is the project being done?
- What activities and procedures are planned for the project to achieve its intended outcomes?
- What is the basis for expecting that the planned activities and procedures will lead to the intended outcomes within the project's particular context?
- How effective are the planned communications and conflict resolution processes?
- What gaps are there in the plan?
- How can the plan be improved?

10.6.1.2 FORMATIVE – PROJECT MANAGEMENT
The following questions might be asked when trying to evaluate and improve the management of a project.

- How effective is the project management?
- Have milestones been met on schedule?
- What is holding up progress?
- What should we do to correct delays?
- How can we fine-tune the project processes to make them more effective?
- How well does the team operate?
- How well is the team managed?
- Are stakeholders supportive?
- To what extent are project outputs meeting stakeholder needs?
- Is project dissemination effective?

10.6.2 Summative Outcomes Evaluation

Depending on the project, and the scope of any evaluation research associated with that project, a project-management evaluation may be concerned with a summative evaluation of the outcomes of the project. This is akin to Owen's (2006) *impact* evaluation form, judging the overall success of the project and its impact on stakeholders.

10.6.2.1 SUMMATIVE – PROJECT PLAN
There is little point in summatively evaluating a project plan. If the project plan was inadequate, the project is likely to have run into problems long before this. Nevertheless, it may be appropriate to evaluate the *implementation* of the project plan, with questions such as 'What processes were planned and what were actually put in place for the project?' This can provide useful information for subsequent projects.

10.6.2.2 SUMMATIVE – PROJECT MANAGEMENT

Funding bodies often require evidence that a project has been carried out efficiently. This can inform any future funding decisions about the same project team. The range of questions to be asked includes:

- Was the project implemented as planned?
- What caused any changes?
- To what extent have the intended outcomes been achieved?
- What factors helped and hindered the achievement of the outcomes?
- What were any unintended outcomes?
- How cost-effective was the project?
- What measures, if any, have been put in place to promote sustainability of the project's focus and outcomes?
- What benefits are there for stakeholders?
- What would we do differently next time?
- What lessons have been learned from this project and how might these be of assistance to other institutions?

We conclude this chapter with some general comments about the role of the project evaluator. According to common practice, many funding bodies require a summative evaluation at the end of a project. However, this is changing, in line with the arguments presented here. For example, the 2009 Grants Scheme Guidelines of the Australian Learning and Teaching Council (ALTC) contained the following requirement for project evaluation: "All projects provided with funding of greater than $150,000 must commission a formal independent evaluation *at the conclusion* of the project." In the 2010 guidelines, the words "at the conclusion" were excised from this requirement. This change resonates with our argument that it is much more appropriate to formatively evaluate the conduct of a project while it is underway – so that project funds can be expended wisely.

A further aspect of the ALTC requirement is worth discussing: that the project evaluation be formal and independent. This is usually interpreted by saying that the evaluator should be external to the project and 'at arm's length'. However, recent experience by one of the authors has revealed that an alternative approach to project-management evaluation might be more effective. Rather than performing a purely summative role, or a formative role from a middle stage of the project, the evaluator acted as a participant observer from the outset of the project. He was 'embedded' as a critical friend of the project team throughout. He attended most project group meetings, reviewed drafts of plans and documents, and debriefed with team members at various stages. This provided a richer understanding of the conduct of the project than did other approaches, and simplified the writing of the evaluation reports.

Self-reflection reports from that project evaluation commented that the involvement of the evaluator as a participant observer led to continuous improvement of project processes, for instance, by drawing the team back to the original proposal. For example:

> [The evaluator's] regular monitoring and input has also been very valuable. I am not aware of another project where the evaluator plays such an active and useful role. (Phillips, 2010)

The final point to make about project-management evaluation is that like "the project itself, the evaluation can also be evaluated, using the same principles and procedures" (Jackson, 2005, p. 59).

10.7 Summary

In this chapter, we have argued that project-management evaluation makes judgements about, and suggests improvements to, the *conduct* of an e-learning development project. We suggested that project-management evaluation is primarily interested in processes, rather than outcomes, and it is primarily concerned with formative evaluation, although we also discussed summative elements. We further broke down our analysis by considering both the development of a project plan, and the hard and soft aspects of actually managing a project.

In the following chapter we consider factors which impact on the sustainability of e-learning initiatives.

11
Using Evaluation-research Results
An Overview of Impact Issues Beyond the Confines of a Single Project

11.1 Introduction

This chapter draws together the practical parts of this book, and looks at some broader issues impacting on the effectiveness of e-learning. In previous chapters, we have used divide-and-conquer techniques to break down complex processes into manageable parts, starting with the process of conducting an evaluation-research study (Chapter 7). We have articulated five different evaluation forms that are appropriate at different stages of the e-learning life cycle (Chapter 8), and summarized questions and data sources which might be appropriate for each form. In Chapter 9, we discussed data and methods, before drawing the threads together through an overview of analysis and interpretation in evaluation research.

Our intention was to assist readers to develop and carry out an e-learning effectiveness study so they can use the findings to improve e-learning practice. We are not saying this is easy – indeed, in this book, we have hopefully made it clear how difficult it is to do e-learning evaluation research well. However, there is a real need to develop evidence-based practice in technology-enhanced learning. Globally, despite large investments over the last two decades, there is little evidence of the effectiveness of e-learning, other than convenience and flexibility. The emerging e-learning field needs to demonstrate a more mature approach to e-learning development, evaluation and research.

Claims have been made with each new cycle of technology innovation that the new technology would revolutionize pedagogy. There is little evidence of this. It is incontrovertible that e-learning uptake has been high worldwide, but this uptake has tended to replicate traditional practice rather than building on the affordances of technology. In Chapters 1 and 3, we outlined the salient points from current research about learning, and made the point that educational technology can be used to facilitate learner-centred, constructivist, deep approaches to learning. Crucially, we took a whole-of-curriculum approach, seeing e-learning artefacts as tools within a broader learning environment.

There is a tension between the traditional approaches to teaching and learning, including the use of technology-enhanced learning, and the learner-centred, outcomes-based and deep-learning approach developed from research into education. Jackson (1998) has drawn a comparison between this tension and Argyris' (1976) concepts of "theory-in-use" and "espoused theory", developed in the context of leadership education for adults. Argyris found that the majority of adults who had been taught, and theoretically understood, the concepts of the espoused theory were not able to apply it but, instead, reverted to their pre-programmed theory-in-use. Jackson (1998) claimed that this disjunction also occurs in university teaching, with the teacher-directed and content-centred approach remaining as the theory-in-use, despite the evidence in support of the learner-centred, deep-learning espoused theory. We will return to Argyris' work later in this chapter.

There are two issues that inhibit more effective use of educational technology. One issue is that e-learning has not been developed to take the most advantage of its possibilities (and e-learning developments haven't built particularly well on principles derived from e-learning evaluation research). A second issue is that, even when e-learning environments are designed and implemented in innovative ways in line with espoused theory, there are barriers to their long-term sustainability. We will address these barriers in the following sections.

11.2 Sustainability of an e-Learning Initiative

Much of this book has been written with individual teachers and/or course teams in mind, with the thesis that, through designing and enacting an evaluation-research plan matched to phases of the e-learning life cycle, the learning environment will be enhanced, and learners will have an optimized learning experience and, hopefully, enriched learning outcomes.

Sustainability relates to the likelihood that the innovation or redesign will continue in future cycles. Our argument is that good e-learning development involves an investment of time and effort. If the implemented e-learning environment that is the focus of evaluation research is not sustainable, then this means that there is a low return on the investment of the development resources. What we are suggesting is that issues of sustainability provide a strong incentive for planning to have a number of iterations of development and evaluation research. The job does not stop once the e-learning environment is used with learners in a 'live' course for the first time.

There are some examples of e-learning projects that are highly sustainable. One good example is the veterinary microbiology project described in section 4.6. The underlying technology is now web-based but the course in which the e-cases are used has a similar learning design, with the same e-cases, 20 years after it commenced.

However, it is rare for an e-learning innovation to be sustainable over such a long period. Many e-learning grants are for individual projects that do not result in university-wide benefits, let alone system-wide ones. These projects, devised by enthusiastic individuals often working in isolation from their colleagues, usually receive short-term funding and evaluation is limited to the requirements of a project report produced in a relatively short timeframe. Many such projects are not sustainable past the initial project funding.

One almost never hears about ineffective e-learning projects because tales of disaster are rarely published. Two exceptions were reviews by McNaught, Lam, Cheng, Kennedy and Mohan (2009) and Alexander et al., (1998), which examined more than a hundred e-learning initiatives across universities in Hong Kong and Australia. These reviews (see also Kirschner, 2005) identified factors which can lead to sustainable project outcomes, in terms of three categories: educational design, project management and sustainability. The project-management factors were discussed as part of developing a project plan in section 10.3, while educational design and sustainability factors are summarized in Table 11.1. Educational design factors can be addressed through solid baseline analysis and design evaluation (Chapter 8), while sustainability issues are discussed here.

Often, an e-learning project may be deemed successful, after an e-learning environment is developed on time and on budget, and the formative evaluation

Table 11.1 Factors which can lead to sustainable e-learning developments

Factor	Characteristics
Educational design	The project: • aims to address a specific area of learner need; • uses a learning design/strategy which has been well thought through; • is integrated into the learning experience; • prepares learners for new learning experiences. The designers: • modify assessment of learning; • realize that learners are unwilling to engage in higher-level learning activities, especially when they are not related to assessment; • do not utilize technology for its own sake; • evaluate both usability and learning.
Sustainability	• Staff are supported through access to technical support and educational software-development expertise. • Learners have access to appropriate hardware, software and support. • Projects are embedded in the department's normal teaching. • Funding is available for implementation and maintenance of the project. • The head of department and the dean are supportive of the project. • Copyright and intellectual property issues are resolved. • Promotion and tenure policies recognize teaching developments.

looks positive. However, many factors impact on the sustainability of that 'successful' project.

- Is it likely that the e-learning environment will be used over an extended period?
- Do the educational benefits of the e-learning environment outweigh ongoing maintenance costs?
- How well is the e-learning environment integrated into the structure of the program learners are enrolled in?
- Is the use of the e-learning environment so attractive to learners, or does it require them to work so hard, that they neglect other studies?
- Are the peak loads on support staff in setting up the e-learning environment interfering with the needs of other units of study?
- What do colleagues think about the e-learning initiative?
- What do learners think about the e-learning initiative?

The following sections will explore some of these questions, from the perspective of the department in which a teacher works and within the broader institutional context.

11.2.1 The Departmental Context

Just because an e-learning environment for a unit of study is well established, with its effectiveness justified by a solid evidence base, does not mean that it is sustainable within the department in which it is situated. If other people in the department know little about the initiative, or are sceptical about its worth, then there is a risk that it will not be sustained. Less innovative colleagues may not agree with the innovation and may, passively or actively, resist it. This is particularly important where change in one unit of study may impact on other units of study, for example, in curriculum articulation and assessment. If this doesn't occur, then innovations have been known to fail.

The views of learners about the value of an innovation can also impact on sustainability. The introduction of problem-based learning into one unit of study across a veterinary program initially appeared promising (Thomas & Pospisil, 2000). However, the different cognitive requirements of the new unit (working holistically, rather than memorizing content) was challenging to learners. Their concerns were reinforced by more senior learners who lauded the benefits of the traditional method in a very competitive learner cohort. This learner resistance spelled the end of the sustainability of this innovation.

The support of the head of department is particularly important in sustainability. If the head of department doesn't appreciate the worth of the innovation, or has other priorities for the department, sustainability of an innovation is particularly problematic. The view of the head of department has a strong influence on how other staff perceive educational innovation, and specific projects in particular.

Even when e-learning innovations have continued for several years, their sustainability can be threatened by staff changes. Two examples are relevant here. During the 1990s a group of staff in a physics department radically changed the way physics was taught by adopting the 'studio physics' model (Wilson, 1994). This approach was demonstrated to be cost-effective and led to better learning outcomes (Zadnik, Deylitz, Yeo, Loss & Treagust, 1999). However, as the key staff progressed in their careers, and new staff became involved in teaching the particular units of study, teaching reverted to traditional approaches. A second example concerns the application of the studio model to a large human biology class (Fyfe, 2000), where large lectures and laboratory sessions were replaced with practicals of 40 to 50 learners. This change was seen as a priority by the head of department, and implemented by a large team, and it was shown to be cost-effective and educationally beneficial. Responsibility for coordinating this unit of study changed four times over a decade, but each time to a member of the original team. The fifth change was to a new staff member who felt that the workload of running the studio approach was too high, despite evidence of the effectiveness of the approach, and reverted to the traditional lecturing approach.

A final example, which used a similar approach in software engineering, was undone by a political decision to merge the department with a larger one. This was an example where the institutional context influenced sustainability – discussed further in the following section.

11.2.2 The Institutional Context

If there are barriers at departmental level, there are also barriers at higher levels. McNaught et al. (2000) conducted a study investigating factors affecting the adoption of educational technology in 28 Australian universities. This report identified a number of factors which, when all present, could lead to widespread adoption of educational technology. Three major themes were identified: the institutional culture, the policy framework and the support infrastructure, which were represented as a Venn diagram, recognizing an overlap between the three components. There was substantial overlap between this work and Bates (2000), including the need to:

- promote and recognize the scholarship of teaching;
- change work practices and workload-management practices;
- recognize and reward staff for innovation;
- develop a policy framework for educational innovation;
- adopt project-management approaches;
- provide adequate technological infrastructure;
- provide support to staff to implement e-learning approaches;
- address intellectual-property issues;
- develop funding strategies;
- facilitate partnerships and collaboration.

As noted above, local contexts can change quite rapidly – for example, through organizational restructures or new program-accreditation criteria. If returns are to be made on investments in educational innovations, then a robust policy and support framework needs to be in place to ensure that developments are sustainable in an environment of change. Higher education is a dynamic playing field.

This also includes a less tangible aspect – the construction of a culture that supports and values a scholarly approach to the use of technology in teaching and learning. In short, the value of evaluation-research data can go well beyond the confines of any single innovation or e-learning project to influence institutional decisions.

Questions concerned with the institutionalization of e-learning projects are rarely addressed in published studies, no doubt because they are difficult to produce evidence for, and because most projects are organizationally 'brittle' – there is little uptake outside of the host department and most projects don't survive the departure of the project champion.

Some relevant questions which might be asked at an institutional level are as follows.

- Are improvements in grade distributions in units of study reflected in retention, progress and pass rates for the degree program?
- What evidence is there that institutional grants for e-learning are improving learning?
- Have there been any flow-back benefits from uptake in other departments or institutions (e.g. enhancements, cost-recovery)?
- Is it possible to trace improvements in generic learning outcomes to the influence of particular e-learning initiatives?
- Have benefits been detected in the workplace, for example, in work placements or postgraduate employment?
- What scholarly benefits have accrued from publication about e-learning initiatives?
- Is the e-learning infrastructure at the university adequate for staff and learner needs?
- Is the pattern of use of e-learning infrastructure changing over time?
- How does this institution compare with similar institutions elsewhere in the use of e-learning?

This section has hopefully demonstrated that it is not sufficient simply to develop exemplary e-learning environments that function as designed, and to build up a solid evidence base. There is a need to go beyond technology issues, to recognize that it is important for others to know what has been done, and what its value is (dissemination). Furthermore, it is important to recognize and adapt to the organizational change factors which impact on sustainability – in other words, to engage with research into the barriers to systemic change.

11.3 Dissemination

When the Carrick Institute for Learning and Teaching (now the Australian Learning and Teaching Council (ALTC)) was being set up in Australia in 2005, systemic change and the embedding of project results were seen as crucial to gaining a return on investment. Two reviews of dissemination practice were conducted (McKenzie, Alexander, Harper & Anderson, 2005; Southwell, Gannaway, Orrell, Chalmers & Abraham, 2005), and refined into the ALTC (2008) 'dissemination framework', which guides grants recipients to address wider adoption issues.

While 'disseminate' is currently used to indicate the opening up of a subject for widespread discussion, its original etymology refers to scattering seeds, as in sowing a crop. The ALTC interpretation goes beyond scattering seeds of ideas to preparing the metaphorical soil, and fertilizing, watering and tending the resultant 'crop'. Dissemination, in this sense, is closely linked to sustainability.

> Dissemination is more than distribution of information or making it available in some way. While embracing this aspect, dissemination also requires that some action has been taken to embed and upscale the innovation within its own context (discipline or institution) and/or to replicate or transform an innovation in a new context and to embed the innovation in the new context. (ALTC, 2008)

Dissemination can apply at various scales: with colleagues or stakeholders in the same department or faculty; with colleagues or stakeholders within the institution; or through global dissemination through scholarly channels. The third of these is the one which comes most readily to mind for most university academics. The outcomes of a project are submitted for peer review in the literature, hopefully with the level of rigour that we discussed in Chapters 5 and 6. This type of dissemination, although valuable career-wise, does not address Stokes' 'consideration of use' well. The findings of the evaluation research are published and available, but a level of serendipity is required for them to be found by others – others who may not necessarily be interested in trawling the e-learning literature.

For dissemination (using the term as we have here) to be effective, a more proactive approach needs to be taken. This involves carefully 'preparing the ground' and 'tending the crop' through activities such as:

- identifying stakeholders and potential users within the department, other parts of the university and at other universities;
- developing a plan to engage with stakeholders throughout the project development and to sell the project outcomes to them;
- carrying out strategies to enable each identified group of potential users to become aware of the benefits of the innovation and how it might be used in their context;

- engaging with intended users during the project development both to get feedback about the evolving e-learning environment and to encourage their 'buy-in' to the initiative;
- continuing to engage with stakeholders after the initial project has concluded about ongoing evaluation-research results.

These activities will serve to mitigate the risks of unsustainability which we summarized in section 11.2. Without evaluation research, there is insufficient evidence for dissemination. If colleagues and managers are clearly aware of the work being done, and the evidence which shows its value, then there is a better chance that an e-learning innovation will become sustainable and deliver a return on investment.

In addition to evidence, a clear description of context is essential. One of the reasons dissemination does not result in uptake is that the context of the innovation is not always clear and potential users may be disappointed when they try to reuse a strategy or some courseware (King, 2003). Dissemination is not just slick marketing; it needs to be done in a transparent and open fashion.

Of course, even with a superbly implemented dissemination plan, there is a risk that organizational change issues will affect sustainability. Without institutional support, re-use issues of scalability and associated financial needs cannot be addressed.

11.4 Issues in Organizational Change

We should not underestimate the difficulties involved in innovation and change. Marris (1986) paralleled the sense of loss during bereavement to the resistance one can feel when letting go of known ways of doing things and embarking on new strategies. For many academics, the increasing emphasis on the use of technology for administration, research and teaching is challenging. We need to recognize these fears and devise plans that build staff confidence and motivation, and provide adequate support and training opportunities. Changing educational practices and styles can produce many negative reactions and this negativity needs to be acknowledged and managed effectively.

The culture of the organization needs to be able to embrace change while offering staff opportunities to manage their own levels of comfort with the change. One factor that emerged strongly from McNaught et al.'s (2000) study of barriers to the uptake of e-learning in universities was that teachers' investments in engaging in scholarly evidence-based innovations in teaching and learning are not sufficiently rewarded. So, while good teachers continue to invest time in good teaching, they often see their focus as being local – with their own learners in their own courses.

11.4.1 The Double-loop Learning Model Applied to Institutional e-Learning

In the literature on organizational learning (e.g. Argyris & Schön, 1978, 1996; Senge, 1990), the distinction between single-loop and double-loop learning is often made. Senge argued that the modern organization needs not only knowledge at all operational levels, but also the capacity to learn. Argyris (1991) discussed how relatively simple models of problem solving, such as action learning, do not go far enough because they focus on "identifying and correcting errors in the external environment" (p. 99). He suggested that the way problems are perceived and defined needs attention as well. His model of a 'learning organization' draws on the work of Argyris and Schön on single- and double-loop learning: single-loop learning is simple problem solving; double-loop learning looks at fundamental organizational structure and "embeds individuals' discoveries, inventions and evaluations in organizational memory" (Argyris & Schön, 1978, p. 19). For Senge, teams are the learning agents that can achieve double-loop learning and translate individual work into new theories of action for the organization.

Double-loop learning builds in organizational self-understanding as an integral step in each cycle – hence the often-used term 'the learning organization'. Swieringa and Wierdsma (1992) called this "collective learning" as opposed to "individual learning". This is outlined in Figure 11.1 in the context of the institutionalization of e-learning.

A number of studies (e.g. McKenzie et al., 2005, in Australia; Gibbs, Holmes & Segal, 2002, in the UK) have emphasized the need for projects to be relevant, well constructed, pragmatic, adaptable, scholarly, and also well supported at both faculty and university levels.

11.4.2 International Benchmarking of Institutional e-Learning Practice

One way to ensure a robust institutional e-learning strategy is to benchmark practices at one's own university with universities elsewhere. The use of international benchmarking is an emerging trend that can assist institutions to

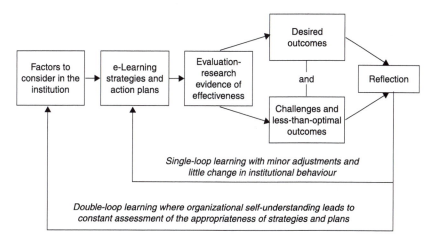

Figure 11.1 Single-loop and double-loop learning in the context of the institutionalization of e-learning.

see how their own practice compares with that of broadly similar institutions elsewhere. Benchmarking projects can be set up by individual institutions wishing to reflect holistically across a number of issues in order to prioritize resource allocation, or can be set up as specific collaborative projects seeking best practice in the field. Some recent and influential models are as follows.

- The Australasian Council on Open, Distance and E-Learning (ACODE) benchmarks were first piloted in 2004. They include 74 questions separated into eight areas such as planning, policy, staff development, staff support, learner support, etc. (ACODE, 2007a, b). The model guides an institution to identify the potential improvement areas through self-assessment and/or collaborative assessment with other institutions (Sankey et al., 2009).
- Another Australasian model is the e-Learning Maturity Model (eMM), first compiled in 2003, which focuses on assessment of e-learning capability using 35 process areas within five process categories (Marshall, 2007). It provides the opportunity for institutions to observe and evaluate the maturity of institutional processes, but it is quite resource-intensive (Adamson & Plenderleith, 2008).
- The UK model, Embedding Learning Technologies Institutionally (ELTI), was begun in 2003 with funding from the Joint Information Systems Committee (JISC); it contains 12 factors in three general areas (Institute of Learning and Research Technology (ILRT), 2003a). It suggests multiple operational processes for an institution (ILRT, 2003b) and it includes a range of open-ended questions to be completed by people with different roles across the institution (ILRT, 2003a).
- The Pick & Mix model, which looks for commonalities of approach, was developed by a benchmarking consultant, Paul Bacsich, in early 2005 (Bacsich, 2006a, b). The design of this approach was based on an extensive literature review and the adoption of other frameworks and benchmarking methodologies. The details of the benchmarking coverage and processes of this approach are regularly updated (Bacsich, 2009). Apart from the 30 suggested domains in version 2.5, there are also another 57 optional domains. It is a relatively comprehensive model, but users are given the flexibility to choose what they would like to study based on their needs and particular situation (Adamson & Plenderleith, 2007).

11.5 Chapter Summary

The central argument of this chapter is that the remit of evaluation research extends beyond the confines of a single project. Evaluation-research evidence for cases of effective technology-enhanced learning needs to be shared locally, institutionally and more broadly. This dissemination will not only support the sustainability of the local initiative but can also impact more widely in terms of contributing to the formation of robust e-learning policies, and models of teaching and learning in higher education.

11.6 The End of the Journey. Or is it the Beginning?

As we reach the end of this book, we would like to provide a 'take-home' message for our readers. We believe we have useful ideas for a range of staff involved in university education – researchers, practitioners, staff in leadership positions, and technical administrators in charge of e-learning policy and infrastructure. We decided that a useful way to provide a summary would be to provide a set of the 'top ten' points that we think are the key messages in this book.

1. e-Learning evaluation research is complex, but is essential for designing optimal learning environments.
2. Given that e-learning artefacts are artificial, rather than natural, phenomena, they can be changed and improved, and they need to be researched appropriately.
3. Studies of the effectiveness of e-learning environments involve a mixture of evaluation (making judgements) and research (seeking understanding), and an investigation can be placed anywhere along the evaluation–research continuum, depending on its goals.
4. It is important for each researcher or practitioner to consider what paradigm s/he is working within, and how the chosen methodology matches it.
5. We identified five evaluation forms that have different emphases when applied at different phases of the e-learning life cycle. These are: baseline analysis, design evaluation, formative evaluation, effectiveness research and project-management evaluation.
6. When undertaking evaluation research, evidence that the e-learning environment functions as designed should be established before conducting summative effectiveness research.
7. Often the pragmatic, mixed-methods paradigm of inquiry works well in evaluation research.
8. While not the only approach, design-based research is a useful framework for guiding evaluation-research studies.
9. We advocate the use of an evaluation-research matrix, to help coordinate the complexity inherent in evaluation research; this will often lead to the development of an explicit evaluation plan.
10. The results of an evaluation-research study should have the purposes of both informing and improving practice, and contributing to design principles and improved theoretical understanding in the field.

Readers will note that many of the issues discussed in this book are broader than the e-learning context – they can be applied to other types of teaching and learning innovation. As a consequence, the models and methods we propose here should apply to a range of contexts and technologies. Mature case-based multimedia scenarios, existing immersive virtual worlds (such as Second Life), and emerging gesture-based computing projects obviously have different characteristics; however, in all cases, similar evaluation-research questions and strategies can be used. This book is about evaluation research of technologies within a learning environment, and its messages and strategies should be useful to anyone interested and involved in the design and improvement of learning environments, and the re-use of effective design ideas and e-learning artefacts.

We have enjoyed the process of articulating our combined ideas and experience, and look forward to the robust dialogues that we hope will be engendered with us and between our readers.

References

ACODE *see* Australasian Council on Open, Distance and E-Learning.

Adamson, V. & Plenderleith, J. (2007). Higher Education Academy/JISC e-Learning Benchmarking Exercise Phase 1 Review. Retrieved 28 October 2010, from http://elearning.heacademy.ac.uk/weblogs/benchmarking/wp-content/uploads/2007/07/2_EDSuTBenchmarking Phase1Report.pdf

Adamson, V. & Plenderleith, J. (2008). Higher Education Academy/JISC e-Learning Benchmarking Exercise Phase 2 Review (EDSuT). Retrieved 28 October 2010, from http://elearning.heacademy.ac.uk/weblogs/benchmarking/wp-content/uploads/Benchmarking2Summary Report21April08F.pdf

Advanced Distributed Learning website (2003). *Advanced distributed learning.* Retrieved 20 September 2010, from www.adlnet.org

Alexander, S. (1999). An evaluation of innovation projects involving communication and information technology in higher education. *Higher Education Research & Development, 18*(2), 173–183.

Alexander, S. & Hedberg, J. G. (1994). Evaluating technology-based learning: which model? In K. Beattie, C. McNaught & S. Wills (Eds.), *Interactive multimedia in university education: Designing for change in teaching and learning.* Amsterdam: Elsevier, pp. 233–244.

Alexander, S., McKenzie, J. & Geissinger, H. (1998). *An evaluation of information technology projects for university learning.* Canberra: Australian Government Publishing Service.

Allan, J. (1996). Learning outcomes in higher education. *Studies in Higher Education, 21*(1), 93–108.

ALTC *see* Australian Learning and Teaching Council (2008).

Amory, A. (2007). Game object model version II: A theoretical framework for educational game development. *Educational Technology Research and Development, 55*(1), 51–77.

Anderson, L. W. & Krathwohl, D. R. (2001). *A taxonomy for learning, teaching, and assessing: A revision of Bloom's taxonomy of educational objectives.* New York: Longman.

Anderson, T. (2005). Distance learning – Social software's killer app? In *Breaking the boundaries: The international experience in open, distance and flexible education.* ODLAA 17th Biennial Conference. Adelaide: Open and Distance Learning Association of Australia. Retrieved 20 September 2010, from http://citeseerx.ist.psu.edu/viewdoc/download?doi=10.1.1.95.630 &rep=rep1&type=pdf

Argyris, C. (1976). Theories of action that inhibit individual learning. *American Psychologist, 31,* 638–654.

Argyris, C. (1991). Teaching smart people to learn. *Harvard Business Review,* May/June, 199–209.

Argyris, C. & Schön, D. (1978). *Organisational learning: A theory of action perspective.* Reading, MA: Addison Wesley.

Argyris, C. & Schön, D. (1996). *Organisational learning II: Theory, method and practice.* Reading, MA: Addison Wesley.

Au Yeung, M., Lam, P. & McNaught, C. (2009). Student-creation of e-cases for clinical reasoning in pharmacy. *Australasian Journal of Peer Learning, 1,* 26–39.

Australasian Council on Open, Distance and E-Learning (ACODE) (2007a). ACODE benchmarks for e-learning in universities and guidelines for use. Retrieved 28 October 2010, from http://www.acode.edu.au/resources/acodebmguideline0607.pdf

Australasian Council on Open, Distance and E-Learning (ACODE) (2007b). ACODE benchmarks. Retrieved 20 September 2010, from www.acode.edu.au/benchmarks.php

Australian Learning and Teaching Council (2008). ALTC dissemination framework. Retrieved 24 October 2010, from www.altc.edu.au/system/files/dissemination_altcframework_ 2008.pdf

Bacsich, P. (2006a). Benchmarking e-learning in HEIs – the Pick & Mix approach: Second update (13 April 2006) – Release 1.2, April 2006. Retrieved 28 October 2010, from http://elearning.heacademy.ac.uk/weblogs/benchmarking/wp-content/uploads/2006/04/eLBPilot PaulBacsich-rev2-final.doc

Bacsich, P. (2006b), Pick & Mix mapping into MIT90s, September 2006. Retrieved 28 October 2010, from http://elearning.heacademy.ac.uk/weblogs/benchmarking/wp-content/uploads/2006/09/PicknMix-MIT90s-20060925.doc

Bacsich, P. (2009). Benchmarking e-learning in UK universities: Lessons from and for the International Context. *International Council for Open and Distance 23rd World Conference*, June. Retrieved 28 October 2010, from http://www.openpraxis.com/files/Bacsich%20et%20al.pdf

Bain, J. D. (1999). Introduction to special issue on learning-centred evaluation of innovation in higher education. *Higher Education Research and Development, 18*(2), 165–172.

Bain, J. D. & McNaught, C. (2006). How academics use technology in teaching and learning: Understanding the relationship between beliefs and practice. *Journal of Computer Assisted Learning, 22*(2), 99–113.

Ballard, B. & Clanchy, J. (1988). Literacy in the university: An 'anthropological' approach. In G. Taylor (Ed.), *Literacy by degrees* (pp. 7–23). Milton Keynes, UK: The Society for Research into Higher Education and Open University Press.

Bannan-Ritland, B. (2003). The role of design in research: The integrative learning design framework. *Educational Researcher, 32*(1), 21–24.

Barab, S. & Squire, K. (2004). Design-based research: Putting a stake in the ground. *The Journal of the Learning Sciences, 13*(1), 1–14.

Barrie, S. (2005). Rethinking generic graduate attributes. *HERDSA News, 27*(1), 1–6. Retrieved 20 September 2010, from www.herdsa.org.au/wp-content/uploads/2007/06/1_herdsa_news_april_2005.pdf

Bates, A. W. (1981). Towards a better research framework for evaluating the effectiveness of educational media. *British Journal of Educational Technology, 3*(12), 215–233.

Bates, A. W. (2000). *Managing technological change: Strategies for college and university leaders*. San Francisco, CA: Jossey-Bass.

Baume, C. & Martin, P. (2002). Introduction and overview. In C. Baume, P. Martin & M. Yorke (Eds.), *Managing educational development projects: Effective management for maximum impact*. London: Kogan Page, pp. 1–11.

Baume, C., Martin, P. & Yorke, M. (2002). *Managing educational development projects: Effective management for maximum impact*. London: Kogan Page.

Becher, T. (1989). *Academic tribes and territories: Intellectual enquiry and the cultures of disciplines*. Buckingham, UK: Open University Press/Society for Research into Higher Education.

Beetham, H. (2004). Review: Developing e-learning models for the JISC practitioner communities. *JISC pedagogies for e-learning programme*, January, 1–15. Retrieved 20 September 2010, from www.jisc.ac.uk/uploaded_documents/Review%20Models.doc

Beetham, H. (2007). Evaluating the learner experience: Some guidelines for e-learning projects. In JISC, *Resources to support learner-centred evaluation*. Retrieved 20 September 2010, from www.jisc.ac.uk/media/documents/programmes/elearningcapital/learnereval-guide.doc

Bell, P. (2004). On the theoretical breadth of design-based research in education. *Educational Psychologist, 39*(4), 243–253.

Berg, B. L. (2009). *Qualitative research methods for the social sciences* (7th ed.). Boston, MA: Allyn & Bacon.

Bernard, R. M., Abrami, P. C., Borokhovski, E., Wade, C. A., Tamim, R. M., Surkes, M. A. & Bethel, E. C. (2009). A meta-analysis of three types of interaction treatments in distance education. *Review of Educational Research, 79*, 1243–1289.

Biggs, J. B. (1989). Approaches to the enhancement of tertiary teaching. *Higher Education Research and Development, 8*(1), 7–25.

Biggs, J. B. (1993). From theory to practice: A cognitive systems approach. *Higher Education Research and Development, 12*(1), 73–85.

Biggs, J. B. (1999). What the student does: Teaching for enhanced learning. *Higher Education Research and Development, 18*, 57–75.

Biggs, J. B. (2003). *Teaching for quality learning at university: What the student does* (2nd ed.). Buckingham, UK and Philadelphia, PA: Society for Research into Higher Education and Open University Press.

Biggs, J. B. & Collis, K. F. (1982). *Evaluating the quality of learning: The SOLO taxonomy (Structure of the Observed Learning Outcome)*. New York: Academic Press.

Bloom, B. S. (Ed.). (1956). *Taxonomy of educational objectives: The classification of educational goals – Handbook I, Cognitive domain*. New York: Longman & Green.

Botturi, L. & Stubbs, T. (Eds.). (2008). *Handbook of visual languages for instructional design: Theories and practices.* Hershey, PA: Information Science Reference.

Boyer, E. L. (1990). *Scholarship reconsidered. Priorities of the professoriate.* Princeton, NJ: Carnegie Foundation for the Advancement of Teaching.

Boyer, E. L. (1996). The scholarship of engagement. *Journal of Public Outreach, 1*(1), 11–20.

Bransford, J. D., Brown, A. L. & Cocking, R. R. (Eds.). (1999). *How people learn: Brain, mind, experience, and school.* Washington, DC: National Academy Press.

Bransford, J. D., Brown, A. L. & Cocking, R. R. (Eds.). (2000). Executive summary of *How people learn: Brain, mind, experience, and school.* Washington, DC: National Academy Press. Retrieved 20 September 2010, from //www.nap.edu/openbook.php?record_id=6160&page=R1

Brown, J. S., Collins, A. & Duguid, P. (1989). Situated cognition and the culture of learning. *Educational Researcher, 18*(1), 32–42.

Burkhardt, H. (2006). From design research to large scale impact: Engineering research in education. In J. van den Akker, K. Gravemeijer, S. McKenney & N. Nieveen (Eds.), *Educational design research.* Abingdon, UK: Routledge, pp. 121–150.

Canby Mugg, J. (1996). Team-building strategies for multimedia teams. *Performance and Instruction, 35*(6), 10–11.

Chesterton, P. & Cummings, R. C. (2007). *ALTC grants scheme – Evaluating projects.* Retrieved 20 September 2010, from www.altc.edu.au/extras/altc-gsep/evaluation_plan.pdf

Chickering, A. W., & Gamson, Z. (1987). Seven principles for good practice in undergraduate education. *American Association for Higher Education Bulletin, 39*(7), 3–7.

Clarke, A. & Dawson, R. (1999). *Evaluation research: An introduction to principles, methods and practice.* London: SAGE.

Cobb, P., Confrey, J., DiSessa, A., Lehrer, R. & Schauble, L. (2003). Design experiments in educational research. *Educational Researcher, 32*(1), 9–13.

Conole, G. & Oliver, M. (2007a). Introduction. In G. Conole & M. Oliver (Eds.), *Contemporary perspectives in e-learning research: Themes, methods and impact on practice.* Abingdon, UK: Routledge, pp. 3–20.

Conole, G. & Oliver, M. (Eds.) (2007b). *Contemporary perspectives in e-learning research: Themes, methods and impact on practice.* Abingdon, UK: Routledge.

Conole, G., Oliver, M. Falconer, I., Littlejohn, A., & Harvey, J. (2007). Designing for learning. In G. Conole & M. Oliver (Eds.), *Contemporary perspectives in e-learning research: Themes, methods and impact on practice* (pp. 101–120). Abingdon, UK: Routledge.

Corderoy, R. M., Harper, B. M. & Hedberg, J. G. (1993). Simulating algal bloom in a lake: an interactive multimedia implementation. *Australian Journal of Educational Technology, 9,* 115–129.

Creswell, J. W. (2009). *Research design: Qualitative and quantitative approaches* (3rd ed.). Thousand Oaks, CA: SAGE.

Cronbach, L. J. & Suppes, P. (Eds.). (1969). *Research for tomorrow's schools: Disciplined inquiry for education.* New York: Macmillan.

Crotty, M. (1998). *The foundations of social research.* Sydney: Allen and Unwin.

Dalziel, J. (2003). Implementing learning design: The learning activity management system (LAMS). In G. Crisp, D. Thiele, I. Scholten, S. Barker & J. Baron (Eds.), *Interact, integrate, impact* (pp. 593–596). Proceedings of the 20th annual conference of the Australasian Society for Computers in Learning in Tertiary Education conference. Adelaide, Australia, 7–10 December. Retrieved 20 September 2010, from www.ascilite.org.au/conferences/adelaide03/docs/pdf/593.pdf

Daniel, H., Lockwood, P., Stewart, C. & McLoughlin, C. (2002). An investigation of the enabling features of the Oz Soils CD program to scaffold transfer of conceptual understandings from independent learning contexts to laboratory and real-life contexts. In R. A. Phillips (Ed.), *Learning-centred evaluation of computer-facilitated learning projects in higher education* (pp. 79–92). Perth, Western Australia: Committee for University Teaching and Staff Development, Commonwealth of Australia. Retrieved 20 September 2010, from www.tlc.murdoch.edu.au/archive/cutsd99/finalpdfreports/Ch6Daniel.pdf

Dawson, S. (2006a). The impact of institutional surveillance technologies on student behaviour. *Surveillance and Society, 4*(1/2), 69–84.

Dawson, S. (2006b). Relationship between student communication interaction and sense of community in higher education. *Internet and Higher Education, 9*(3), 153–162.

Dawson, S., Bakharia, A. & Heathcote, E. (2010). SNAPP: Realising the affordances of real-time SNA within networked learning environments. In L. Dirckinck-Holmfeld, V. Hodgson, C.

Jones, M. de Laat, D. McConnell & T. Ryberg (Eds.), *Proceedings of the 7th International Conference on Networked Learning.*

Dawson, S., McWilliam, E. & Tan, J. P. L. (2008). Teaching smarter: How mining ICT data can inform and improve learning and teaching practice. In R. Atkinson & C. McBeath (Eds.), *Hello! Where are you in the landscape of educational technology?* (pp. 221–230). Proceedings of the 25th annual Australasian Society for Computers in Learning in Tertiary Education 2008 conference, Deakin University, Melbourne, 30 November–3 December. Retrieved 20 September 2010, from http://ascilite.org.au/conferences/melbourne08/procs/dawson.pdf

De Souza, M., Fardon, M. & Phillips, R. A. (2002). An evaluation of tertiary language learning through student-constructed multimedia: The interactive stories approach. *Australian Journal of Educational Technology, 18*(2), 127–146.

Design-Based Research Collective. (2003). Design-based research: An emerging paradigm for educational inquiry. *Educational Researcher, 32*(1), 5–8.

Doran, G. T. (1981). There's a S.M.A.R.T. way to write management's goals and objectives. *Management Review, 70*(11), 35–36.

Draper, S. W. (1996). Observing, measuring, or evaluating courseware: A conceptual introduction. In G. Stoner (Ed.), *Implementing learning technology* (pp. 58–65). Edinburgh: Learning Technology Dissemination Initiative (LTDI). Retrieved 20 September 2010, from www.icbl.hw.ac.uk/ltdi/implementing-it/measure.pdf

Draper, S. W. (1997). Prospects for summative evaluation of CAL in higher education. *ALT-J, 5*(1), 33–39.

Draper, S. W., Brown, M. I., Henderson, F. P. & McAteer, E. (1996). Integrative evaluation: An emerging role for classroom studies of CAL. *Computers in Education, 26*(1), 17–32.

Duncan, W. (Ed.) (1996). *A guide to the project management body of knowledge.* Upper Darby, PA: Project Management Institute.

Dyke, M., Conole, G., Ravenscroft, A. & de Freitas, S. (2007). Learning theory and its application to e-learning. In G. Conole & M. Oliver (Eds.), *Contemporary perspectives in e-learning research: Themes, methods and impact on practice.* Abingdon, UK: Routledge, pp. 82–97.

Edelson, D. C. (2002). Design research: What we learn when we engage in design. *Journal of the Learning Sciences, 11*(1), 105–121.

Edelson, D. C. (2006). Balancing innovation and risk: Assessing design research proposals. In J. van den Akker, K. Gravemeijer, S. McKenney & N. Nieveen (Eds.), *Educational design research.* Abingdon, UK: Routledge, pp. 100–106.

Edwards, D., Rai, S., Phillips, R. A. & Fung, L. C. C. (2007). A framework for interoperable learning objects for e-Learning. In A. Koohang & K. Harman (Eds.), *Learning objects and instructional design.* Santa Rosa, CA: Informing Science Press, pp. 437–470.

Eisner, E. W. (1979). *The educational imagination: On the design and evaluation of school programs.* New York: Macmillan.

Eisner, E. W. (1985). *The art of educational evaluation: A personal view.* London: Falmer.

Eisner, E. W. (1991). Taking a second look: Educational connoisseurship revisited. In M. McLaughlin & D. C. Phillips (Eds.), *Evaluation and education: At quarter century.* Ninetieth year book of National Society for the Study of Education Part II. Chicago, IL: University of Chicago Press, pp. 169–187.

Ellis, R. & Goodyear, P. (2009). *Students' experiences of e-learning in higher education: The ecology of sustainable innovation.* New York: Routledge.

Engeström, Y. (1987). *Learning by expanding: An activity-theoretical approach to developmental research.* Helsinki, Finland: Orienta-Konsultit Oy.

Engeström, Y., Miettinen, R., & Punamäki, R.-L. (1999). (Eds.). *Perspectives on activity theory.* New York: Cambridge University Press.

England, E. & Finney, A. (1999). *Managing multimedia* (2nd ed.). Harlow, UK: Addison Wesley Longman.

Entwistle, N., Hanley, M. & Hounsell, D. (1979). Identifying distinctive approaches to studying. *Higher Education, 8*, 365–380.

Flagg, B. N. (1990). *Formative evaluation for educational technologies.* Hillsdale, NJ: L. Erlbaum Associates.

Flyvbjerg, B. (2004). Five misunderstandings about case-study research. In C. Seale, G. Gobo, J. F. Gubrium & D. Silverman (Eds.), *Qualitative research practice.* London and Thousand Oaks, CA: Sage, pp. 420–434.

Foreman-Peck, L. & Winch, C. (2010). *Using educational research to inform practice: A practical guide to practitioner research in universities and colleges.* Abingdon, UK: Routledge.

Fraser, S. P. & Bosanquet, A. M. (2006). The curriculum? That's just a unit outline, isn't it? *Studies in Higher Education, 31*(3), 269–284.

Friesen, N. (2009). *Re-thinking e-learning research: Foundations, methods and practices.* New York: Peter Lang.

Funnell, S. (1997). Program logic: An adaptable tool for designing and evaluating programs. *Evaluation News and Comment, 6*(1), 5–17.

Fyfe, G. M. (2000). Active learning for understanding in introductory human biology. In A. Herman & M. Kulski (Eds.), *Flexible futures in tertiary teaching.* Proceedings of the 9th Annual Teaching Learning Forum. Perth: Curtin University of Technology. Retrieved 24 October 2010, from http://otl.curtin.edu.au/tlf/tlf2000/fyfeg.html

Garstang, M. (1994). Checklists for training project management: The team's perspective. *Journal of Instruction Delivery Systems, 8*(1), 29–32.

Gibbs, G. (1992). The nature of quality in learning. In G. Gibbs (Ed.), *Improving the quality of student learning.* Bristol, UK: Technical and Educational Services Ltd, pp. 1–11.

Gibbs, G., Holmes, A. & Segal, R. (2002). Funding innovation and disseminating new teaching practices. Milton Keynes, UK: NQEF National Coordination Team. Retrieved 20 September 2010, from www.heacademy.ac.uk/assets/York/documents/resources/web0261_funding_innovation_and_disseminating_new_teaching_practices.pdf

Glass, G. V. & Worthen, B. R. (1971). Educational evaluation and research: similarities and differences. *Curriculum Theory Network, 8/9,* 149–165.

Goldstein, P. J. & Katz, R. N. (2005). Academic analytics: The uses of management information and technology in higher education. *EDUCAUSE Center for Applied Research.* Retrieved 20 September 2010, from http://net.educause.edu/ir/library/pdf/ecar_so/ers/ers0508/EKF0508.pdf

Goodyear, P. (2009). *Teaching, technology and educational design: The architecture of productive learning environments.* Sydney: Australian Learning and Teaching Council.

Goodyear, P. & Ellis, R. A. (2010). Expanding conceptions of study, context and educational design. In R. Sharpe, H. Beetham & S. de Freitas (Eds.), *Rethinking learning for the digital age: How learners shape their own experiences.* New York: Routledge.

Goodyear, P. & Retalis, S. (2010). Learning, technology and design. In P. Goodyear & S. Retalis (Eds.), *Technology-enhanced learning: Design patterns and pattern languages Vol. 2.* Rotterdam: Sense Publishers, pp. 1–28.

Gravemeijer, K. & Cobb, P. (2006). Design research from a learning design perspective. In J. van den Akker, K. Gravemeijer, S. McKenney & N. Nieveen (Eds.), *Educational design research.* Abingdon, UK: Routledge, pp. 17–51.

Guba, E. G. (1990). The alternative paradigm dialog. In E. C. Guba (Ed.), *The paradigm dialog.* Newbury Park, CA: Sage, pp. 17–27.

Guba, E. G. & Lincoln, Y. S. (1981). *Effective evaluation: Improving the usefulness of evaluation results through responsive and naturalistic approaches.* San Francisco: Jossey Bass Publishers.

Guba, E. G. & Lincoln, Y. S. (1989). *Fourth generation evaluation.* Newbury Park, CA: SAGE Publications.

Guba, E. G. & Lincoln, Y. S. (1994). Competing paradigms in qualitative research. In N. K. Denzin & Y. S. Lincoln (Eds.), *Handbook of qualitative research.* London: SAGE Publications, pp. 105–117.

Guest, G., Bunce, A. & Johnson, L. (2006). How many interviews are enough? An experiment with data saturation and variability. *Field Methods, 18*(1), 59–82.

Gunn, C. (1999). They love it, but do they learn from it? Evaluating the education impact of innovations. *Higher Education Research & Development, 18*(2), 185–199.

Hannafin, M. J., Hannafin, K. M., Land, S. M. & Oliver, K. (1997). Grounded practice and the design of constructivist learning environment. *Educational Technology Research and Development, 45*(3), 101–117.

Harasim, L., Hiltz, S. R., Teles, L. & Turoff, M. (1995). *Learning networks: A field guide to teaching and learning online.* Cambridge, MA: The MIT Press.

Harper, B., Hedberg, J., Corderoy, B., & Wright, R. (2000). Employing cognitive tools within interactive multimedia applications In P. S. Lajoie (Ed.), *Computers as cognitive tools, Vol 2: No more walls.* Mahwah, NJ: Lawrence Erlbaum Associates, pp. 227–246.

Harper, B., Hedberg, J., Wright, R. & Corderoy, R. (1995). Multimedia reporting in science problem solving. *Australian Journal of Educational Technology, 11*(2), 23–37.

Harrow, A. (1972). *A taxonomy of psychomotor domain: A guide for developing behavioral objectives.* New York: David McKay.

Harvey, J. (1998). *Evaluation cookbook*. Retrieved 20 September 2010, from www.icbl.hw.ac.uk/ltdi/cookbook/cookbook.pdf

Heerkens, G. R. (2002). *Project management*. New York: McGraw-Hill.

Herrington, J. & Oliver, R. (2000). An instructional design framework for authentic learning environments. *Educational Technology Research and Development, 48*(3), 23–48.

Herrington, J., Reeves, T. C. & Oliver, R. (2009). *A guide to authentic e-learning*. New York and London: Routledge.

Hestenes, D. & Wells, M. (1992). A mechanics baseline test. *Physics Teacher, 30*(3), 159–166.

Hestenes, D., Wells, M. & Swackhammer, G. (1992). Force concept inventory. *Physics Teacher, 30*(3), 141–151.

Hicks, O. (2007). Curriculum in higher education in Australia – Hello? Paper presented at *Enhancing higher education, theory and scholarship, 30th HERDSA annual conference*. Adelaide: Higher Education Research and Development Society of Australasia. Retrieved 20 September 2010, from www.altcexchange.edu.au/system/files/Curriculum%20in%20Higher%20Education%20-%20HERDSA%20Full%20Paper.doc

Howell, G. T. (1992). *Building hypermedia applications: A software development guide*. New York: McGraw-Hill.

Hutchings, P. & Shulman, L. S. (1999). The scholarship of teaching: New elaborations, new developments. *Change: The Magazine of Higher Learning, 31*(5), 10–15.

IMS Global Learning Consortium (2010). *Learning design specification – IMS learning design information model*. Retrieved 20 September 2010, from www.imsglobal.org/learningdesign/ldv1p0/imsld_infov1p0.html

Institute of Learning and Research Technology (2003a). *The ELTI audit tools*. University of Bristol. Retrieved 29 October 2010, from www.jisc.ac.uk/uploaded_documents/Workshop_pack_audit_tools_v5.doc

Institute of Learning and Research Technology (2003b). *The ELTI facilitator's guide*. University of Bristol. Retrieved 28 October 2010, from www.jisc.ac.uk/media/documents/programmes/jos/workshop_pack_facilitator_v5.pdf

Interactive Multimedia Learning Laboratory. (1996). Exploring the Nardoo: Classroom edition. Retrieved 20 September, 2010, from www.impty.com/docs/classrom.pdf

Jackson, B. (1998). Evaluation of learning technology implementation. In N. Mogey (Ed.), *LTDI Evaluation Studies*. Edinburgh: Learning Technology Dissemination Initiative, pp. 117–136. Retrieved 24 October 2010, from www.icbl.hw.ac.uk/ltdi/evalstudies/cont.htm

Jackson, K. (2005). *Project evaluation toolkit*. Retrieved 20 September 2010, from www.utas.edu.au/pet/pdf/fullcontents.pdf

Jensen, R. A. & Kiley, T. J. (2005). *Teaching, leading and learning in prek-8 settings: Strategies for success* (2nd ed.). Boston, MA: Houghton Mifflin.

Joint Committee on Standards for Educational Evaluation (1994). *The program evaluation standards*. Thousand Oaks, CA: SAGE.

Joint Information Systems Committee (2008). *JISC project management guidelines*. Retrieved 20 September 2010, from www.jisc.ac.uk/media/documents/funding/project_management/projectmanagementguidelines.pdf

Jones, C., Dirckinck-Holmfeld, L. & Lindström, B. (2006). A relational, indirect, meso-level approach to CSCL design in the next decade. *International Journal of Computer-Supported Collaborative Learning, 1*(1), 35–56.

Jones, C., Zenios, M. & Griffiths, J. (2004). Academic use of digital resources: Disciplinary differences and the issue of progression. In *The 4th Networked Learning Conference*. Lancaster University, UK. Retrieved 20 September 2010, from http://hal.archives-ouvertes.fr/docs/00/19/02/71/PDF/Jones-Chris-2004c.pdf

Judd, T. & Kennedy, G. (2001). Extending the role of audit trails: A modular approach. *Journal of Educational Multimedia and Hypermedia, 10*(4), 377–396.

Judd, T., Kennedy, G. & Cropper, S. (2010). Using wikis for collaborative learning: Assessing collaboration through contribution. *Australasian Journal of Educational Technology, 26*(3), 341–354.

Kelly, A. E. (2006). Quality criteria for design research: Evidence and commitments. In J. van den Akker, K. Gravemeijer, S. McKenney & N. Nieveen (Eds.), *Educational design research*. Abingdon, UK: Routledge, pp. 107–118.

Kember, D., Ma, R., McNaught, C. & 18 exemplary teachers. (2006). *Excellent university teaching*. Hong Kong: Chinese University Press.

Kember, D. & McNaught, C. (2007). *Enhancing university teaching: Lessons from research into award-winning teachers.* Abingdon, UK.: Routledge.

Kemmis, S. & McTaggart, R. (2000). Participatory action research. In N. K. Denzin & Y. S. Lincoln (Eds.), *Handbook of qualitative research* (2nd ed.). London: Sage, pp. 567–605.

Kennedy, G., Dalgarno, B., Bennett, S., Gray, K., Waycott, J., Judd, T., Bishop, A., Maton, K., Krause, K. & Chang, R. (2009). Educating the net generation: A handbook of findings for policy and practice. Retrieved 24 September 2010, from www.netgen.unimelb.edu.au/downloads/handbook/NetGenHandbookAll.pdf

Kennedy, G. E. & Judd, T. S. (2004). Making sense of audit trail data. *Australasian Journal of Educational Technology, 20*(1), 18–32.

Kenny, J. (2004). A study of educational technology project management in Australian universities. *Australasian Journal of Educational Technology, 20*(3), 388–404.

Kincheloe, J. L. & McLaren, P. L. (1994). Rethinking critical theory and qualitative research. In N. K. Denzin & Y. S. Lincoln (Eds.), *Handbook of qualitative research.* Thousand Oaks, CA: Sage.

King, H. (2003). Disseminating educational developments. In P. Kahn & D. Baume (Eds.), *A guide to staff and educational development.* London: Staff and Educational Development Association & Kogan Page, pp. 96–115.

Kirschner, P. (2005). *Determinants for failure and success of innovation projects: The road to sustainable educational innovation.* Amsterdam: Open University of the Netherlands.

Kothari, C. R. (2008). *Research methodology: Methods and techniques.* New Delhi: New Age International.

Kozma, R. B. (1994). Will media influence learning? Reframing the debate. *Educational Technology Research and Development, 42*(2), 7–19.

Krathwohl, D. R. (2002). A revision of Blooms' taxonomy: An overview. *Theory into Practice, 41*(4), 212–218.

Krathwohl, D. R., Bloom, B. S. & Masia, B. B. (1964). *Taxonomy of educational objectives: The classification of educational goals. Handbook II: The affective domain.* New York: David McKay.

Kuhn, T. S. (1996). *The structure of scientific revolutions* (3rd ed.). Chicago, IL: University of Chicago Press.

Lam, P., McNaught, C. & Cheng, K. F. (2008). Pragmatic meta-analytic studies: Learning the lessons from naturalistic evaluations of multiple cases. *ALT-J, 16*(2), 61–79.

Laurillard, D. (1999). A conversational framework for individual learning applied to the learning organisation and the learning society. *Systems Research and Behavioural Science, 16,* 113–122.

Laurillard, D. M. (2002a). Personal communication.

Laurillard, D. M. (2002b). *Rethinking university teaching: A conversational framework for the effective use of learning technologies* (2nd ed.). London: Routledge.

Liaw, T., Kennedy, G., Keppell, M., Marty, J. & McNair, R. (2000). Using multimedia to assist students with communication skills and biopsychosocial integration: An evaluation. *Australian Journal of Educational Technology, 16*(2), 104–125.

Lincoln, Y. S. & Guba, E. G. (1985). *Naturalistic inquiry.* Beverly Hills, CA: Sage.

Littlejohn, A. & Pegler, C. (2007). *Preparing for blended e-learning.* Abingdon, UK: Routledge.

Lockyer, L., Bennett, S., Agostinho, S. & Harper, B. (2009). *Handbook of research on learning design and learning objects: Issues, applications, and technologies.* Hershey, PA: Information Science Reference.

Luca, J. & Mcloughlin, C. (2004). Using online forums to support a community of learning. In L. Cantoni & C. McLoughlin (Eds.), *ED-MEDIA 2004* (pp. 1468–1474). Proceedings of the 16th Annual World Conference on Educational Multimedia, Hypermedia & Telecommunications, Lugano, Switzerland, 21–26 June. Norfolk VA: Association for the Advancement of Computers in Education.

Marris, P. (1986). *Loss and change.* London: Routledge & Kegan Paul.

Marshall, L. (2006). *A Learning companion: Your guide to practising independent learning* (4th ed.). Sydney: Pearson Education Australia.

Marshall, L. & Rowland, F. (2006). *A guide to learning independently* (4th ed.). Sydney: Pearson Education Australia.

Marshall, S. (2007). e-Learning Maturity Model process descriptions. Retrieved 28 October 2010, from www.utdc.vuw.ac.nz/research/emm/Publications.shtml

Maslow, A. H. (1970). *Motivation and personality* (2nd ed.). New York: Harper and Row, Publishers, Inc.

Mayer, R. E. (1999). Multimedia aids to problem-solving transfer. *International Journal of Educational Research, 31*, 611–623.

Mayer, R. E., & Chandler, P. (2001). When learning is just a click away: Does simple user interaction foster deeper understanding of multimedia messages? *Journal of Educational Psychology, 93*(2), 390–397.

McDaniel, K. & Liu, M. (1996). A study of project management techniques for developing interactive multimedia programs: A practitioner's perspective. *Journal of Research on Computing in Education, 29*(1), 29–48.

McKenzie, J., Alexander, S., Harper, C. & Anderson, S. (2005). *Dissemination, adoption and adaptation of project innovations in higher education*. Report for the Carrick Institute for Learning and Teaching in Higher Education. Retrieved 24 October 2010, from www.altc.edu.au/resource-dissemination-adoption-uts-2005

McNaught, C. (2007). Developing criteria for successful learning repositories. In J. Filipe, J. Cordeiro & V. Pedrosa (Eds.), *Web information systems and technologies,* Dordrecht: Springer, pp. 8–18.

McNaught, C. (2011). Who said Chinese students don't want to discuss ideas? Strategies for using online forums with Chinese learners. In A. Edmundson (Ed.), *Cases on globalized and culturally appropriate e-learning: Challenges and solutions*. Hershey, PA: IGI Global, pp. 25–26.

McNaught, C., Cheng, K-F. & Lam, P. (2006). Developing evidence-based criteria for the design and use of online forums in higher education in Hong Kong. In N. Lambropoulos & P. Zaphiris (Eds.), *User-centered design of online learning communities*. Hershey, PA: Information Science Publishing, pp. 161–184.

McNaught, C., Lam, P., Cheng, K.-F., Kennedy, D. M. & Mohan, J. B. (2009). Challenges in employing complex e-learning strategies in campus-based universities. *International Journal of Technology Enhanced Learning, 1*(4), 266–285.

McNaught, C., Phillips, P., Rossiter, D. & Winn, J. (2000). Developing a framework for a usable and useful inventory of computer-facilitated learning and support materials in Australian universities. Evaluations and Investigations Program Report 99/11. Canberra: Higher Education Division Department of Employment, Education, Training and Youth Affairs. Retrieved 20 September 2010, from www.dest.gov.au/highered/eippubs1999.htm

McNaught, C. & Vogel. D. (2006). The fit between eLearning policy and institutional culture. *International Journal of Learning Technology, 2*(4), 370–385.

McNaught, C., Burd, A., Whithear, K., Prescott, J. & Browning, G. (2003). It takes more than metadata and stories of success: Understanding barriers to reuse of computer-facilitated learning resources. *Australian Journal of Educational Technology, 19*(1), 72–86.

McNaught, C., Whithear, K. & Browning, G. (1994). The role of evaluation in curriculum design and innovation: A case study of a computer-based approach to teaching veterinary systematic bacteriology and mycology. In K. Beattie, C. McNaught & S. Wills (Eds.), *Interactive multimedia in university education: Designing for change in teaching and learning* (pp. 295–308). Amsterdam: Elsevier.

McNaught, C., Whithear, K. & Browning, G. (1999). Systems not projects: Focusing on evaluating overall student experience, rather than isolated innovations. *Higher Education Research & Development, 18*(2), 247–259.

McNiff, J., Lomax, P. & Whitehead, J. (2003). *You and your action research project* (2nd ed.). London: RoutledgeFalmer.

Means, B., Toyama, Y., Murphy, R., Bakia, M. & Jones, K. (2009). *Evaluation of evidence-based practices in online learning: A meta-analysis and review of online learning studies*. US Department of Education & Office of Planning, Evaluation, and Policy Development. Retrieved 20 September 2010, from www.hakoled.org.il/webfiles/fck/File/tikshuv_usa.pdf

Miles, M. B. & Huberman, A. M. (1994). *Qualitative data analysis* (2nd ed.). Thousand Oaks, CA: Sage Publications.

Misanchuk, E. R., & Schwier, R. (1993). Representing interactive multimedia and hypermedia audit trails. *Journal of Educational Multimedia and Hypermedia, 1*(3), 355–372.

Moreno, R. & Mayer, R. E. (2005). Role of guidance, reflection and interactivity in an agent-based multimedia game. *Journal of Educational Psychology, 97*(1), 117–128.

Murphy, E., Dingwall, R., Greatbatch, D., Parker, S. & Watson, P. (1998). Qualitative research methods in health technology assessment: A review of the literature. *Health Technology Assessment, 2*(16): iii–ix, 1–274.

Nieveen, N., McKenney, S. & van den Akker, J. (2006). Educational design research: The value of variety. In J. van den Akker, K. Gravemeijer, S. McKenney & N. Nieveen (Eds.), *Educational design research*. Abingdon, UK: Routledge, pp. 151–158.

O'Reilly, M., Lefoe, G., Philip, R. & Parrish, D. (2010). Designing for user engagement: The ALTC exchange for higher education. *International Journal on E-Learning, 9*(2), 251–277.

Oblinger, D. G. & Campbell, J. P. (2007). *Academic analytics*. Retrieved 20 September 2010, from http://net.educause.edu/ir/library/pdf/PUB6101.pdf

Oliver, M. (1999). The B.P. evaluation of learning technology project: A review. *B.P. ELT Report no. 9*. London: University of North London.

Oliver, M. (2003). *Curriculum design as an acquired social practice: A case study of UK higher education*. Paper presented at the 84th annual meeting of the American Educational Research Association, Chicago, IL.

Oliver, M., Harvey, J., Conole, G. & Jones, A. (2007). Evaluation. In G. Conole & M. Oliver (Eds.), *Contemporary perspectives in e-learning research: Themes, methods and impact on practice*. Abingdon, UK: Routledge, pp. 203–216.

Oliver, M., Roberts, G., Beetham, H., Ingraham, B., Dyke, M. & Levy, P. (2007). Knowledge, society and perspectives on learning technology. In G. Conole & M. Oliver (Eds.), *Contemporary perspectives in e-learning research: Themes, methods and impact on practice*. Abingdon, UK: Routledge, pp. 21–37.

Oliver, R. (1999). Exploring strategies for online teaching and learning. *Distance Education, 20*(2), 240–254.

Owen, J. M. (2006). *Program evaluation: Forms and approaches* (3rd ed.). Crows Nest, Australia: Allen and Unwin.

Paivio, A. (1971). *Imagery and verbal processes*. New York: Holt, Rinehart & Winston.

Paivio, A. (1986). *Mental representations*. Oxford: Oxford University Press.

Palloff, R. & Pratt, K. (1999). *Building learning communities in cyberspace: Effective strategies for the online classroom*. San Fransisco, CA: Jossey Bass.

Patton, M. Q. (1990). *Qualitative evaluation and research methods* (2nd ed.). Newbury Park, CA: Sage.

Patton, M. Q. (1997). *Utilization-focused evaluation: The new century text* (3rd ed.). Thousand Oaks, CA: Sage.

Payne, D. A. (1994). *Designing educational project and program evaluations: A practical overview based on research and experience*. Boston, MA: Kluwer.

Peters, M. & Robinson, V. (1984). The origins and status of action research. *The Journal of Applied Behavioral Science, 20*(2), 113–124.

Phillips, D. C. (2006). Assessing the quality of design research proposals: Some philosophical perspectives. In J. van den Akker, K. Gravemeijer, S. McKenney & N. Nieveen (Eds.), *Educational design research* (pp. 93–99). Abingdon, UK: Routledge.

Phillips, R. A. (1997). *The developer's handbook to interactive multimedia: A practical guide for educational applications*. London: Kogan Page.

Phillips, R. A. (2001). A case study of the development and project management of a web/CD hybrid application. *Journal of Interactive Learning Research, 12*(2/3), 229–247.

Phillips, R. A. (2002a). Innovative use of Microsoft Word and QTVR for teaching radiology and diagnostic imaging. In J. Cook & D. McConnell (Eds.), *Proceedings of the 9th International conference of the association for learning technology*. Sunderland, UK: Association for Learning Technology, pp. 71–81.

Phillips, R. A. (Ed.) (2002b). Executive summary of *Learning-centred evaluation of computer-facilitated learning projects in higher education*. Perth, Western Australia: Committee for University Teaching and Staff Development, Commonwealth of Australia. Retrieved 20 September 2010, from www.tlc.murdoch.edu.au/project/cutsd01.html

Phillips, R. A. (2004). The design dimensions of e-learning. In R. Atkinson, C. McBeath, D. Jonas-Dwyer & R. Phillips (Eds.), *Beyond the comfort zone* (pp. 781–790). Proceedings of the 21st annual Australasian Society for Computers in Learning in Tertiary Education conference, University of Western Australia, 5–8 December. Retrieved 20 September 2010, from www.ascilite.org.au/conferences/perth04/procs/phillips.html

Phillips, R. A. (2005, April 2005a). We can't evaluate e-learning if we don't know what we mean by evaluating e-learning! *Interact: The Learning Technology Support Service Newsletter, 30*.

Phillips, R. A. (2005b). Challenging the primacy of lectures: The dissonance between theory and practice in university teaching. *Journal of University Teaching and Learning Practice, 2*(1), 1–12.

Phillips, R. A. (2010). Clarifying, developing and valuing the roles of Unit Coordinators as informal leaders of learning in higher education. Unpublished final evaluation report. Canberra: Australian Learning and Teaching Council.

Phillips, R. A. & Baudains, C. (2002). *Learning botany: Evaluation of a web-supported unit on plant diversity.* Perth, Western Australia: Murdoch University. Retrieved 20 September 2010, from www.tlc.murdoch.edu.au/project/N265Eval.pdf

Phillips, R. A. & Gilding, T. (2002). Approaches to evaluating the effect of ICT on student learning. *ALT starter guide.* Retrieved 20 September 2010, from www.alt.ac.uk/docs/eln015.pdf

Phillips, R. A. & Luca, J. (2000). Issues involved in developing a project-based online unit which enhances teamwork and collaboration. *Australian Journal of Educational Technology, 16*(2), 147–160.

Phillips, R. A., Bain, J., McNaught, C., Rice, M. & Tripp, D. (2000). *Handbook for learning-centred evaluation of computer-facilitated learning projects in higher education.* Retrieved 20 September 2010, from www.tlc.murdoch.edu.au/archive/cutsd99/handbook/handbook. html

Phillips, R. A., Baudains, C. & van Keulen, M. (2002). An evaluation of student learning in a web-supported unit on plant diversity. In A. Williamson, C. Gunn, A. Young & T. Clear (Eds.), *Winds of change in the sea of learning* (pp. 525–534). Proceedings of the 19th annual Australasian Society for Computers in Learning in Tertiary Education 2002 conference, UNITEC Institute of Technology, Auckland, New Zealand, 8–11 December. Retrieved 20 September 2010, from www.ascilite.org.au/conferences/auckland02/proceedings/papers/161.pdf

Phillips, R. A., Pospisil, R. & Richardson, J. L. (2001). The use of a QTVR image database for teaching veterinary radiology and diagnostic ultrasound to distance education students. *Australian Journal of Educational Technology, 17,* 96–114.

Phillips, R. A., Scott, M. & Richardson, J. L. (2003). Learning diagnostic imaging: The use of ICT in an image-based distance education subject. *Proceedings of Apple University Consortium Conference 2003.* Adelaide: University of Adelaide.

Pintrich, P. R. & Schrauben, B. (1992). Students' motivational beliefs and their cognitive engagement in classroom academic tasks. In D. H. Schunk & J. Meece (Eds.), *Student perceptions in the classroom.* Hillsdale, NJ: Lawrence Erlbaum, pp. 149–179.

Pintrich, P. R., Smith, D. A. R., Garcia, T. & McKeachie, W. (1991). A manual for the use of the motivated strategies for learning questionnaire (MSLQ). University of Michigan, National Center for Research to Improve Postsecondary Teaching and Learning, Ann Arbor, MI.

Pratt, D. D. and Associates (1998). *Five perspectives on teaching in adult and higher education.* Malabar, FL: Krieger Publishing.

Preece, J., Rogers, Y., Sharp, H., Benyon, D., Holland, S. & Carey, T. (1994). *Human–computer interaction.* Wokingham, UK: Addison-Wesley.

Ramsden, P. (1988). Studying learning: Improving teaching. In P. Ramsden (Ed.), *Improving learning: New perspectives.* London: Kogan Page, pp. 13–31.

Ramsden, P. (1992). *Learning to teach in higher education.* London: Routledge.

Ray, W. & Ravizza, R. (1985). *Methods* (2nd ed.). Belmont, CA: Wadsworth Publishing.

Reason, P. & Bradbury, H. (2006). *Handbook of action research: Participative inquiry and practice.* London: Sage.

Reeves, T. C. (1989). The role, methods, and worth of evaluation in instructional design. In K. A. Johnson & Foa, L. J. (Eds.), *Instructional design: New alternative for effective education and training.* Macmillan: American Council on Education & Oryx Press, pp. 157–181.

Reeves, T. C. (1993). Pseudoscience in computer-based instruction: The case of learner control research. *Journal of Computer-based Instruction, 20*(2), 39–46.

Reeves, T. C. (1995). Questioning the questions of instructional technology research. In M. R. Simonson & M. Anderson (Eds.), *Proceedings of the Annual Conference of the Association for Educational Communications and Technology, Research and Theory Division* (pp. 459–470). Anaheim, CA. Retrieved 20 September 2010, from http://citeseerx.ist.psu.edu/viewdoc/download?doi=10.1.1.83.2842&rep=rep1&type=pdf

Reeves, T. C. (1997). Established and emerging evaluation paradigms for instructional design. In C. R. Dills & A. J. Romiszowski (Eds.), *Instructional development paradigms.* Englewood Cliffs, NJ: Educational Technology Publications, pp. 163–178.

Reeves, T. C. (1999). A research agenda for interactive learning in the new millennium. In B. Collis & R. Oliver (Eds.), *ED-MEDIA 2009* (pp. 15–20). Proceedings of the 11th World Conference on Educational Multimedia, Hypermedia and Telecommunications, Seattle, 19–24 June. Chesapeake, VA: Association for the Advancement of Computers in Education (AACE).

Reeves, T. C. (2000a). Enhancing the worth of instructional technology research through 'design experiments' and other development research strategies. Paper presented at the *International perspectives on instructional technology research for the 21st Century*. New Orleans. Retrieved 20 September 2010, from www.teknologipendidikan.net/wp-content/uploads/2009/07/Enhancing-the-Worth-of-Instructional-Technology-Research-through3.pdf

Reeves, T. C. (2000b). Socially responsible educational technology research. *Educational Technology*, 40(6), 19–28.

Reeves, T. C. (2005). No significant differences revisited: A historical perspective on the research informing contemporary online learning. In G. Kearsley (Ed.), *Online learning: Personal reflections on the transformation of education*. Englewood Cliffs, NJ: Educational Technology Publications, pp. 299–308.

Reeves, T. C. (2006a). Design research from a technology perspective. In J. van den Akker, K. Gravemeijer, S. McKenney & N. Nieveen (Eds.), *Educational design research*. London: Routledge, pp. 52–66.

Reeves, T. C. (2006b). How do you know they are learning? The importance of alignment in higher education. *International Journal of Learning Technology*, 2(4), 294–309.

Reeves, T. C. & Hedberg, J. G. (2003). *Interactive learning systems evaluation*. Englewood Cliffs, NJ: Educational Technology Publications.

Reeves, T. C. & Lent, R. M. (1984). Levels of evaluation for computer-based instruction. In D. F. Walker & R. D. Hess (Eds.), *Instructional software: Principles and perspectives for design and use*. Belmont, California: Wadsworth, pp. 188–203.

Reeves, T. C. & Reeves, P. (1997). Effective dimensions of interactive learning on the world wide web. In B. Khan (Ed.), *Web-based instruction*. Englewood Cliffs, New Jersey: Educational Technology Publications, pp. 59–66.

Reeves, T. C., Herrington, J. & Oliver, R. (2005). Design research: A socially responsible approach to instructional technology research in higher education. *Journal of Computing in Higher Education*, 16(2), 97–116.

Research Assessment Exercise. (2008). *Research Assessment Exercise 2008: Guidance on submissions*. Retrieved 20 September 2010, from www.rae.ac.uk/Pubs/2005/03/rae0305.doc

Richey, R. C., Klein, J. D. & Nelson, W. A. (1996). Developmental research: studies of instructional design and development. In D. Jonassen (Ed.), *Handbook of research for educational communications and technology*. London: Macmillan, pp. 1099–1130.

Richey, R. C., Klein, J. D. & Nelson, W. A. (2004). Developmental research: Studies of instructional design and development. In D. Jonassen (Ed.), *Handbook of research for educational communications and technology* (2nd ed.). Mahwah, New Jersey: Lawrence Erlbaum, pp. 1099–1130.

Roblyer, M. D. (2005). *Integrating educational technology into teaching* (4th ed.). Upper Saddle River, NJ: Prentice-Hall.

Robson, C. (2002). *Real world research* (2nd ed.). Maldern, MA: Blackwell.

Ross, S. M. & Morrison, G. R. (1989). In search of a happy medium in instructional technology research: Issues concerning external validity, media replication, and learner control. *Educational Technology Research and Development*, 37(1), 19–33.

Rowe, H. A. (1996). I.T. is failing to revolutionise the curriculum, because to date we have failed to evaluate its benefits in context. Paper presented at the *Annual Conference of the Australian Computers in Education conference*, Canberra. Retrieved 20 September 2010, from www.cpe.ied.edu.hk/newhorizon/abstract/2004n/page16.pdf

Russell, T. L. (1999). *The no significant difference phenomenon*. Raleigh, NC: North Carolina State University.

Salmon, G. (2003). *E-moderating: The key to teaching and learning online* (2nd ed.). London; New York: RoutledgeFalmer.

Salomon, G. (1991). Transcending the qualitative-quantitative debate: The analytic and systemic approaches to educational research. *Educational Researcher*, 20(6), 10–18.

Sankey, M., Taylor, J., Lawson, R., Galligan, L., Smith, A., Craig, S., Lambert, M. A., Brosnan, S. & Russell, T. (2009). *Program revitalization. Technology enhanced learning and flexible delivery project: ACODE benchmarking*. Deakin benchmarking activity final report, 2008.

Retrieved 28 October 2010, from www.usq.edu.au/~/media/USQ/learnedeach/ADS/ACODEBMprojectreportDeakinFinalpdf

Schon, D. A. (1982). *The reflective practitioner: How professionals think in action*. New York: Basic Books.

Senge, P. (1990). *The fifth discipline: The art and practice of the learning organisation*. London: Random Century Group.

Shavelson, R. J. (1988). *Statistical reasoning for the behavioural sciences* (2nd ed.). Needham Heights, MA: Allyn and Bacon.

Shavelson, R. J., Phillips, D. C., Towne, L. & Feuer, M. J. (2003). On the science of education design studies. *Educational Researcher, 32*(1), 25–28.

Shulman, L. S. (1988). Disciplines of inquiry in education: An overview. In R. M. Jaeger (Ed.), *Complementary methods for research in education*. Washington: AERA, pp. 3–17.

Shulman, L. S. (2005). Pedagogies of uncertainty. *Liberal Education, 91*(2), 18–25.

Simon, H. A. (1969). *The sciences of the artificial*. Cambridge, MA: MIT Press.

Soltis, J. F. (1992). Inquiry paradigms. In M. C. Alkin (Ed.), *Encyclopedia of educational research*. New York: Macmillan, pp. 620–622.

Southwell, D., Gannaway, D., Orrell, J., Chalmers, D. & Abraham, C. (2005). Strategies for effective dissemination of project outcomes. Report for the Carrick Institute for Learning and Teaching in Higher Education. Retrieved 24 October 2010, from www.altc.edu.au/resource-strategies-dissemination-uq-2005

Spiro, R. J., Coulson, R. L., Feltovich, P. J. & Anderson, D. K. (1988). Cognitive flexibility theory: Advanced knowledge acquisition in ill-structured domains. In V. Patel (Ed.), *Proceedings of the 10th Annual Conference of the Cognitive Science Society*. Hillsdale, NJ: Erlbaum, pp. 375–383. Retrieved 20 September 2010, from http://en.scientificcommons.org/18470488

Steel, C. (2009). Reconciling university teacher beliefs to create learning designs for LMS environments. *Australasian Journal of Educational Technology, 25*(3), 399–420.

Stern, E. (1990). The evaluation of policy and the politics of evaluation. *The Tavistock Institute of Human Relations Annual Review*. London: Tavistock Institute, pp. 28–30.

Stokes, D. E. (1997). *Pasteur's Quadrant: Basic science and technological innovation*. Washington, DC: The Brookings Institution.

Sweller, J. (1988). Cognitive load during problem solving: Effects on learning. *Cognitive Science, 12*, 257–285.

Swieringa, J. & Wierdsma, A. (1992). *Becoming a learning organization: Beyond the learning curve*. Wokingham, UK: Addison Wesley.

Tabachnick, B. G. & Fidell, L. S. (1996). *Using multivariate statistics* (3rd ed.). New York: Harper Collins.

Tesch, R. (1990). *Qualitative research. Analysis types and software tools*. New York: Falmer Press.

The Cambridge Online Dictionary (n.d.). *Definition of learning*. Retrieved 20 September 2010, from http://dictionary.cambridge.org

The Design-Based Research Collective (2003). Design-based research: An emerging paradigm for educational inquiry. *Educational Researcher, 32*(1), 5–8.

Thomas, J. & Pospisil, R. (2000). Developing a cross-cultural perspective in science students. *Flexible learning for a flexible society: Proceedings of the ASET-HERDSA Conference 2000*. Toowoomba: University of Southern Queensland, 2–5 July. Retrieved 24 October 2010, from www.ascilite.org.au/aset-archives/confs/aset-herdsa2000/procs/thomas.html

Trochim, W. M. K. (2006). *Introduction to evaluation*. Retrieved 20 September 2010, from www.socialresearchmethods.net/kb/intreval.htm

van den Akker, J. (1999). Principles and methods of development research. In J. van den Akker, R. M. Branch, K. Gustafson, N. Nieveen & T. Plomp (Eds.), *Design approaches and tools in education and training*. Dordrecht: Kluwer Academic, pp. 1–14.

van den Akker, J., Gravemeijer, K., McKenney, S. & Nieveen, N. (2006). *Educational design research*. Abingdon, UK: Routledge.

Varnava, T. (2002). Managing resources: The art of the possible. In C. Baume, P. Martin & M. Yorke (Eds.), *Managing educational development projects: Effective management for maximum impact*. Birmingham, UK: Staff and Educational Development Association, pp. 63–78.

Viera, A. J. & Garrett, J. M. (2005). Understanding interobserver agreement: The kappa statistic. *Family Medicine Journal, 37*(5), 360–363.

Von Brevern, H. (2004). Cognitive and logical rationales for e-learning objects. *Educational Technology & Society, 7*(4), 2–25.

Wang, F. & Hannafin, M. J. (2005). Design-based research and technology-enhanced learning environments. *Educational Technology Research and Development, 53*(4), 5–23.

Watson, R. K., Pattison, P. E. & Finch, S. (1993). *Beginning statistics for psychology.* Sydney: Prentice-Hall.

Waycott, J., Bennett, J., Kennedy, G., Dalgarno, B. & Gray, K. (2010). Digital divides? Student and staff perceptions of information and communication technologies. *Computers and Education, 54*(4), 1202–1211.

Wenger, E. (1998). *Communities of practice: Learning, meaning, and identity.* Cambridge: Cambridge University Press.

Wills, S. & McNaught, C. (1996). Evaluation of computer based learning in higher education. *Journal of Computing in Higher Education, 7*(2), 106–128.

Wilson, J. M. (1994). The CUPLE Physics Studio. *The Physics Teacher, 32*, 518–523.

Worthen, B. R., Sanders, J. R. & Fitzpatrick, J. L. (1997). *Program evaluation: Alternative approaches and practical guidelines* (2nd ed.). New York: Longman.

Zadnik, M. G., Deylitz, S., Yeo, S., Loss, R. & Treagust, D. (1999). Teaching *really* difficult concepts: How we did it and what the students say. In K. Martin, N. Stanley & N. Davison (Eds.), *Teaching in the disciplines/Learning in context: Proceedings of the 8th Annual Teaching Learning Forum* (pp. 480–483). Perth: The University of Western Australia. Retrieved 24 October 2010, from http://otl.curtin.edu.au/tlf/tlf1999/zadnik.html

Author Index

Subject Index

O

observation *see* method, observation
ontology 71, 73, 75–6, 78
open data 92, 95
open educational resource 11, 125, 130
organizational change issues 174,
    176–7
outcomes: generic, academic 35–8, 125,
    174; personal, transferrable 35,
    37; subject-based 35–7

P

paradigm: critical theory 75–7, 79–81,
    84, 88; interpretivist 74–5, 77,
    79–81, 84; positivist 72–4, 77,
    79–81, 84, 96, 99; postpositivist
    74; pragmatic 77–9, 81, 84, 86,
    93, 108
paradigm of: inquiry 65, 69–82, 84, 86,
    93, 103–4, 106, 146–7, 152, 179;
    teaching 17
participants 16, 75, 90, 108–12, 141–2,
    145–6, 149, 151, 153, 155, 167
Pasteur's Quadrant 56–8, 60, 62, 65, 78,
    91, 175
peer review 21, 77, 110, 122–7, 140
phenomenon 16, 65–9, 71, 73, 75, 77,
    81–3, 87, 103–6, 146, 153;
    artificial 66, 74, 87, 105–6; event
    66; natural 66–7, 83, 87, 106
policy framework 9, 173
postmodernism 9, 72, 74–5
pre- and post-tests 19–20, 96
presage, process, product *see* 3–P
    model
problem analysis 114–15, 117–18, 121,
    127
problem space of educational design 28,
    30–1, 33–4, 36, 39–40
program evaluation 9, 43–4, 120
program logic 120
project: definition 44, 112; evaluation 45,
    62, 165, 167; evaluator 165, 167;
    management 12, 48, 53, 157–8,
    160, 162–6, 171, 173; plan
    158–60, 162–3, 165–6, 168, 171;
    scope 159, 162, 166
project management: evaluation 48,
    100, 117–18, 136, 156, 157,

164–8, 179; hard 163–5, 168;
    methodology *see* methodology,
    project management; soft
    163–5, 168
project manager, characteristics 158, 160,
    162–5
prototyping 125, 128, 159–60
pseudo-scientific approaches 89

Q

qualitative analysis software *see* software,
    qualitative analysis
qualitative analysis: coding 150, 152,
    154–5; content 147, 150, 152;
    narrative 151; thematic 140,
    147, 152; themes 146, 150–2,
    155
quest for fundamental understanding,
    Stokes 55–8, 60, 62, 65
questionnaire *see* method, questionnaire
questions: broad 65, 69–71, 79–82, 106–7,
    113, 133, 148, 151–3; closed
    141; open 141, 145, 178; specific
    107–9, 113–16, 118, 121–36,
    140, 165–7, 174

R

randomized controlled trials 19, 73, 96
reconstructive study 94, 121–2
Reeves and Reeves model for interactive
    learning on the web 28, 30, 34,
    36, 39
reflective practitioner 17–18, 88–9
reliability 54, 73, 146, 150, 153–5
reporting 111–12, 147, 153, 155–6, 163–4,
    167
requirements analysis 12, 114, 121
research designs: comparison 19–20,
    95–8; experimental *see*
    methods, experimental;
    quasi-experimental *see*
    methods, quasi-experimental
research goals 65, 69, 78, 81, 84–6, 94,
    106, 132, 151
research paradigm *see* Paradigm of
    Inquiry
research process 53–4, 57, 69–70, 76,
    80, 86, 90, 94, 100, 103–4, 109,
    111–12, 113, 116, 119

type II development research 94
types of e-learning artefacts *see* e-learning
    artefact, types

U

understanding, research 50–8, 60, 65, 108,
    132,
usability testing 48–9, 51, 60, 62, 84–5,
    116, 120, 128, 141, 171
usage log *see* method, usage log

V

validity 73–4, 75–6, 78, 94, 146, 153–5
video-stimulated recall *see* method,
    video-stimulated recall
virtual learning environment 10

W

Web 2.0 systems 11, 61, 83
Wiki 61, 62, 80, 94, 143